78-2884

P9-AER-838

THE LEGACY OF
HOLMES AND BRANDEIS

Da Capo Press Reprints in

AMERICAN CONSTITUTIONAL AND LEGAL HISTORY

GENERAL EDITOR: LEONARD W. LEVY

Claremont Graduate School

THE LEGACY OF HOLMES
AND BRANDEIS

A Study in the Influence of Ideas

by Samuel J. Konefsky

DA CAPO PRESS • NEW YORK • 1974

Library of Congress Cataloging in Publication Data

Konefsky, Samuel Joseph, 1915-
   The legacy of Holmes and Brandeis.

   (Da Capo Press reprint in American constitutional and legal history)
   Reprint of the ed. published by Macmillan, New York.
   1. Holmes, Oliver Wendell, 1841-1935. 2. Brandeis, Louis Dembitz,
1856-1941. 3. United States. Supreme Court. I. Title.
[KF8748.K65 1974]   347'.73'26   78-157828
ISBN 0-306-70215-0

This Da Capo Press edition of *The Legacy of Holmes and Brandeis is an*
unabridged republication of the first edition published in New York in 1956,
This edition is reprinted by arrangement with Macmillan Publishing Co., Inc.

Published by Da Capo Press, Inc.
A Subsidiary of Plenum Publishing Corporation
227 West 17th Street, New York, N.Y. 10011

Manufactured in the United States of America

The Legacy of HOLMES
and BRANDEIS

By Samuel J. Konefsky

CHIEF JUSTICE STONE AND THE SUPREME COURT

THE LEGACY OF HOLMES AND BRANDEIS:
  A STUDY IN THE INFLUENCE OF IDEAS

Edited by Samuel J. Konefsky

THE CONSTITUTIONAL WORLD OF MR. JUSTICE FRANKFURTER:
  SOME REPRESENTATIVE OPINIONS

THE LEGACY OF HOLMES
AND BRANDEIS

A Study in the Influence of Ideas

by Samuel J. Konefsky

New York, 1956

THE MACMILLAN COMPANY

KF
8748
.K65
1974

Library of Congress catalog card number: 56-11835

To Abraham Flexner
For his Ninetieth Birthday

A Note of Thanks

So many exceedingly generous persons and groups have contributed to the writing of this book that it will be quite impossible to thank them adequately in this brief space. Yet on the theory that nothing gets finished which does not get started, I am bound to say that my first obligation is to Mr. Henry Allen Moe and the John Simon Guggenheim Memorial Foundation. Their award of two Fellowships enabled me to launch the research, most of which I carried on at Yale University. The Social Science Research Council and the American Philosophical Society aided other phases of the project, and a grant from the Rockefeller Foundation enabled me to complete it.

Some of these grants afforded me the opportunity to interview many of the former law clerks to Justices Holmes and Brandeis as well as other eminent scholars and jurists. While I absolve them of any responsibility for my interpretations, the least I can do is to acknowledge my great debt to all of them: Dean Acheson, Thomas H. Austern, Robert M. Benjamin, Mr. Justice Hugo L. Black, Zechariah Chafee, Jr., W. Graham Claytor, Jr., Felix S. Cohen, Edward S. Corwin, Laurence Curtis, Mr. Justice William O. Douglas, Warren G. Ege, Judge Jerome N. Frank, Mr. Justice Felix Frankfurter, Paul A. Freund, Lon L. Fuller, Henry M. Hart, Jr.,

Mark DeWolfe Howe,` J. Willard Hurst, Mr. Justice Robert H.
Jackson, Louis L. Jaffe, James M. Landis, Judge Calvert Magruder,
Alpheus Thomas Mason, Nathaniel L. Nathanson, James M. Nicely,
Roscoe Pound, Thomas Reed Powell, Mr. Justice Stanley F.
Reed, David Riesman, Mr. Justice Owen J. Roberts, Horace
Chapman Rose, Harry Shulman, Arthur E. Sutherland, Jr., Carl
Brent Swisher, Judge Charles E. Wyzanski, Jr.

I shall not even attempt to speak of the many reasons for my profound gratitude to Dr. Abraham Flexner, whose friendship I like
to think of as one of the miracles in my life. Thanks to his magic, I
also have had the support of private benefactors at crucial stages in
the preparation of this book. Mrs. David M. Levy, Mr. Lessing J.
Rosenwald and Mr. Paul Mellon have been truly magnanimous, and
I am deeply grateful to them.

Professor Samuel E. Thorne, Law Librarian at Yale University,
encouraged me to come to New Haven, and I am indebted to him
for facilitating my work there. The staff of the Brooklyn College
Library was of enormous help to me whenever called upon, and I
want them to know that I appreciate their genial cooperation.
Lionel J. Coen, one of my finest students and now Librarian of the
New York Law Institute, has extended to me all the services of the
Institute. He must know how much I value his aid.

I have been fortunate to have had the help of several earnest and
able assistants—Robert A. Petito, Arthur B. Frommer, Morris M.
Wilhelm, Burton N. Scholl—and I wish to thank them publicly
for the spirit in which they served me. Mrs. Elsie Stein prepared the typescript and Miss Edith Axelrod worked on the
proofs and index. To both of them I am grateful for the extraordinary care and patience with which they executed their tedious tasks.

For placing at my fingertips materials not otherwise available in
braille, I am indebted to many devoted transcribers and those who
direct their labors. Mrs. Anne Ritter, of the Brooklyn Braille Bindery,
has for years so completely dedicated herself to meeting my special
research needs that she has been, in a very real sense, my personal
braillist. I cannot thank her enough. Miss Dorothy S. Knight of the

New York Association for the Blind; Mr. Bernard M. Krebs, Librarian of the New York Guild for the Jewish Blind; Mrs. Rose F. Maged of the Brooklyn Braille Center; and Mrs. Ralph G. Stone of the Plymouth Church Braille Group—all have earned my lasting gratitude for their magnificent service.

What the writing of this book has cost my suffering wife and children only they know. It is good to be able to answer the children's plaintive query: "When will you finish?" To describe my wife's role I can do no better than to repeat what I said in the preface to my first book—"It could not have been written without her indispensable assistance and unfailing encouragement."

S. J. K.

August 1956

Contents

1

"The men I should be tempted to commemorate"

In the spacious domain of constitutional jurisprudence, there has always been ample room for the achievement of judicial eminence in greatly varying ways. Perhaps this is due in part to the nature of the United States Constitution itself. For in essaying nothing more ambitious than the barest outline of general powers and limitations, it cast upon oncoming generations the unavoidable task of adapting old provisions and dogmas to new problems and needs. And by confronting the future with the claims of the past, it was bound to test the ability and wisdom of men in meeting the challenge of social change.

This is not to say that "continuity with the past" is a unique attribute of American civilization. "The law, so far as it depends on learning," Holmes told a Harvard Law School audience in 1895, "is indeed, as it has been called, the government of the living by the dead." Acknowledging that it was probably inevitable that "the living should be so governed," he hastened to add a timeless admonition: "The present has a right to govern itself so far as it can; and it ought always to be remembered that historic continuity with the past is not a duty, it is only a necessity." [1] These words of Holmes were but an echo of Thomas Jefferson's sterner warning earlier in the century:

[1] Oliver Wendell Holmes, *Speeches* (Boston: Little, Brown and Company, 1918), pp. 67–68.

1

2 THE LEGACY OF HOLMES AND BRANDEIS

Some men look at constitutions with sanctimonious reverence, and deem them like the ark of the covenant, too sacred to be touched. They ascribe to the men of the preceding age a wisdom more than human, and suppose what they did to be beyond amendment . . . laws and institutions must go hand in hand with the progress of the human mind. As that becomes more developed, more enlightened, as new discoveries are made, new truths disclosed, and manners and opinions change with the change of circumstances, institutions must advance also, and keep pace with the times.[2]

Yet what Jefferson deplored and Holmes accepted does have special relevance in the study of American institutions. Our written Constitution not only has set limits to innovation but has led us to weigh public policies in the scales of legal precepts. One result has been that the Supreme Court of the United States was able to establish itself, without significant or effective resistance, as the final arbiter of constitutional controversies. In thus becoming the "living oracles" of the Constitution, to borrow a phrase from Blackstone,[3] the members of this tribunal have been in a position to exert a powerful influence on the shaping of America's destiny, so far, at least, as law can determine the direction in which a society moves. But constitutional interpretation, even as law generally, is not always in step with social necessities.

If in performing the ordinary functions of courts judges have been slow to accept the need for change, how much more fertile are the opportunities for blocking progress in the exercise of the power of judicial review. The right to pass judgment on the validity of governmental action has inevitably drawn into the vortex of the adjudicatory process the deepest issues dividing the American people. By the manner in which they have used this great prerogative judges have revealed, of course, their own stature as statesmen. The Justices have been engaged in statecraft; but not all of them have been statesmen, any more than have all those who have exercised the other powers of government.

That the work of the Supreme Court calls more for wisdom and

[2] Ford (ed.), *The Writings of Thomas Jefferson*, X, 42–43.
[3] William Blackstone, *Commentaries*, I, 69.

ideas than for mere legal erudition is plain from the roster of the
really great jurists. In Joseph Story, Marshall had a colleague whose
scholarship certainly overshadowed his own. But the reasons which
have entitled Marshall to the simple characterization of "the great
Chief Justice" help to illumine the measure of judicial statesmanship. His able and lucid exposition of momentous public questions
is hardly the chief factor. Above everything else, it was Marshall's
prescient awareness of the needs of a growing republic and his
articulation of the necessary intellectual weapons for their realization which justify the homage of posterity. One of our finest judicial
biographers has summarized the matter in these realistic terms:

John Marshall has a prominent place in American history not because as a
Federalist he stood alone among men, or not because he phrased new
conceptions of federalism, but because he was able persuasively to read
into constitutional law the conceptions of a powerful group in the society
of his time which were to retain and increase their popularity during the
years to come.[4]

As applied to Justices Holmes and Brandeis, however, such a criterion of greatness may be misleading. Their reputation for judicial
objectivity does not quite comport with the picture of Marshall's
boldness in striving to vindicate his vision of America's future. A
former law clerk to Justice Brandeis has posed the problem in the
course of suggesting some criteria for assessing greatness in the
appellate judge:

We put Holmes on our list of greats in large part because of the value we
put on his irreverence toward judicial pretense. The problem of intellectual integrity is a peculiarly challenging one in the case of the judge,
because typically he is called on to assume the burdens of impartiality
after a long training in being the partisan. The moral hazard of the
lawyer is that he will justify his means by his particular end. Here, then,
is a prime problem for the student of such a man as Brandeis. As practitioner, a feared opponent and valiant champion, master of technique
and not mastered by it, daring, adroit, sometimes ruthless in attack, yet
holding to principle: what in the practice of such a man must the biog-

[4] Carl B. Swisher, "The Judge in Historical Perspective," *24 Ind. L. J. 381*,
382 (1949).

rapher find to explain why the judge could cast off the partisan robe so completely? [5]

But quite apart from a judge's appreciation of the forward-pushing impulses of his time, the truly seminal mind has been the mark of preeminence in judicial labor even as it is in other creative fields. In our own century and in the realm of judicial thinking, of none is this true more than of Justices Holmes and Brandeis. "The men I should be tempted to commemorate," Holmes once remarked, "would be the originators of transforming thought." [6]

Modern psychology has done much in exploring the contradictory impulses in human nature which often propel men to resist or reject the very things which really attract or interest them. Perhaps therein is to be found the explanation for the chief irony of Justice Holmes' intellectual life. The man who could speak so cynically of excessive generalization was forever setting matters in a general frame, even if in the name of perspective. "I am glad that a philosopher is interested in the law," Holmes wrote in his first letter to Morris R. Cohen; and he added, "I hardly should be interested in it—if it did not open a wide door to philosophizing—and enable me to illustrate another of my chestnuts that the chief end of man is to frame general ideas—and that no general idea is worth a straw." [7] Though not a builder of formal systems of abstract thought, Holmes was constantly preoccupied with the unifying principles which account for or grow out of particular events or situations. Surely such a thinker has every right to be called philosopher, however much the appellation may be unpalatable to him.

The ambivalence persisted. Writing to Sir Frederick Pollock from Washington in 1905, Holmes confessed that while he was "inclined to belittle the doings of the philosophers," he thought "philosophy the end of life." [8] He voiced this conflict even more pungently many

[5] Willard Hurst, "Who is the 'Great' Appellate Judge?" 24 Ind. L. J. 394, 398 (1949).
[6] Holmes, op. cit., p. 90.
[7] "The Holmes-Cohen Correspondence," edited with a Foreword by Felix S. Cohen, IX Journal of the History of Ideas 1, 8 (Jan., 1948).
[8] Mark DeWolfe Howe (ed.), Holmes-Pollock Letters (Cambridge: Harvard Univ. Press, 1941), I, 122.

years later: "I always say the chief end of men is to form general propositions—adding that no general proposition is worth a damn." [9] Holmes liked to think of himself as an "evolutionist"; and an evolutionist in the law, he believed, "will hesitate to affirm universal validity for his social ideals." [10] Indeed, he regarded it as nothing short of disastrous for a judge to decide cases purely on the basis of personal predilections: "It is a misfortune if a judge reads his conscious or unconscious sympathy with one side or the other prematurely into the law, and forgets that what seem to him to be first principles are believed by half his fellow men to be wrong." [11] But the jurist who reputedly refrained from indulging his own social sympathies could not altogether escape the temptation to hold forth on the fundamental issues of the civilization of which he was a part. To be sure, less may be learned about his philosophy of life and of law from the outcome in the concrete case and far more from his more general utterances, whether embodied in formal legal essays, an occasional public address, or his letters. When all sources are scanned, there emerges a mind which is much tougher in its convictions about the good society than has been the wont of some to depict. The very felicity of his speech makes us miss at times the seriousness of his purpose. Nor is it true that his deep distrust of "panaceas" and "nostrums" was merely the fruit of his broadly philosophical outlook. Actually, he had a good many strongly felt affirmative preferences, even though they were sometimes cast in the "language of cynicism," to use his own phrase.[12]

But if Holmes was wary of philosophic abstractions, how much

---

[9] *Ibid.*, II, 13. Three other expressions of a similar vein may be of interest: "Too broadly generalized conceptions are a constant source of fallacy." Lorenzo v. Wirth, 170 Mass. 598 (1898). "For the incompetent, it sometimes is true, . . . that an interest in general ideas means an absence of particular knowledge." *Collected Legal Papers* (New York: Harcourt, Brace and Co., 1920), p. 201. "Philosophy may have gained by the attempt in recent years to look through the fiction to the fact and to generalize corporation, partnership and other groups into a single conception. But to generalize is to omit, . . ." Donnell v. Herring-Hall-Marvin Safe Co., 208 U.S. 267, 273 (1908).

[10] Holmes, *Collected Legal Papers*, p. 186.

[11] *Ibid.*, p. 295.

[12] *Ibid.*, p. 170.

more was the aversion characteristic of the thinking of his esteemed friend and colleague, Louis Dembitz Brandeis. Brandeis always insisted that he had no "rigid social philosophy." [13] Yet the fact remains that his views on American society and government represent such a fundamental and creative attack on the central problem of the twentieth century as to make of him a truly significant political thinker, in the American sense, at least. His sustained effort to reconcile modern economic forces with the ideals of responsible democratic government revealed a depth of understanding and a capacity for social invention which well justify the assertion that "No man can more reasonably be acclaimed the prophet of our industrial era." [14] We have the word of another of his contemporaries that during the presidential campaign of 1912, Brandeis was "the most powerful intellect assisting Mr. Wilson to expound the principles of democracy applied to the problems of a machine age." [15] Brandeis may have differed from Holmes in temperament, outlook and method, but both were men whose basic assumptions and values were clearly reflected in their behavior as judges.

It is easier, however, to recognize an original mind than to assess its influence on others. As David Riesman—whose unusual career has included a year with Justice Brandeis—has said so aptly while speaking about the impact of Freud's thought: "where a man's thought and action do not lead to creation of a new institution but mingle in a general climate of opinion, the tracing of the consequences of his work is even more a shadowy and impalpable task: no Mendelian law governs the unembodied transmission of ideas." [16] Even after Holmes and Brandeis had come to be universally respected and widely quoted, the effect of their contribution to public thinking about constitutional questions remained a matter of conjecture.

[13] Alpheus Thomas Mason, *Lawyer and Judge in the Modern State* (Princeton: Princeton Univ. Press, 1933), p. 183.
[14] George R. Farnum, "Louis D. Brandeis—A Chapter Closed," 2 *American Lawyer* 8 (April, 1939).
[15] Norman Hapgood, "Justice Brandeis: Apostle of Freedom," 125 *The Nation* 330, 331 (October 5, 1937).
[16] Riesman, *Individualism Reconsidered* (Glencoe, Illinois: The Free Press, 1954), p. 365.

Indeed, very sharply differing opinions have been expressed with respect to their intellectual influence.

Writing in 1941, Robert H. Jackson presented one view:

Justices such as Holmes and Brandeis have not only furnished the highest expression but they have been the very source and the intellectual leaders of recent liberalism in the United States.[17]

A quite different estimate was advanced by Morris Raphael Cohen just six years earlier:

. . . he [Holmes] did not in his own lifetime exert any highly effective influence on the law and life of our country. Except in the matter of civil rights, he has not, like Marshall or Taney, changed the current of our constitutional law, nor for that matter left any permanent impress on any other branch of our law, as lesser men, like Story, did in admiralty, or conflict of laws. Holmes was a lone, though a titanic, figure, and the currents of our national life have swept by and around him.[18]

Benjamin N. Cardozo, then Chief Judge of the New York Court of Appeals and soon to be Holmes' successor on the Supreme Court, voiced a much more generous sentiment in 1931:

He [Holmes] is today for all students of the law and for all students of human society the philosopher and the seer, the greatest of our age in the domain of jurisprudence, and one of the greatest of the ages.[19]

An equally optimistic view of Brandeis was contemporaneously expressed by the man who ultimately became Brandeis' official biographer: "The prophet has indeed come into honor in his own country and in his own time." [20]

[17] Jackson, *The Struggle for Judicial Supremacy* (New York: Alfred A. Knopf, 1941), p. 312.
[18] Cohen, "Justice Holmes," 82 *New Republic* 206 (April 3, 1935). When Professor Cohen came to edit this article some years later for inclusion in a collection of his own occasional papers, he appended this footnote: "This essay was written in 1935, before the considerable changes in the personnel and fundamental attitude of the Supreme Court. Since then Holmes's views on constitutional law have been pretty generally followed by the majority of the Court." *Faith of a Liberal* (New York: Henry Holt and Co., 1946), p. 21.
[19] Felix Frankfurter (ed.), *Mr. Justice Holmes* (New York: Coward-McCann, Inc., 1931), p. 5.
[20] Mason, *op. cit.*, p. 69.

Nor is the influence exerted by Justices Holmes and Brandeis the only debatable point about their juristic contribution. Of even greater interest is the question as to whether the two men shared a common philosophy. An able publicist has put the problem in these words:

> After he joined the Supreme Court, Brandeis was often associated with Justice Holmes in dissent. Because of this, the American public spoke of them, almost interchangeably, as liberals. Actually, their liberalism was by no means identical. . . . They shared a common devotion to the ideals of democracy and individual liberty. They saw life as a conflict of forces, and defined the function of government as the production of a just equilibrium. But notwithstanding this basic unity of view, the area of their difference greatly exceeded that of their agreement.[21]

The characterization of the two Justices as molders of the liberal faith raises anew an old and elusive question in political definitions: What is liberalism, especially in a judge? Another of Justice Brandeis' law secretaries has shared with us an interesting experience not without some illumination on this conundrum. This is the story Professor Louis L. Jaffe tells:

> Sometime ago I spoke with a friend of mine, then a government servant, now a law professor. "Every time," said he, "that I run across another Holmes decision which I didn't know before, I wonder how he came by his reputation as a liberal." "You mean that the results don't square with liberal policy. But is it the judge's function to decide according to the tenets of a certain policy?" "Why surely!" he replied, "the judge wherever choice is possible should bring about the result most in accord with progressive policy. That is the test of a good judge, a liberal judge." [22]

Yet only the unsophisticated—those who have not been initiated into the complexities of judicial motivation—would seriously maintain that the measure of liberalism in a constitutional judge is that simple. One of our most erudite observers of the legal scene, who himself appears to be of the liberal persuasion, has sketched the

[21] Lloyd Morris, *Postscript to Yesterday* (New York: Random House, 1947), p. 365.
[22] Jaffe, "The Constitutional Universe of Mr. Justice Frankfurter," *62 Harv. L. Rev. 357, 358* (1949).

difficulty in a rather challenging fashion. "It is particularly difficult to assess the liberalism of a judge," writes William Seagle, and the reason he gives is this: "the legal and political aspects of a question often have no common denominator; liberalism is a political faith, while legal issues are enmeshed in principles and precedents; thus judges may decide against their personal inclinations and sympathies." [23]

Obviously, then, the effort to explore the ferment in American constitutional thought for which Holmes and Brandeis are presumably responsible will entail at least two major inquiries. That is to say, not only will it be necessary to examine the fundamental character of their conception of what Justice Brandeis termed "the constitutional function of judicial review," [24] but its fate at the hands of the interpreters and the disciples will also have to be considered. Maitland's injunction that history be written "backwards" [25] is thus not without relevance for the study of legal institutions in America. Viewed in this light, the present volume is an attempt to illumine the constitutional ideology to which the Supreme Court as reorganized by Franklin D. Roosevelt was heir. As a body of precepts and attitudes, it was no more completely coherent or consistent in the days when it was a gospel of criticism than it has been since attaining the status of official creed.

Shortly before his own appointment to the Supreme Court, Justice Felix Frankfurter said: "About a year ago the old views of Mr. Justice Holmes began to be the new constitutional direction of the Court." [26] Writing three years later—by which time the Court was composed almost entirely of Roosevelt appointees—Max Lerner reported on the "triumph" of Holmes:

It is well recognized among the lawyers that the new doctrinal direc-

[23] Seagle, *Men of Law: From Hammurabi to Holmes* (New York: The Macmillan Company, 1947), pp. 347–48.
[24] Dissenting in Burns Baking Co. v. Bryan, 264 U.S. 504, 517, at 534 (1924).
[25] H. A. L. Fisher (ed.), *The Collected Papers of Frederic William Maitland* (London: Cambridge Univ. Press, 1911), I, 493.
[26] Frankfurter, *Mr. Justice Holmes and the Supreme Court* (Cambridge: Harvard Univ. Press, 1938), p. 44.

tions of the present Supreme Court spell a return to Holmes. Five years
ago those who followed the New Deal constitutional crisis were overcome by a sense of sadness at what seemed the decisive defeat of the
Holmes tradition. But to-day when the Court assembles for conference
the true Chief Justice is the image of Holmes that all but one or two of
its members carry in their thinking. Rarely has a more certain defeat
been followed by a more complete triumph.[27]

But as is by now well known, the bright new day was soon to be
beclouded by the appearance of serious conflicts among the new
Justices. Nevertheless, while disagreeing with one another on many
vital issues, most of the New Deal Justices continued to speak as
apostles of the Holmes-Brandeis philosophy of law. One member
of the Court is the most avid of Holmes' admirers; another is known
to feel that his special mission is to advance the liberalism of Louis
D. Brandeis; all have invoked the words and wisdom of the two
"masters."

C. Herman Pritchett—one of our leading analysts of the Supreme
Court since its reconstruction by Presidents Roosevelt and Truman
—has suggested that one reason why the "judicial honeymoon" soon
degenerated into "a domestic wrangle" was that the legacy of
judicial liberalism on which the Roosevelt Court was drawing was a
confused one. What Professor Pritchett says about the divergence
between Holmes and Brandeis is particularly pertinent:

A . . . factor in the Roosevelt Court's difficulties was that the liberal
judicial tradition it inherited was a divided one. Lerner, in accepting
Holmes as the spiritual father of the New Court, was overlooking the
great judge's long-time partner in dissent, Justice Brandeis. His image
was likewise present in the thinking of the Roosevelt Court, and his version of liberalism was not identical with that of Holmes, . . . The
Roosevelt Court has thus had not one but two preceptors from whom to
take its liberal line.[28]

In a widely discussed recent article—calling on the members of

[27] Lerner, *Ideas for the Ice Age* (New York: The Viking Press, 1941), pp.
100–101.
[28] Pritchett, *The Roosevelt Court* (New York: The Macmillan Company,
1948), p. 266. See also Professor Pritchett's article, "Justice Holmes and a Liberal Court," *24 Va. Quar. Rev. 43* (Winter, 1948).

the Supreme Court to recognize that the "high function" they perform is "for the most part an institutional rather than an individual function"—Professor Carl Brent Swisher also relates contemporary judicial discord to the "heresy" initiated by Holmes and Brandeis. His assessment of personal blame is quite direct. "Holmes and Brandeis were the original troublemakers for the conservatives. . . . The continuing strife over social issues and the power of government to deal with them, and over exposure of the nature of the judicial function itself, created a permanent rift in the Court such as it had not known since before the Civil War." [29]

The claims of a common discipleship by men so often found divided on basic questions would suggest that there is need for a systematic study of the exact nature of the intellectual heritage which is loosely summed up by the phrase, "the Holmes-Brandeis tradition." Such an exploration should afford an excellent opportunity for testing the validity of one of Justice Holmes' most apt aphorisms: "The man of action has the present, but the thinker controls the future." [30]

[29] Swisher, "The Supreme Court—Need for Re-evaluation," *40 Va. L. Rev. 837, 842* (1954).
[30] Holmes, *Speeches*, p. 43.

2

"Speaking as a political economist"

I

When Louis D. Brandeis took his seat on the Supreme Court on June 5, 1916, Justice Holmes had been a member of the tribunal for almost fourteen years. On March 8th, Holmes had reached his seventy-fifth birthday, and some of the law journals marked the happy occasion by "gratefully" dedicating issues to him and by offering warm tributes. The editors of the *Harvard Law Review* assembled for their April number articles by both American and European jurists and scholars which dealt with him or his ideas.[1] Only one of these contributions was concerned with the Justice's work on the Supreme Court, and even that one was confined to a consideration of his constitutional opinions.[2]

"That English, European, and American jurists should join in this tribute, despite the sorrows and distractions of the great war," the editors observed, "shows how deeply the legal philosophy of the civilized world feels itself indebted to him." It is worth noting, however, that in listing the achievements upon which Holmes' en-

---

[1] The contributors were Frederick Pollock, Eugene Ehrlich, John H. Wigmore, Learned Hand, Roscoe Pound, and Felix Frankfurter. 29 *Harv. L. Rev.* 565 (April, 1916).

[2] Felix Frankfurter, "The Constitutional Opinions of Mr. Justice Holmes," *ibid.*, p. 683.

viable reputation rested, they did not include his service on the nation's highest court. "In England and on the Continent," the dedicatory statement continued, "his immortal work 'The Common Law,' has already brought him renown beyond that of any other American jurist since Story. To Americans, perhaps, the creative labors of his twenty years on the bench, woven permanently into the fabric of our common law, a part of our life and of the life of coming generations, present an even greater claim to gratitude and admiration." [3]

The editors of another law journal ignored the Justice's judicial labors altogether and took note of the occasion by printing several pages of quotations from his speeches. They justified their particular form of celebration by citing the need for reminding the younger members of the legal profession that "his wisdom is not all enfenced within the pages of his judicial opinions. It is a benevolent act to introduce them to his philosophy of life—wider even than his philosophy of law—as dispensed in his various speeches to the fortunate audiences." [4]

No one familiar with the luminous pages of Holmes' famous book on the common law, or the profound insights lurking in his legal essays, or the subtle eloquence in which he clothed his public addresses, will ever object to their free use on all suitable occasions. It may even be, as one of his admirers has suggested, that he was a greater scholar than judge: "The judge could scarce have been without the scholar; his greatness is the scholar's. And the scholar's medium is more revealing, less transient, than that of a judge." [5]

Whether one agrees with this estimate or not, it is easy to understand the emphasis on his career as a state judge in any discussion of his significance in the history of Anglo-American common law. It was true of Holmes as of Cardozo, Max Lerner has reminded us, "that even if he had remained on the state bench and had never

[3] *Ibid.*, p. 703.
[4] *10 Ill. L. Rev. 617* (April, 1916).
[5] Hessel E. Yntema, "Mr. Justice Holmes' View of Legal Science," *40 Yale L. J. 696* (1931).

reached the national, he would still have been a first-rate figure. . . .
Holmes belongs with the half-dozen most important figures in the
state judicial history of America." [6] Roscoe Pound includes Holmes
in his list of the ten judges "who must be ranked first in American
judicial history." [7] But the score of years Holmes spent on the
Massachusetts Court are significant more for his influence in the
various fields of private law—torts, crimes, contracts—and less for the
part he played in the shaping of the American constitutional
tradition.

Writing soon after Holmes' death, Sir Frederick Pollock appealed
to the late Justice's countrymen not to forget his "service" to the
common law. At the same time, he discerned the aspect of Justice
Holmes' work valued most by the American people:

> There may be a shade of difference, not in substance but in emphasis,
> between his American and his English admirers, in their remembrance of
> his achievements. His own people, for whom the decisions of the Su-
> preme Court are matters of practical concern, may naturally think of him
> in the first place as the greatest expounder of the Constitution since John
> Marshall, . . . That work was great; but here in England we are a little
> anxious that it should not overshadow Holmes's service to the Common
> Law on its proper ground, most of which lies farther back in his career.
> He has been hailed, and justly, as the classical successor to Blackstone
> and Kent.[8]

Apart from the impact of the rare qualities of his personality,
there can be little question that it was the constitutional philosophy
of Justice Holmes which helped establish his hold on the popular
imagination. Even if it is true, in Felix Frankfurter's phrase, that
Holmes' special gift was "great utterance," [9] literary felicity alone—
no more than immense learning—could scarcely account for the
ultimate vindication of his ideas. In the setting of the social con-

---

[6] Lerner, *The Mind and Faith of Justice Holmes* (Boston: Little, Brown and
Company, 1943), p. 90.
[7] Pound, *The Formative Era of American Law* (Boston: Little, Brown and
Company, 1938), p. 30.
[8] Pollock, *51 Law Quar. Rev.* 263 (1935).
[9] Frankfurter, *Mr. Justice Holmes and the Supreme Court*, p. 31.

flicts in twentieth-century America, it was probably inevitable that many of his views should have been seized upon by contending forces. But Holmes was no partisan of social amelioration, however much his name was enlisted in its cause. His approach to public questions was the logical outgrowth of his unique conception of the judicial function. This is perhaps the reason it was so widely misunderstood, if only because it was so incredible. In an age of growing tensions, such detachment was bound to be suspect.

II

It is not surprising, therefore, to find that some of those who welcomed the appointment of Holmes to the Supreme Court of the United States felt constrained to defend him against the charge of radicalism. An editorial in the *Boston Herald* had commented some years earlier on the source of the criticism: "The quality of a radical is perhaps strikingly shown in his stand on industrial questions, of which he is a student. Strange as it may seem for a man of his environment, his legal opinions have leaned to the side of the laborer." [10]

The rumored "radicalism" was apparently Theodore Roosevelt's main reason for deciding to offer Holmes a place on the Supreme Court. "The labor decisions which have been criticized by some of the big railroad men and other members of large corporations," he wrote to Senator Henry Cabot Lodge, "constitute to my mind a strong point in Judge Holmes' favor." [11] The President went on to praise the Massachusetts jurist for rising above his own class interests:

The ablest lawyers and the greatest judges are men whose past has naturally brought them into close relationship with the wealthiest and most powerful clients, and I am glad when I can find a judge who has been able to preserve his aloofness of mind so as to keep his broad

[10] Quoted in *60 Albany L. J. 118* (August 26, 1899).
[11] Elting E. Morison (ed.), *The Letters of Theodore Roosevelt* (Cambridge: Harvard Univ. Press, 1951), III, 288.

humanity of feeling and his sympathy for the class from which he has
not drawn his clients. I think it eminently desirable that our Supreme
Court should show in unmistakable fashion their entire sympathy with all
proper effort to secure the most favorable possible consideration for the
men who most need that consideration.[12]

Yet when one reads the Massachusetts opinions which led to
the suspicion that Holmes was a radical, it is immediately discernible that they tell us less about his own social sympathies and
infinitely more concerning his view as to the judge's limited role in
constitutional interpretation. Indeed, they foreshadowed the whole
philosophy of judicial self-restraint with which his name was to become so intimately identified in later years. The opinions which
made him seem most the radical found him on the minority side of
his Court, a fact which no doubt contributed to the impression
they were creating in certain circles. "The last two or three years I
have found myself separated from my brethren on some important
constitutional questions," Holmes wrote to Pollock on April 2, 1894,
adding: "among the respectable there are some who regard me as a
dangerous radical!" [13] Though few in number, these prophetic dissents afforded him opportunities for dealing with great constitutional
issues in his own unique fashion.

In Commonwealth v. Perry,[14] a majority of the Court set aside a
law forbidding employers of weavers to withhold wages because of
imperfections in their work. The legislation was held to interfere
with "the right to make reasonable contracts," inferred by the
Court from the right of "acquiring, possessing, and protecting property" guaranteed by Article I of the Massachusetts Bill of Rights.
Unable to see the relevance of this particular provision, Holmes dissented, saying that the protective measure interfered with property
no more than usury or gambling laws. His opinion strongly implied
that his colleagues had come to a contrary conclusion because they
did not like what the legislature had done:

It might be urged, perhaps, that the power to make reasonable laws
impliedly prohibits the making of unreasonable ones, and that this law

[12] *Ibid.*
[13] *Holmes-Pollock Letters,* I, 50.   [14] 155 Mass. 117, 123 (1891).

is unreasonable. If I assume that this construction of the Constitution is correct, and that, speaking as a political economist, I should agree in condemning the law, still I should not be willing or think myself authorized to overturn legislation on that ground, unless I thought that an honest difference of opinion was impossible, or pretty nearly so.

I suppose that this act was passed because the operatives, or some of them, thought that they were often cheated out of a part of their wages under a false pretense that the work done by them was imperfect, and persuaded the Legislature that their view was true. If their view was true, I cannot doubt that the Legislature had the right to deprive the employers of an honest tool which they were using for a dishonest purpose, and I cannot pronounce the legislation void, as based on a false assumption, since I know nothing about the matter one way or the other.[15]

Here, then, is the essence of Justice Holmes' theory of judicial toleration of governmental action. Judges are not free to indulge their preferences as would-be "political economists." Their function, at least in constitutional adjudication, is not to weigh the social wisdom of public policy. A judge's private conviction that a law is foolish or even dangerous, Holmes was implying, is no reason for holding it invalid. Particularly in a debatable area, a legislature is not acting unreasonably when it undertakes to solve a problem by selecting one remedy from among the many conflicting policies urged on it.

A year later, Holmes compressed these views into a single categorical sentence: "The need or expediency of such legislation is not for us to consider." [16] The legislation to which he was referring he had already described as "a step towards Communism." [17] It was a proposal to authorize cities and towns to sell coal and wood through municipal yards. Massachusetts is one of the few states whose highest tribunal enjoys the power to render advisory opinions, opinions which merely "advise" one or both houses of the legislature as to the constitutionality of pending measures. On this particular occasion, the Supreme Judicial Court announced that it

[15] *Ibid.*, at 124–25.
[16] Advisory Opinion of the Justices, *155 Mass. 598, 607* (1892).
[17] *Holmes-Pollock Letters*, I, 42 (April 15, 1892).

considered the tax to raise the money for the operation of the fuel yards unconstitutional because the funds would not serve any public purpose. The opinion which Holmes gave the legislature was quite the reverse:

> I am of opinion that when money is taken to enable a public body to offer to the public without discrimination an article of general necessity, the purpose is no less public when that article is wood or coal than when it is water, or gas, or electricity, or education, to say nothing of cases like the support of paupers or the taking of land for railroads or public markets.[18]

Holmes' ability to reconcile new ways with old principles was especially manifest whenever he found himself unable to agree with his brethren. A striking illustration is a case concerned with an innovation in the governmental machinery itself.[19] Replying to questions presented by the State House of Representatives, a majority of the Massachusetts Court gave as their opinion that it was unconstitutional to provide in an act granting woman suffrage that the law take effect upon its acceptance by a majority of the voters. This was the period when political reformers were preaching the gospel that the cure for the ills of democracy was more democracy, a diagnosis which was leading to the adoption of such schemes as the referendum, the initiative and the direct primary. But four of the seven members of the Massachusetts Court insisted that the state constitution, embodying as it does the will of the people, had placed the responsibility of government upon the representatives, and that the legislative power could not be delegated to any other body. Their contention struck Holmes, who detected excessive borrowing from the *Leviathan,* as "an echo of Hobbes's theory that the surrender of sovereignty by the people was final." He stressed a vital difference: "Hobbes urged his notion in the interest of the absolute power of King Charles I., and one of the objects of the Constitution of Massachusetts was to deny it." [20]

[18] 155 Mass. 598 at 607.
[19] In re Municipal Suffrage to Women, *160 Mass. 586, 593* (1894).
[20] *Ibid.,* at 595.

While agreeing with his colleagues that the State Constitution had established "a representative government, not a pure democracy," Holmes nevertheless called on them not to tie the hands of the legislature by confining it to procedures to which they themselves had grown accustomed. "I think that in construing the Constitution," he cautioned them, "we should remember that it is a frame of government for men of opposite opinions and for the future, and therefore not hastily import into it our own views, or unexpressed limitations derived merely from the practice of the past." [21] This admonition was to become a familiar refrain in his utterances from the Supreme Bench. Merely because the referendum was unknown to the framers of the state constitution, he argued, it did not follow that the legislature lacked the power to pass laws subject to approval by the people.

His brief opinion in this case is Holmes at his logical best. The General Court, as the legislature of Massachusetts is called, was given the whole lawmaking power, and the only question which he deemed pertinent was whether the Constitution, expressly or impliedly, prohibited the legislature from so exercising its discretion as to provide for the different forms of local option. Finding no such ban, he concluded that there was nothing in the document to prevent the body to whom the lawmaking function had been delegated from ascertaining the wishes of those ultimately responsible for the delegation. In other words, the legislature was free to refuse to put a law into effect when it had been rejected by the people. What mattered was that when a law did go into effect, it did so "by the express enactment of the representative body."

III

But if Holmes' opinion affirming the power to use the referendum impressed some of his contemporaries as radical, it was inevitable that his opinions upholding the right to peaceful picketing and the closed shop should strike the business community as the views of a

[21] *Ibid.*, at 594.

pro-labor judge. A judge who refused to enjoin picketing did so because he favored the use of this powerful labor weapon. Those having this suspicion of Holmes could not be expected to see that his now famous dissent in Vegelahn v. Guntner [22] was the effort of a man who, while quite reconciled to the drift of economic forces of his day, was merely seeking to keep them from working for the benefit of only one group in society. "As a Judge and as a good citizen," he once told a labor leader, "I like to understand all phases of economic opinion." [23]

Justice Allen's opinion for the majority in the *Vegelahn* case sustained a sweeping injunction forbidding picketing by strikers. Although there was no evidence of violence, the Court seemed to assume that the mere presence of the pickets necessarily carried with it the threat of force. The attempt to persuade persons looking for jobs not to enter the struck plant was a form of moral intimidation and therefore no part of lawful competition. Holmes, who dissented along with Chief Justice Field, said that he did not think that "two men, walking together up and down a sidewalk and speaking to those who enter a certain shop, do necessarily and always thereby convey a threat of force." He conceded that there was a difference between the activity of a single individual, which may have the effect of injuring another man's business, and the acts of several persons who deliberately conspire to hurt that business. "I take it to be settled, and rightly settled," Holmes went on to summarize the state of the law, "that doing that damage by combined persuasion is actionable, as well as doing it by falsehood or by force." [24] The really crucial question, however, was whether there were circumstances in which the damage suffered by a business was nevertheless lawfully inflicted. As Holmes observed, "It has been the law for centuries that a man may set up a business in a small country town too small to support more than one, although thereby he expects and

[22] 167 Mass. 92, 104 (1896).
[23] *Holmes-Pollock Letters*, I, 44 (Jan. 20, 1893).
[24] 167 Mass. 92, 104, at 105.

intends to ruin someone already there, and succeeds in his intent." [25]

In his discussion of the factors which ought to determine the answer to the question as to justifiable damage, there is revealed much of Holmes' basic economic thinking. Characteristically, he introduced this part of his opinion with some remarks on the inadequacy of general propositions:

The true grounds of decision are considerations of policy and of social advantage, and it is vain to suppose that solutions can be attained merely by logic and the general propositions of law which nobody disputes. Propositions as to public policy rarely are unanimously accepted, and still more rarely, if ever, are capable of unanswerable proof. They require a special training to enable any one even to form an intelligent opinion about them. In the early stages of law, at least, they generally are acted on rather as inarticulate instincts than as definite ideas for which a rational defence is ready.[26]

At the hands of Justice Holmes, the traditional argument against peaceful picketing turned into something of a boomerang. For he refuted it by pointing out that picketing, even if it interfered with business, was part of the price to be paid for the benefits society as a whole derives from free competition. It was time for those who believed in "the policy of allowing free competition" to recognize that the struggle between employers and employees was but a phase of what he called "the battle of trade." To broaden its scope to include employer-employee relations, he suggested that "free struggle for life" might be substituted for the term free competition. "Certainly the policy is not limited to struggles between persons of the same class competing for the same end. It applies to all conflicts of temporal interests." [27]

Holmes found that the pursuit of economic advantage was everywhere leading to business combinations, a tendency which was not only in the main beneficial but which could not be halted. So long

[25] *Ibid.*, at 106.
[26] *Ibid.*
[27] *Ibid.*, at 107.

as it was lawful for businessmen to combine for the purpose of promoting their interests, he thought it was wrong for courts to restrain workers from getting together in furtherance of their own interests. He predicted that the day will come when those opposed to peaceful picketing would accept it as a legitimate labor weapon, even as they had come to reconcile themselves to strikes. The passages in which these ideas were set forth have continued to serve as one of the chief sources of commentary on Holmes' fundamental economic outlook, and for this reason they merit quotation at some length:

It is plain from the slightest consideration of practical affairs, or the most superficial reading of industrial history, that free competition means combination, and that the organization of the world, now going on so fast, means an ever-increasing might and scope of combination. It seems to me futile to set our faces against this tendency. Whether beneficial on the whole, as I think it, or detrimental, it is inevitable, unless the fundamental axioms of society, and even the fundamental conditions of life, are to be changed.

One of the eternal conflicts out of which life is made up is that between the effort of every man to get the most he can for his services, and that of society, disguised under the name of capital, to get his services for the least possible return. Combination on the one side is patent and powerful. Combination on the other is the necessary and desirable counterpart, if the battle is to be carried on in a fair and equal way.[28]

Suggestive of a definite economic philosophy as these observations were, they did not quite convey the whole of it even as of at that time. Alongside them must be placed what he said in a case which is in a very real sense a companion to Vegelahn v. Guntner, though decided four years later. In Plant v. Woods,[29] Holmes once again declined to join his colleagues in affirming a labor injunction. The injunction had been obtained by a new union of painters and decorators, who were seeking to prevent the group from which they had seceded from carrying out a threat that they would use a strike or boycott unless the employer made the deserters return to the old

[28] Ibid., at 108.
[29] 176 Mass. 492, 504 (1900).

union or fire them altogether. In today's parlance, this was a juris-dictional dispute between rival unions.

In one respect, the problem for Holmes in Plant v. Woods was more knotty than in the *Vegelahn* case. The legal issue was, of course, whether the economic harm to be anticipated from the threatened strike and boycott was privileged, in the sense of being justified by the purpose or motive of the action. But it was obvious that the pressure which the old union was bringing to bear on the employers was not directly related to any of the ordinary claims of employees, such as demands for higher wages or better work-ing conditions. The immediate occasion for hostility was the old union's effort to keep itself from being destroyed; the demand for the closed shop was the desperate means to that end. Yet ultimately, only by preserving its integrity as an organization would it be in a position to bargain with employers effectively. Holmes was quick to grasp the logic of the situation and summarized the relation of means to ends in one short sentence: "I think that unity of organiza-tion is necessary to make the contest of labor effectual, and that societies of laborers lawfully may employ in their preparation the means which they might use in the final contest." [30]

At the same time he tried to show that he was not an economic radical. In the course of doing so, he revealed himself to be an unconscious disciple of the wage-fund theory—the assumption that the amount of national income available for distribution as wages cannot be increased. Organized labor has always regarded this doc-trine as both fallacious and reactionary.

Holmes' disclaimer of radicalism and his confession of economic faith are to be found in the concluding paragraph of his opinion in Plant v. Woods:

Although this is not the place for extended economic discussion, and although the law may not always reach ultimate economic conceptions, I think it well to add that I cherish no illusions as to the meaning and effect of strikes. While I think the strike a lawful instrument in the universal

[30] *Ibid.*, at 505.

struggle of life, I think it pure phantasy to suppose that there is a body of capital of which labor as a whole secures a larger share by that means. The annual product, subject to an infinitesimal deduction for the luxuries of the few, is directed to consumption by the multitude, and is consumed by the multitude, always. Organization and strikes may get a larger share for the members of an organization, but, if they do, they get it at the expense of the less organized and less powerful portion of the laboring mass. They do not create something out of nothing. It is only by divesting our minds of questions of ownership and other machinery of distribution, and by looking solely at the question of consumption,—asking ourselves what is the annual product, who consumes it, and what changes would or could we make,—that we can keep the world of realities.[31]

Comparing the *Vegelahn* and *Plant* dissents, Max Lerner has discerned a contradiction which seems to suggest that Holmes' social conservatism may explain why he clung to "economic orthodoxy." Mr. Lerner writes:

Thus the judge becomes in this opinion explicitly the economist, as in the *Vegelahn* opinion he had become explicitly the sociologist and had written a discourse on the struggle for life. If one seeks to connect the two discourses one gets a curious result: every group by the laws of life must seek to better itself—but labor's effort is doomed by some iron law mechanism; nevertheless the law will not deny to the individual workers the arid satisfaction of a struggle among themselves for larger portions of the rigidly restricted total. Thus by following the economic orthodoxy of the wage-fund theory Holmes undoes a good deal of the realism underlying . . . his dissent in the *Vegelahn* case.[32]

IV

For a historian—and he began his career as a legal historian— Holmes was singularly static in his conception of the economic universe. Malthus and Adam Smith were his guides to the verities, and his continued reliance upon their teachings, supplemented by some of the social implications of Darwinism, only served to lend a semblance of pseudo-scientific support for his thinking. But at bot-

[31] *Ibid.*
[32] Lerner, *op. cit.*, p. 119.

tom, his skepticism of social regeneration and his belief in a more or less fixed "annual product" were merely part of his collection of "can't-helps"—as he called his personal prejudices. "When I say that a thing is true, I mean," he explained in 1915, "that I can't help believing it. . . . I therefore define the truth as the system of my limitations and leave absolute truth for those who are better equipped." [33]

He apparently could not help but believe that what mattered was who consumes a nation's wealth and not who owns or controls it. When he wrote to Brandeis in 1919 that in his opinion the poor now had "substantially all there is" and that social experiments were "merely shifting the place of pressure," [34] he was only repeating views he had expressed many times before. What he came to call his "stream of products" idea, first suggested in Plant v. Woods, he had developed more fully in his famous letter on "economic elements" which appeared in 1904.[35] He there observed that "the objections to unlimited private ownership are sentimental or political, not economic" and argued that the work of the great capitalists in increasing worldly goods for all proved that this was so:

The real problem is not who owns, but who consumes, the annual product. The identification of these two very different questions is the source of many fallacies, and misleads many workingmen. The real evil of fifty-thousand-dollar balls and other manifestations of private splendor is that they tend to confirm this confusion in the minds of the ignorant by an appeal to their imagination, and make them think that the Vanderbilts and Rockefellers swallow their incomes like Cleopatra's pearl. The same conception is at the bottom of Henry George's *Progress and Poverty.* He thinks he has finished the discussion when he shows the tendency of wealth to be owned by the landlords. He does not consider what the landlords do with it.

I conceive that economically it does not matter whether you call Rocke-

[33] Holmes, "Ideals and Doubts," in *Collected Legal Papers,* pp. 304–305.
[34] Quoted in Alpheus Thomas Mason, *Brandeis: A Free Man's Life* (New York: The Viking Press, 1946), p. 574.
[35] Holmes, *Collected Legal Papers,* p. 279. See also the *Holmes-Laski Letters,* edited by Mark DeWolfe Howe (Cambridge: Harvard Univ. Press, 1953), I, 88.

feller or the United States owner of all the wheat in the United States, if that wheat is annually consumed by the body of the people; except that Rockefeller, under the illusion of self-seeking or in the conscious pursuit of power, will be likely to bring to bear a more poignant scrutiny of the future in order to get a greater return for the next year.[36]

Though the occasion hardly seemed to call for it, we find the Justice several years later restating this thesis in almost identical language: "We are apt to think of ownership as a terminus, not as a gateway, and not to realize that except the tax levied for personal consumption large ownership means investment, and investment means the direction of labor towards the production of the greatest returns—returns that so far as they are great show by that very fact that they are consumed by the many, not alone by the few." [37]

In retrospect, Holmes' views about the nature of economic power are all the more astounding when it is recalled that he was holding to them so tenaciously during the years which were witnessing an ever-growing concentration of ownership and control. Believing that "every social improvement is immediately absorbed by an increase in the population," [38] he simply doubted the possibility of bettering society "by tinkering with the institution of property." [39] The son of New England's intellectual aristocracy, though occasionally disconcerted by the social crudeness and money-grabbing proclivities of America's new capitalists, nevertheless assumed that their success flowed from superior qualities as proved in the "competition of the market." He greatly admired the men a later generation was to dub "the robber barons" and attributed to them a creative social contribution not unlike the role of the architect in building a house: "It is obvious that the intelligence of an architect contributes more to the change of form which takes place in a house than that of all the laboring hands." [40]

[36] Holmes, *Collected Legal Papers*, pp. 279–80.
[37] *Ibid.*, p. 293.
[38] *Holmes-Laski Letters*, I, 165.
[39] Holmes, *op. cit.*, p. 306.
[40] *Ibid.*, p. 281. See also *Holmes-Pollock Letters*, I, 166–67.

Such, then, were some of the more important "ultimate economic conceptions" of the man who, as a judge, was destined to come to be regarded by millions of Americans as a partisan of social reform —"a flaming champion of the common man." [41]

[41] Charles E. Clark, "Case Study of a Liberal," 6 *Saturday Review of Literature 581* (Dec. 21, 1929).

3

"They need something of Mephistopheles"

At the time Mr. Justice Holmes began his service on the Supreme Court, it was already quite clear that the dominant issue in American constitutional law was the relation of government to business. American capitalism had brought forth conditions and problems which increasingly were becoming the direct concern of government. While the phenomenal advances in transportation, communication and mass production were revolutionizing the life of the people, the economic and social consequences of this development were also having their effect on our legal institutions. The rising tide of economic concentration, the relations between capital and labor, the attempts to protect the consumer through utility regulation, the need to pay for the new costs of government by socially minded uses of the taxing power—these were becoming the chief sources of litigation before the Supreme Court.

In his response to the new issues, Justice Holmes revealed himself to be strikingly aloof from the battles which saw most of his fellow judges taking sides along with most other citizens. "I cannot but believe," he had said in 1897, "that if the training of lawyers led them habitually to consider more definitely and explicitly the social advantage on which the rule they lay down must be justified, they sometimes would hesitate where now they are confident, and see that really they were taking sides upon debatable and often burning questions."[1] In his very first opinion as a member of the Supreme Court,[2] delivered in a case which was argued only three days after he took his place, he made it plain that he would assign a very limited role to the judiciary. The detachment he advocated ripened in time into a virtual school of jurisprudence, at least in the realm of constitutional interpretation.

Though speaking for the majority, Holmes set forth in his opinion in Otis v. Parker ideas which he was forced later to express in dissent. His opinion sustained the validity of a section of the California constitution prohibiting contracts for the sale of mining stock on margin. The principal objection to the provision in question was the argument which had already become monotonously familiar in the legal assault on all protective legislation emanating from the states—that it unduly restricted liberty and property in violation of the Fourteenth Amendment of the Federal Constitution. Conceding that the states were not free to interfere arbitrarily with "private business or transactions," he cautioned judges against the temptation to decide cases on the basis of their own general economic or ethical views. Courts must take into account local experience and even feelings; "a deep-seated conviction on the part of the people concerned" as to what should be done was "entitled to great respect." One paragraph in particular contained the clue to much that was to come from Holmes later with growing sharpness:

It is true, no doubt, that neither a state legislature nor a state constitution can interfere arbitrarily with private business or transactions, and that the mere fact that an enactment purports to be for the protection of public safety, health or morals, is not conclusive upon the courts. . . . But general propositions do not carry us far. While the courts must exercise a judgment of their own, it by no means is true that every law is void which may seem to the judges who pass upon it excessive, unsuited to its ostensible end, or based upon conceptions of morality with which

[1] Holmes, "The Path of the Law," in *Collected Legal Papers*, p. 184.
[2] Otis v. Parker, 187 U.S. 606 (1903).

they disagree. Considerable latitude must be allowed for differences of view as well as for possible peculiar conditions which this court can know but imperfectly, if at all. Otherwise a constitution, instead of embodying only relatively fundamental rules of right, as generally understood by all English-speaking communities, would become the partisan of a particular set of ethical or economical opinions, which by no means are held *semper ubique et ab omnibus.*[3]

To be sure, Otis v. Parker did not concern any of the really controversial manifestations of governmental action in the field of economic or social melioration. But Holmes' opinion presaged the stand he was to take in the more bitterly contested cases. In retrospect, it may be seen as the epitome of the attitude he was to exhibit toward the chief constitutional struggle into which the Court was more and more being drawn—the conflict between the Fourteenth Amendment and the police power of the States. "On both these two basic problems of constitutional law—the power of the States and the power of the Nation," Felix Frankfurter concluded in 1916, "Mr. Justice Holmes's influence has been steady and consistent and growing. His opinions form a coherent body of constitutional law, and their effect upon the development of the law is the outstanding characteristic of constitutional history in the last decade." [4]

Stripped of their legal technicalities, Justice Holmes' police power opinions merge into a significant contribution to the discussion of what is perhaps the deepest and most complex issue for a free society —the relation between public welfare and individual and group rights. In no other branch of constitutional law were the fundamental issues implicit in social control revealed more dramatically than in the numerous due process cases. They mirrored all the deeper influences which were shaping the judicial response to the profound economic and social changes taking place in America in the late nineteenth and early twentieth centuries.

[3] *Ibid.,* at 608–09.
[4] Frankfurter, "The Constitutional Opinions of Mr. Justice Holmes," 29 *Harv. L. Rev. 683, 684.*

II

All too often lawyers and judges were invoking old and outmoded conceptions of individual rights and social needs when dealing with the stern realities of modern industrialism. Thus, at the very moment when powerful economic forces were rendering the individual less and less able to help himself, a robust philosophy of individualism was holding sway over the minds of those who were determining the course of the legal and constitutional accommodations necessitated by the new situation. This curious paradox was once graphically portrayed by Roscoe Pound with the aid of a few telling questions:

Why, then, do courts persist in the fallacy? Why do so many of them force upon legislation an academic theory of equality in the face of practical conditions of inequality? Why do we find a great and learned court in 1908 taking the long step into the past of dealing with the relation between employer and employee in railway transportation, as if the parties were individuals—as if they were farmers haggling over the sale of a horse? Why is the legal conception of the relation of employer and employee so at variance with the common knowledge of mankind? [5]

Seeking to discover the deeper causes of this condition of the law, Pound found them lurking chiefly in English political and legal thinking.[6] And turning to the American scene, he listed first among

[5] Pound, "Liberty of Contract," *18 Yale L. J. 454* (1909); reprinted in *2 Selected Essays on Constitutional Law 208, 209* (1938).

[6] Pound's historical summary will bear quoting: "It [the idea of unlimited freedom of making contracts] began as a doctrine of political economy, as a phase of Adam Smith's doctrine which we commonly call laissez-faire. It was propounded as a utilitarian principle of politics and legislation by Mill. Spencer deduced it from his formula of justice. In this way it became a chief article in the creed of those who sought to minimize the functions of the state, that the most important of its functions was to enforce by law the obligations created by contract. But we must remember that the task of the English individualists was to abolish a body of antiquated institutions that stood in the way of human progress. Freedom of contract was the best instrument at hand for the purpose. They adopted it as a means, made it an end. While this evolution in juristic and political thought was in progress, the common law too had become thoroughly individualistic." *Ibid.*, pp. 210–11.

the factors to which he attributed the apotheosis of the doctrine of liberty of contract, "The currency in juristic thought of an individualistic conception of justice, which exaggerates the importance of property and of contract, exaggerates private right at the expense of public right, and is hostile to legislation, taking a minimum of law-making to be the ideal." [7]

The "great and learned court" to which Pound alluded was, of course, the Supreme Court of the United States, which shared responsibility for the anomaly. The self-restraint urged by Justice Miller when the Fourteenth Amendment was before the Tribunal for the first time—the importance of keeping the Court from becoming "a perpetual censor upon all legislation of the States" [8]—was in time completely disregarded. "The Court in its early fear for the federal balance," Edward S. Corwin has written, "denied the Fourteenth Amendment practically all efficacy as a limitation upon State power, save in the interest of racial equality before the law. Subsequently, however, the Court found reason to abandon its early conservative position and in the interest of private and particularly of property rights to take a greatly enlarged view of its supervisory powers over State legislation. . . . The history of this change is the history particularly of the development of the phrase 'due process of law.'" [9]

The shift in the interpretation of due process of law—from what Professor Corwin has called a concept "having to do with the enforcement of law" to a test of its "making" or substance—was greatly facilitated, in the view of another scholar, by the addition of five new justices between 1875–85. "When Mr. Justice Miller died in 1890 he left behind him on the bench but one colleague who had sat with him in the *Slaughter House Cases*, and that colleague, Mr. Justice Field, had from the outset been an outspoken and dogmatic apostle of the new faith." [10] But the more basic ex-

[7] *Ibid.*, p. 211.
[8] The *Slaughter-House Cases*, 16 Wall. 36, at 78 (1873).
[9] Corwin, "The Supreme Court and the Fourteenth Amendment," 7 *Mich. L. Rev. 643*, 672 (1909).
[10] Robert E. Cushman, "The Social and Economic Interpretation of the Fourteenth Amendment," 20 *Mich. L. Rev. 737*, 742 (1922).

planation for the failure of Justice Miller's injunction against judicial censorship of legislation and for the eventual triumph of Justice Field's conception of due process must be sought elsewhere:

When that Amendment [the Fourteenth] first came before the Supreme Court in the *Slaughter-House Cases,* four dissenting Justices, under the lead of Mr. Justice Field, sought to encrust upon the undefined language of the due process clause the eighteenth century "law of nature" doctrines. As the new protection of the Fourteenth Amendment was persistently invoked by counsel against the growing efforts of the states to regulate economic enterprise, the rejected dissents of Mr. Justice Field gradually established themselves as the views of the Court.[11]

Not too many years were to elapse before the emergence of due process as a source of limitation upon the substance of legislation was to furnish the Supreme Court with a potent weapon for controlling public policy, particularly in the economic field. Liberty of contract, though nowhere to be found in the Constitution itself, became the most pervasive of the abstractions in the arsenal of judicially developed criteria for testing the constitutionality of legislation. And when corporations came to be treated as "persons" within the meaning of the constitutional guarantees whose historic purpose was the protection of the rights of individuals, the resulting jurisprudence greatly enhanced the power of the courts. This was so because American business was more and more coming to be conducted in corporate form. Inevitably, therefore, momentous questions of governmental policy came to be weighed in judicial scales and in an atmosphere dominated by theoretical considerations and syllogistic reasoning.

III

Part of Mr. Justice Holmes' service to constitutional law was to rescue it from the unreal world of absolute concepts. No one was more aware of the tentative and experimental character of public policies or of the conflict of private interests out of which govern-

[11] Frankfurter (ed.), *Mr. Justice Holmes*, pp. 77–78.

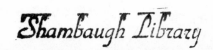

mental action grows. To him we are indebted for a definition of the police power which is one of the most sweeping ever to have been enunciated by the Court, a definition which was to be characterized by Harold J. Laski two decades later as "the modern charter of the federal state." [12] Laski was recalling the decision in Noble State Bank v. Haskell,[13] in which the Court by unanimous vote held valid a law passed by Oklahoma following the Panic of 1907 which required all banks to contribute to a fund intended to guarantee bank deposits.

In determining whether or not state legislation deprived anyone of liberty or property without due process of law, Holmes maintained, judges must be careful not to push the broad language of the Fourteenth Amendment "to a drily logical extreme." Because all laws restrict liberty or property to some degree and because there were "few scientifically certain criteria of legislation," they should not stand in the way of changes deemed necessary by legislatures: "Judges should be slow to read into the latter [the Constitution] a *nolumus mutare* as against the law-making power." [14]

Difficult though it was to fix the limits of the police power, the least that could be said was that it "extends to all great public needs." "It may be put forth," Holmes added, "in aid of what is sanctioned by usage, or held by the prevailing morality or strong or preponderant opinion to be greatly and immediately necessary to the public welfare." And in his opinion denying the petition for a rehearing is to be found this observation: "We fully understand . . . the very powerful argument against the wisdom of the legislation, but on that point we have nothing to say, as it is not our concern." [15] He insisted that his analysis of the police power "was intended to indicate an interpretation of what has taken place in the past, not to give a new or wider scope to the power."

As a description of the general drift of judicial exposition this

[12] *Ibid.*, p. 144.
[13] 219 U.S. 104 (1911).
[14] *Ibid.*, at 110.
[15] 219 U.S. 575 (1911).

claim was accurate enough, even if it glossed over the cases in which the Court had resorted to rather narrow views of the police power. Yet it was the Court's more extreme interpretations which had stirred Holmes to some of his most pungent protests against the abuse of judicial power and which were giving him his reputation as a "liberal." The most celebrated of these protests in the early period was doubtless his dissenting opinion in Lochner v. New York.[16]

This is the case in which by a bare majority of five to four the Supreme Court set aside a New York law which had provided that bakery workers were not to labor for more than ten hours a day or sixty hours a week. Justice Peckham's opinion for the majority certainly demonstrates that the courts were not unconcerned with the wisdom of legislation. The opposite was often the case, as an observer of the contemporary scene boldly stated:

Despite disavowal that the policy of legislation is not the courts' concern, there is an unmistakable dread of the class of legislation under discussion. Intense feeling against the policy of the legislation must inevitably have influenced the result in the decisions. In truth this presents the point of greatest stress in our constitutional system, for it requires minds of unusual intellectual disinterestedness, detachment, and imagination to escape from the too easy tendency to find lack of power where one is convinced of lack of wisdom.[17]

The debate in the Lochner case—between Justice Peckham and the dissenters, Holmes, Harlan, White and Day—continues to serve as a most instructive lesson in the intellectual tug of war which the police power cases were bringing to the fore. In pointing up the possibility that the different notions as to the "liberty" guaranteed by the Constitution were the fundamental cause of division in the Court, it enhanced our understanding of the real roots of judicial decisions. "Statutes of the nature of that under review, limiting the hours in which grown and intelligent men may labor to earn their

[16] 198 U.S. 45, 65, 74 (1905).
[17] Frankfurter, "Hours of Labor and Realism in Constitutional Law," 29 *Harv. L. Rev.* 353 (1916); reprinted in 2 *Selected Essays 699*, 707.

living," Peckham proclaimed, "are mere meddlesome interferences with the rights of the individual." [18] A similar note of defiance—a virtual declaration of war upon the prevailing legislative mood— was sounded two years later by the New York Court of Appeals when it struck down a law forbidding women to work in factories at night: "The tendency of legislatures, in the form of regulatory measures, to interfere with the lawful pursuit of citizens, is becoming a marked one in this country, and it behooves the courts, firmly and fearlessly, to interpose the barriers of their judgments, when invoked to protest against legislative acts plainly transcending the powers conferred by the Constitution upon the legislative body." [19]

The *Lochner* case has all the elements which characterized the course of constitutional decisions on liberty of contract. On the one hand, it may be seen as the culmination of that doctrinaire interpretation of due process which was turning the United States Constitution into a bulwark for laissez-faire. From this standpoint, Justice Peckham's definition of the liberty guaranteed by the Fourteenth Amendment, a statement he had formulated some years earlier, pretty much disposed of the case:

The liberty mentioned in that Amendment means not only the right of the citizen to be free from the mere physical restraint of his person, as by incarceration; but the term is deemed to embrace the right of the citizen to be free in the enjoyment of all his faculties; to be free to use them in all lawful ways; to live and work where he will; to earn his livelihood by any lawful calling; to pursue any livelihood or avocation, and for that purpose to enter into all contracts which may be proper, necessary and essential to his carrying out to a successful conclusion the purposes above mentioned.[20]

But on the other hand, the decision was wholly inconsistent with the attitude exhibited by the Court in Holden v. Hardy,[21] a case decided only seven years before and which sustained a Utah statute establishing an eight-hour day for mine workers. One sentence from Jus-

[18] 198 U.S. 45, at 61.
[19] People v. Williams, *189 N.Y. 131, 135* (1907).
[20] Peckham was quoting from his own opinion for the Court in Allgeyer v. Louisiana, 165 U.S. 578, at 598 (1897).
[21] 169 U.S. 366 (1898).

tice Brown's opinion will suffice: "These employments, when too
long pursued, the legislature has judged to be detrimental to the
health of the employes, and, so long as there are reasonable grounds
for believing that this is so, its decision upon this subject cannot be
reviewed by the Federal courts." [22] In the light of the outcome in
Holden v. Hardy, Roscoe Pound was entirely justified in saying that
the *Lochner* decision was "reactionary" even for its day.[23]

Since the *Lochner* case was also concerned with a law intended
to protect the health of employees by limiting their hours of labor,
how can one explain the Court's failure to adhere to the logic of its
decision in Holden v. Hardy? A technically correct answer might be
that the majority concluded that bakers had a constitutional right
to contract to work for as long as they pleased. But the Court's
dilemma stemmed from the fact that its decisions recognized the
right of the States to restrict the individual's freedom of contract in
the interest of the public. What, then, were the Court's reasons for
refusing to treat the ten-hour law as either a health law or one
intended to safeguard the public? Justice Peckham addressed himself to both issues:

There is no contention that bakers as a class are not equal in intelligence
and capacity to men in other trades or manual occupations, or that they
are not able to assert their rights and care for themselves without the
protecting arm of the State, interfering with their independence of judgment and of action. They are in no sense wards of the State. Viewed in
the light of a purely labor law, with no reference whatever to the question
of health, we think that a law like the one before us involves neither the
safety, the morals nor the welfare of the public, and that the interest of
the public is not in the slightest degree affected by such an act. The law
must be upheld, if at all, as a law pertaining to the health of the individual engaged in the occupation of a baker. It does not affect any other
portion of the public than those who are engaged in that occupation.
Clean and wholesome bread does not depend upon whether the baker
works but ten hours per day or only sixty hours a week.[24]

Peckham went further. He did not content himself with the mere

[22] *Ibid.*, at 395.
[23] Pound, *op. cit.*, 2 *Selected Essays 208, 230.*
[24] 198 U.S. 45, at 57.

assertion that bakery employees were quite capable of protecting themselves without the help of government—an assertion which could have been dismissed as one more manifestation of sterile individualism. Much more serious, because of its implications for the technique of defending the validity of protective legislation, was his insistence that there was no relation between the health of bakers and the number of hours they worked. Turning medical expert, Peckham stated that "We think that there can be no fair doubt that the trade of the baker, in and of itself, is not an unhealthy one to that degree which would authorize the legislature to interfere with the right to labor and with the right of free contract on the part of the individual, either as employer or employee, . . . To the common understanding, the trade of a baker has never been regarded as an unhealthy one." [25]

In attenuation of judicial opinions such as Peckham's, it has sometimes been said that in those days counsel failed to acquaint courts with the social facts underlying regulatory measures. No such charitable explanation can be offered for the result in the *Lochner* case. All one need do is to read Justice Harlan's painstaking dissent to realize that the Supreme Court did have before it highly persuasive evidence establishing the need for the legislation. Harlan relied heavily on a report by the New York Bureau of Labor Statistics and other scientific publications pointing to the low resistance and short life of bakers and showing that they suffered from sore eyes and from chronic inflammation of the lungs and bronchial tubes. He ended his factual refutation with a vigorous attack upon the majority's abuse of their power:

I take leave to say that the New York statute, in the particulars here involved, cannot be held to be in conflict with the Fourteenth Amendment, without enlarging the scope of the Amendment far beyond its original purpose and without bringing under the supervision of this court matters which have been supposed to belong exclusively to the legislative departments of the several States when exerting their conceded power to guard the health and safety of their citizens by such regulations as they

[25] *Ibid.,* at 59.

in their wisdom deem best. . . . A decision that the New York statute is void under the Fourteenth Amendment will, in my opinion, involve consequences of a far-reaching and mischievous character; for such a decision would seriously cripple the inherent power of the States to care for the lives, health and well-being of their citizens. Those are matters which can be best controlled by the States. The preservation of the just powers of the States is quite as vital as the preservation of the powers of the General Government.[26]

IV

Because of its eloquence and its insight into the deeper philosophic issue, Holmes' dissent has proved to be the more memorable one. Described by Roscoe Pound shortly after its delivery as the "best exposition" of sociological jurisprudence, it soon vindicated his judgment that it deserved to become "classical." [27] The dissent will bear quoting even at this late date:

This case is decided upon an economic theory which a large part of the country does not entertain. If it were a question whether I agreed with that theory, I should desire to study it further and long before making up my mind. But I do not conceive that to be my duty, because I strongly believe that my agreement or disagreement has nothing to do with the right of a majority to embody their opinions in law. . . . The liberty of the citizen to do as he likes so long as he does not interfere with the liberty of others to do the same, which has been the shibboleth for some well-known writers, is interfered with by school laws, by the Post Office, by every state or municipal institution which takes his money for purposes thought desirable, whether he likes it or not. The Fourteenth Amendment does not enact Mr. Herbert Spencer's Social Statics. . . . Some of these laws embody convictions or prejudices which judges are likely to share. Some may not. But a constitution is not intended to embody a particular economic theory, whether of paternalism and the organic relation of the citizen to the State or of *laissez-faire*. It is made for people of fundamentally different views, and the accident of our finding certain opinions natural and familiar or novel and even shocking ought not to conclude our judgment upon the question whether statutes embodying them conflict with the Constitution of the United States.

[26] *Ibid.*, at 73–74.
[27] Pound, *op. cit.*, in 2 *Selected Essays 208, 231.*

General propositions do not decide concrete cases. The decision will depend on a judgment or intuition more subtle than any articulate major premise. . . . I think that the word liberty in the Fourteenth Amendment is perverted when it is held to prevent the natural outcome of a dominent opinion, unless it be said that a rational and fair man necessarily would admit that the statute proposed would infringe fundamental principles as they have been understood by the traditions of our people and our law. It does not need research to show that no such sweeping condemnation can be passed upon the statute before us. A reasonable man might think it a proper measure on the score of health. Men whom I certainly could not pronounce unreasonable would uphold it as a first installment of a general regulation of the hours of work.[28]

These sentences have become so familiar that the view they advance has escaped critical analysis. Perhaps the most serious distortion is the use of the *Lochner* dissent as proof of Holmes' humanitarianism. The seeds may have been sown by Pound himself. In his now famous article on liberty of contract he had written:

Jurisprudence is the last in the march of the sciences away from the method of deduction from predetermined conceptions. The sociological movement in jurisprudence, the movement for pragmatism as a philosophy of law, the movement for the adjustment of principles and doctrines to the human conditions they are to govern rather than to assumed first principles, the movement for putting the human factor in the central place and relegating logic to its true position as an instrument, has scarcely shown itself yet in America. Perhaps the dissenting opinion of Mr. Justice Holmes in Lochner v. New York is the best exposition of it we have.[29]

Yet one will search in vain for any display of humanitarian passion in the *Lochner* dissent. Indeed, there was no reason for Holmes to file a separate opinion if he were merely interested in showing the need for the health law; Harlan had done that. Holmes seems to have been driven to dissent because he felt that his brethren were not paying sufficient heed to what he regarded as the essence of constitutional interpretation—the limited range of judicial power

[28] 198 U.S. 45, 74, at 75–76.
[29] Pound, in 2 *Selected Essays 208, 217.*

and the spaciousness of the Constitution, "the great theme of his judicial life," as Felix Frankfurter once phrased it.[30] In laying bare the real roots of judicial decisions, Holmes was furnishing the critics of judicial reaction with powerful intellectual weapons. As Professor Corwin wrote in 1909, comparing the Harlan and Holmes dissents in the *Lochner* case, "Justice Holmes' dissent is still more trenchant, cutting as it does through the momentary question of policy to the deeper, though inarticulate, major premise underlying all preference for or against the political will when it appears arrayed against private rights." [31] It is to be noted, however, that Holmes himself was not at all critical of the view of due process which made it possible for judges to read their economic preferences into the Constitution. It was left for Professor Corwin to put this criticism most bluntly:

. . . he [Holmes] accepts in toto the present day view of due process of law. Moreover his "rational and fair man" without a social philosophy of some kind and, equally, his Constitution devoid of preconceptions are the veriest fictions. And certainly it was ungracious on Justice Holmes' part to imply a lack of rationality on the part of his majority brethren. The truth is that, the moment the Court, in its interpretation of the Fourteenth Amendment, left behind the definite, historical concept of "due process of law" as having to do with the *enforcement* of law and not its *making*, the moment it abandoned, in its attempt to delimit the police power of the State, its ancient maxim that the possibility that a power may be abused has nothing to do with its existence, that moment it committed itself to a course that was bound to lead, however gradually and easily, beyond the precincts of judicial power, in the sense of the power to ascertain the law, into that of legislative power, which determines policies on the basis of facts and desires. Moreover, and this is another point at which Justice Holmes seems to blink the truth, the feeling instigating the first step was the same as that which prompted the last, viz.: a fear of popular majorities, which fear, however, lies at the very basis of the whole system of judicial review, and indeed of our entire constitutional system.[32]

At no time did Holmes challenge the conception of due process which enabled courts to pass upon the policies embodied in legisla-

[30] Frankfurter, *Mr. Justice Holmes and the Supreme Court,* p. 50.
[31] Corwin, *op. cit.,* p. 669.
[32] *Ibid.,* p. 670.

tion. His psychological analysis was not altogether free from self-contradiction. For if it were true that the ultimate source of a judicial decision may be "a judgement or intuition more subtle than any articulate major premise," did it not follow that avowed constitutional doctrines or "propositions" were serving merely as rationalizations for unexpressed economic or social preferences? Since Holmes was criticizing his colleagues for wantonly reading laissez-faire into the Constitution, his conclusion should have been that "general propositions" do indeed "decide concrete cases." Henry Steele Commager is certainly justified in reminding us that at the time Holmes observed that "the Fourteenth Amendment does not enact Herbert Spencer's Social Statics," the Justice "was obviously wrong." [33] The ironic fact is that Peckham, too, thought he was guiding himself by the test of reasonableness:

In every case that comes before this court, . . . where legislation of this character is concerned and where the protection of the Federal Constitution is sought, the question necessarily arises: Is this a fair, reasonable and appropriate exercise of the police power of the State, or is it an unreasonable, unnecessary and arbitrary interference with the right of the individual to his personal liberty or to enter into those contracts in relation to labor which may seem to him appropriate or necessary for the support of himself and his family? [34]

Strictly speaking, therefore, what separated Holmes from the majority in the Lochner case was a matter of degree, a difference of view as to whether the New York legislature was justified in curtailing freedom of action in the circumstances disclosed by the case. Moreover, since Holmes saw no need for research to establish the reasonableness of the New York law, his dissent may fairly be described as altogether lacking in constructive criticism. In a fundamental sense, it was no more than a moral preachment, an earnest plea for judicial self-restraint. Holmes was asking his fellow judges to curb their predilections and fears, lest they confuse a necessary

[33] Commager, The American Mind (New Haven: Yale Univ. Press, 1950), p. 373.
[34] 198 U.S. 45, at 56.

social adjustment with a basic attack on the society in which they believed. He was perhaps tempted to add what he actually allowed himself to say not too many years later: "Judges are apt to be naif, simple-minded men, and they need something of Mephistopheles. We too need education in the obvious—to learn to transcend our own convictions and to leave room for much that we hold dear to be done away with short of revolution by the orderly change of law." [35]

While Holmes was not exactly a lone voice, he may have helped to stem the tide of judicial reaction, even if only temporarily. For the fact is that his dissents served to dramatize the extent to which the laws being annulled by the Court could be squared with the Constitution and sound reasoning. Actually, as Roscoe Pound has pointed out, "After 1900, the pendulum had clearly begun to swing the other way." [36] Still, it is possible to exaggerate the "reactionary" course of Supreme Court decisions during the first decade of the present century.

Alarmed by the growing agitation for judicial reform which was part of the Progressive ferment, one student of the Supreme Court set about to correct the impression that the Court was blocking social legislation. "The reformers who claim that the Court stands as an obstacle to 'social justice' legislation," Charles Warren wrote in 1913, "if asked to specify where they find the evil of which they complain and for which they propose radical remedies, always take refuge in the single case of *Lochner v. New York, . . .* Yet a single case does not necessarily prove the existence of an evil." [37]

It was true, of course, that the cases in which state laws were held invalid under the Fourteenth Amendment were not as numerous as some supposed. But the "evil" of which the *Lochner* decision became a symbol cannot be understood or measured by mere statistics; exceptions are sometimes more revealing than the general rule. The

[35] Holmes, "Law and the Court," (1913), in *Collected Legal Papers,* p. 295.
[36] Pound, in *2 Selected Essays 208, 229.*
[37] Warren, "The Progressiveness of the United States Supreme Court," *13 Col. L. Rev. 294* (1913). See also his "A Bulwark to the State Police Power—The United States Supreme Court," *13 Col. L. Rev. 667* (1913).

spectacle of the country's highest tribunal losing all sense of reality about a vital human and social problem was bound to hurt the Court's standing with the public. If the resulting dissatisfaction damaged the Court as an institution, one may borrow the language of Charles Evans Hughes and say that the wound was "self-inflicted." [38]

[38] Hughes, *The Supreme Court of the United States* (Long Island: Garden City Publishing Co., 1936), p. 50.

4

"The pulse of the machine"

I

"It is not far from the mark," one of Holmes' law secretaries has written, "to conclude that his thinking in the field of economics stopped at twenty-five." [1] If this is a fair and accurate estimate, it obviously would be a grave indictment of a judge generally hailed for his learning and sagacity. But even if it were only an exaggeration suggestive of the basic truth, it would merit careful exploration.

Holmes' alleged failure to grow in economic understanding is all the more serious when one thinks of the revolutionary transformations that had taken place in the structure of the American economy between the time he completed his formal education at Harvard and the time he began sitting in judgment on the issues precipitated by these changes. Whether his views about the economic foundations of American society were unaffected by post-Civil-War events is thus a question of the profoundest importance. Is it true that he was "curiously uncritical," in Mr. Biddle's words, "about the orthodox economic axioms on which he was brought up?" [2]

However much Holmes may have shared Adam Smith's faith in the benign influence of the untrammelled economic order, his

[1] Francis Biddle, *Mr. Justice Holmes* (New York: Charles Scribner's Sons, 1942), pp. 86–87.
[2] *Ibid.*, p. 88.

view of the play of economic forces was hardly naive. For him there were two great truths about the economic world. One was that the economic order was marked by conflict of interests and the other that it worked more or less automatically to the advantage of society as a whole. Charles A. Beard might well have included Holmes among the leaders of American thought who appreciated "the economic basis of politics." [3] For in his view of the sources of modern legislation Holmes merely echoed Madison's classic statement in the tenth number of the *Federalist*:

Those who hold and those who are without property have ever formed distinct interests in society. Those who are creditors, and those who are debtors, fall under a like discrimination. A landed interest, a manufacturing interest, a mercantile interest, a moneyed interest, with many lesser interests, grow up of necessity in civilized nations, and divide them into different classes, actuated by different sentiments and views. The regulation of these various and interfering interests forms the principal task of modern legislation, and involves the spirit of party and faction in the necessary and ordinary operations of government. [4]

Compare this language with the following passage from Holmes' famous article on "The Gas-Stokers' Strike," which appeared in 1873:

This tacit assumption of the solidarity of the interests of society is very common, but seems to us to be false . . . in the last resort a man rightly prefers his own interest to that of his neighbors. And this is as true in legislation as in any other form of corporate action. All that can be expected from modern improvements is that legislation should easily and quickly, yet not too quickly, modify itself in accordance with the will of the *de facto* supreme power in the community, and that the spread of an educated sympathy should reduce the sacrifice of minorities to a minimum. [5]

Because Holmes believed that struggle and competition were the sources of social strength and progress, he continued to regard conflict as inevitable and efforts to modify the basic organization of

[3] *The Economic Basis of Politics* is the title of a little volume Beard wrote in 1934. (New York: Alfred A. Knopf.)

[4] *The Federalist* (New York: The Heritage Press, 1945), p. 57.

[5] *VII Amer. L. Rev. 582, 583 (1873).*

society as futile. Hence the contradictory qualities of dogmatism and
tolerance in his approach to economic problems. The author of the
famous generalization that "to have doubted one's own first principles is the mark of a civilized man" [6] suffered from few doubts
concerning the virtues of American capitalism, which he seems to
have equated with freedom of competition. "The name of Holmes'
economic God," Louis B. Boudin has written, "was not property,—
which is reactionary, because static and concerned with vested interests, that is, perpetuation of the past. It was Competition,—an
evolutionary God, slow but progressive, who keeps a steady forward
course by constant adjustment to changing conditions." [7]

So confident was Holmes that in the long run the economic
process would operate for the good of all, that he often failed to
reckon with the impact of the forces which were destroying the very
equilibrium in which he believed. "I don't read the papers or otherwise feel the pulse of the machine," he confessed to Pollock in 1906.
"I agree," he added, "that there are great wastes in competition, due
to advertisement, superfluous reduplication of establishments, etc.
But those are the very things the trusts could get rid of." [8]

Thus, at the very time when leading spokesmen for political progressivism were almost obsessed with the threat to American
democracy stemming from the growth of trusts and monopolies,
Holmes was quite unconcerned with the new phenomenon. There
is nothing among his utterances to compare even remotely with
Henry Demarest Lloyd's declaration that "Liberty and monopoly
cannot live together";[9] or Brandeis' query whether in the long run
political democracy and industrial absolutism "can co-exist in the
same community";[10] or Woodrow Wilson's nostalgic regret that

[6] Holmes, "Ideals and Doubts," in *Collected Legal Papers*, p. 307.
[7] Boudin, "Justice Holmes and his World," *Lawyers Guild Rev.* vol. III, #4,
p. 24, 37 (1943).
[8] *Holmes-Pollock Letters*, I, 124.
[9] Lloyd, *Wealth Against Commonwealth* (New York: Harper & Brothers,
1894), p. 519.
[10] Brandeis, *Business—A Profession* (Boston: Hale, Cushman & Flint, 1933),
p. 342.

"American industry is not free, as it once was free" or his further
assertion that "Monopoly means the atrophy of enterprise." [11]

Holmes felt that it was futile to resist the trend of the times
toward business organization, which he saw as an unavoidable by-
product of competition. The "ever-increasing might and scope of
combination" which was leading to the "organization of the world"
was but part of the "struggle for life." All of this he made quite
clear before coming to Washington. In the *Vegelahn* case Holmes
supported the right of workingmen to combine to defend themselves
in their struggle with employers, and for this reason his opinion is
sometimes cited as proof of his liberal or pro-labor attitude. However, not all of Holmes' admirers have appreciated the curious fact
which at least one of them has pointed out with much acuteness.
Speaking of the "liberal strain" in the *Vegelahn* dissent, Max Lerner
has noted that precisely the same basic economic ideas led him to
write the "pro-monopoly" dissent in the *Northern Securities* case.[12]
"For Holmes saw, as did few others, that 'free competition' in the
economic system actually meant having freedom for combination in
order to have a competitive chance." [13]

II

Looking back to the effect of his dissent on the man who had but
recently put him on the Court, Holmes always believed that it broke
up his "incipient friendship" with Theodore Roosevelt who, he
thought, viewed the dissent "as a political departure (or, I suspect
more truly, couldn't forgive anyone who stood in his way)." [14]
Roosevelt's disappointment is quite understandable. "The Northern
Securities suit is one of the great achievements of my administration," he boasted to his campaign manager in 1904, adding, "I look

[11] Wilson, *The New Freedom* (New York: Doubleday, Page & Company,
1913), pp. 15, 286.
[12] Northern Securities Co. v. United States, 193 U.S. 197, 364, 400 (1904).
[13] Lerner, *The Mind and Faith of Justice Holmes*, p. 110.
[14] *Holmes-Pollock Letters*, II, 63–64.

back upon it with great pride, for through it we emphasized in signal fashion, as in no other way could be emphasized the fact that the most powerful men in this country were held to accountability before the law." [15] Holmes voted with Chief Justice Fuller and Justices White and Peckham in denying the right of the Government to dissolve the Northern Securities Company, and had Justice Brewer—who was known also to be opposed to the Rooseveltian trust policies—joined them, the most spectacular of Roosevelt's "trust-busting" projects would have been frustrated.

The Northern Securities Company had been organized by J. P. Morgan and James J. Hill for the purpose of securing control of the Great Northern and Northern Pacific railroads, two roads which had hitherto been competitors. At Roosevelt's direction, Attorney General Knox instituted a suit asking the courts to dissolve this holding company as a monopoly in restraint of trade, alleging that it had been formed in violation of the Sherman Anti-Trust Act.[16] The Company's lawyers relied in the main on the Supreme Court's decision in United States v. E. C. Knight Co.[17]—the famous *Sugar Trust* case of 1895—in which the Sherman Act was held not to apply to business combinations organized for the purpose of monopolizing production—a conclusion which led Justice Harlan, the lone dissenter in the case, to charge that "While the opinion of the Court in this case does not declare the act of 1890 to be unconstitutional, it defeats the main object for which it was passed." [18] Conceding that the offending concern had acquired "nearly complete control of the manufacture of refined sugar in the United States"—98 per cent, to

[15] *Letters of Theodore Roosevelt*, IV, 886.

[16] Section 1 of the Sherman Act of 1890 reads as follows: "Every contract, combination in the form of trust or otherwise, or conspiracy, in restraint of trade or commerce among the several States, or with foreign nations, is hereby declared illegal. Every person who shall make any such contract or engage in any such combination or conspiracy, shall be deemed guilty of a misdemeanor, and, on conviction thereof, shall be punished by fine not exceeding five thousand dollars, or by imprisonment not exceeding one year, or by both said punishments, in the discretion of the court."

[17] 156 U.S. 1, 18 (1895).

[18] *Ibid.*, at 42.

be exact—the Court nevertheless had ruled that the Sherman Act did not cover the transaction. This was so because its object was "private gain in the manufacture of the commodity" and manufacturing was a purely local process.

To be sure, the Hill-Morgan combine involved in the *Northern Securities* case had nothing to do with manufacturing. However, its legal defenders found the ruling in the *Sugar Trust* case both relevant and useful in support of their contention that the Sherman Act did not reach all restraints of trade. Their principal argument was that the Northern Securities Company had come into being as the result of a stock transaction, not in itself commerce, and that Congress had no power to prohibit corporations chartered by a state from acquiring and disposing of shares.

This time speaking for a majority of the Court, Justice Harlan wrote a sweeping opinion in the *Northern Securities* case, sustaining the Justice Department's claim that the Company had been formed in violation of the Sherman Act. Pointing out that Congress had adopted a national policy of free competition, the wisdom or propriety of which was not for the Court to weigh, he held that the Sherman law prohibited all contracts, combinations or conspiracies in restraint of trade, which "directly or necessarily" operated to restrain interstate commerce. "Whether the free operation of the normal laws of competition is a wise and wholesome rule for trade and commerce is an economic question which this Court need not consider or determine." Harlan accused the country's monopolies of seeking "shelter behind the reserved rights of the States and even behind the constitutional guaranty of liberty of contract." The Sherman Act did not infringe the rights of the states and freedom of contract did not confer "a right to deprive the public of the advantages of free competition in trade and commerce." As for the view that the federal government was meddling in local affairs because the Northern Securities Company was organized under state law, Harlan emphatically rejected any implication that Congress "must act in subordination to the will of the States." He summarized the Court's holding in these words:

No State can, by merely creating a corporation, or in any other mode, project its authority into other States, and cross the continent, so as to prevent Congress from exerting the power it possesses under the Constitution over interstate and international commerce, or so as to exempt its corporations engaged in interstate commerce from obedience to any rule lawfully established by Congress for such commerce. It cannot be said that any State may give a corporation, created under its laws, authority to restrain interstate or international commerce against the will of the nation as lawfully expressed by Congress. Every corporation created by a State is necessarily subject to the supreme law of the land.[19]

In the opinion of Justice Edward D. White, one of the Court's most confirmed individualists, the judgment announced by Justice Harlan tended to extend federal power to "all subjects essentially local" and to subject to the "regulating power" of Congress "the sum of property to be acquired by individuals or by corporations." In a vein which was to become a familiar refrain in the days of the New Deal's troubles with the judiciary, White contemplated the fearful consequences that would inevitably follow: "If it were judged by Congress that the farmer in sowing his crop should be limited to a certain production because overproduction would give power to affect commerce, Congress could regulate that subject." When that day comes, both the state and federal governments will have been destroyed, and upon their "ruins" will rise "a government endowed with arbitrary power to disregard the great guaranty of life, liberty and property and every other safeguard upon which organized civil society depends."[20]

It is clear from the alignments and debate in the *Northern Securities* case that the underlying issue dividing the Justices was not their disagreement over the scope of Congress's constitutional power to suppress monopolies. Harlan's views on the trust problem, it must be noted, did not command majority support on the Court. At the time he still believed that the Sherman Anti-Trust Act made illegal all restraints on interstate trade, whether they were reasonable or not. "The Act is not limited to restraints of interstate and

[19] 193 U.S. 197, at 345–46.
[20] *Ibid.*, at 387.

international trade or commerce that are unreasonable in their nature," he wrote, "but embraces all direct restraints, reasonable or unreasonable, imposed by any combination, conspiracy or monopoly upon such trade or commerce." [21]

Brewer, on the other hand, voted to dissolve the Northern Securities Company solely because he was convinced that it was an "unreasonable combination" of interstate trade. If through the medium of a holding company Morgan and Hill were permitted to obtain control of two competing railway systems, they would then be able (through the purchase of stock of other railroads) to place the control of the entire transportation system of the country in a single corporation. Although he could not believe that such far-reaching monopolization of interstate business was either reasonable or lawful, Brewer took occasion to criticize the Court for going too far in its recent interpretations of the Sherman law. Commenting on those anti-trust cases in which he had sided with the majority, he made it known that he had since come to have a different view as to the scope of the statute: "Instead of holding that the Anti-Trust Act included all contracts, reasonable or unreasonable, in restraint of interstate trade, the ruling should have been that the contracts there presented were unreasonable restraints of interstate trade, and as such within the scope of the Act." Brewer felt obliged to explain his vote and to clarify his position "for fear" that the "broad and sweeping language" of Harlan's opinion might serve to "unsettle" legitimate business arrangements and reasonable contracts.[22]

[21] *Ibid.*, at 331.

[22] *Ibid.*, at 364. Brewer was thus anticipating the action taken by the Supreme Court in 1911 when it read the rule of reason into the application of the Sherman Act. See Chief Justice White's opinion in the *Standard Oil* and *American Tobacco Company* cases, 221 U.S. 1, and 221 U.S. 106. Henceforth, the provision declaring "every contract in restraint of trade" to be illegal was to extend only to such contracts as were in fact "unreasonable." Holmes supported these decisions.

III

These differences among the Justices supporting the Court's judgment are no doubt what Holmes had in mind when he remarked,
rather sarcastically, "I am happy to know that only a minority of
my brethren adopt an interpretation of the law which, in my opinion,
would make eternal the *bellum omnium contra omnes* and disinte-
grate society so far as it could into individual atoms." [23] Much more
so than in the *Sugar Trust* case, the really fundamental problem in
the *Northern Securities* case was the question, as Justice Harlan had
phrased it in the former, "what, in a legal sense, is an unlawful
restraint of trade?" Harlan's opinion for the Court, Brewer's separate
opinion concurring in the result, the interminable dissent by White
and the shorter dissent by Holmes—all of them can be read as essays
in economic philosophy, though they are, strictly speaking, technical
discussions of constitutional and statutory interpretation. At the start
of his dissenting opinion, Holmes insists that he was "no friend of
artificial interpretation"; but his contemporaries might well have
retorted that the judge "protesteth too much." Compared with
Harlan's informed and exhaustive discussion of the trust problem,
Holmes' treatment of the basic issues in the case strikes one as quite
narrow and unrealistic—an exercise in syllogistic logic. His intro-
ductory remarks at once reveal his impatience with the mood of
the country—the popular agitation over trusts and monopolies:

Great cases like hard cases make bad law. For great cases are called
great, not by reason of their real importance in shaping the law of the
future, but because of some accident of immediate overwhelming interest
which appeals to the feelings and distorts the judgment. These immediate
interests exercise a kind of hydraulic pressure which makes what previously was clear seem doubtful, and before which even well settled principles of law will bend. . . . Furthermore, while at times judges need for
their work the training of economists or statesmen, and must act in view
of their foresight of consequences, yet when their task is to interpret and
apply the words of a statute, their function is merely academic to begin

[23] 193 U.S. 197, 400, at 411.

with—to read English intelligently—and a consideration of consequences comes into play, if at all, only when the meaning of the words used is open to reasonable doubt.[24]

The very way in which Holmes formulated the question raised by the case is a clue to his rather artificial answer. The question before the Court was, as he saw it, whether it was unlawful "if several men unite to form a corporation for the purpose of buying more than half the stock of each of two competing inter-state railroad companies." To Holmes it made no difference that the restraint of interstate trade complained of was the work of financial giants. Granted that the Northern Securities Company was set up to end competition between two great railway systems, a proper use of the Sherman law required the Court to read its words "as if the question were whether two small grocers shall go to jail." This simple analogy is perhaps the most revealing symptom of his attitude—it was a mistake to construe the Sherman anti-trust law as though it were directed against certain great combinations; the law itself "does not say so."

Holmes' irritation with the Government's approach to the monopoly problem seems to have exerted enough "hydraulic pressure" on his thinking to make him emerge with a view of the federal commerce power most uncharacteristic of him. He supposed that under some circumstances Congress might regulate business contracts the effect of which on interstate commerce was only "indirect," but their effect would still have to be "certain and very great" to justify national regulation. After quoting with approval Fuller's pronouncement in the *Sugar Trust* case that "the fact that trade or commerce might be indirectly affected was not enough to entitle complainants to a decree," he expressed the fear that "no part of the conduct of life" would be immune from federal intrusion if the Sherman Act were to be enforced in keeping with the logical implications of the Government's argument. "Commerce depends upon population, but Congress could not, on that account, undertake to regulate marriage and divorce" was his caustic reply. He re-

[24] *Ibid.*, at 400–401.

garded the "effect" of the formation of the holding company upon the competition between the Great Northern and the Northern Pacific as quite "remote" and the stock transaction itself as "an ordinary incident of property and personal freedom." [25]

Yet it was not constitutional theory but common law precepts which seem to have led Holmes astray in the *Northern Securities* case. Refusing to agree that the maintenance of competition was the "expressed object" of the Sherman Act, he doggedly insisted that the common law concept of "restraint of trade" did not apply to combinations that are entered into voluntarily and that are not directed against a third party, not a party to the combination. "Contracts in restraint of trade, I repeat, were contracts with strangers to the contractor's business, and the trade restrained was the contractor's own." [26] Holmes emphasized that the common law objection to contracts in restraint of trade never applied to partnerships or any other arrangement for "substituting a community of interest where there had been competition."

Turning to "combinations or conspiracies" in restraint of trade,

[25] *Ibid.*, at 402. Not the least interesting fact about these rigid views of the federal commerce power is that less than a year later Holmes was to be the Court's spokesman for what for its time was probably the broadest conception of the commerce power as applied to trusts and monopolies. Swift and Co. v. United States, 196 U.S. 375 (1905). The case grew out of a suit brought by the Roosevelt Administration in 1902 seeking to enjoin a large number of companies from continuing practices by means of which they had succeeded in dominating the meat packing industry. By emphasizing that the "direct object" of the conspiracy was to control the meat industry throughout the country, Holmes was able to distinguish this case from the *Sugar Trust* case: "The case is not like United States v. E. C. Knight Co., . . . where the subject-matter of the combination was manufacture and the direct object monopoly of manufacture within a State. However likely monopoly of commerce among the States in the article manufactured was to follow the agreement it was not a necessary consequence nor a primary end. Here the subject matter is sales and the very point of the combination is to restrain and monopolize commerce among the States in respect to such sales." (At 397.) Ironically enough, Holmes' opinion in the Swift case contains a much quoted passage which is often cited as an illustration of the broad interpretation of the national commerce power: "commerce among the States is not a technical legal conception, but a practical one drawn from the course of business." (At 398.) Chief Justice Taft was later to characterize the *Swift* case as a "milestone in the interpretation of the commerce clause." Board of Trade v. Olsen, 262 U.S. 1, at 35 (1923).

[26] 193 U.S. 197, 400, at 404.

he pointed out that as "defined" by the common law they were "combinations to keep strangers to the agreement out of the business." It was their effect in restricting the market available to the general public, not their impact upon the parties to the contract, which was considered to be the evil, and such contracts were frowned upon as contrary to public policy. On the basis of his knowledge of the common law and his reading of the "plain language" of the Sherman Act, Holmes was certain that it did not apply to the Northern Securities Company. The objection to the trusts, he argued, "was not the union of former competitors but the sinister power exercised . . . by the combination in keeping rivals out of the business and ruining those who already were in." Every business concern "monopolizes" that part of business in which it is engaged, and it is of course true that by creating the Northern Securities Company Hill and Morgan secured control of a large area. Holmes asked that it be remembered, however, that the statute makes no distinction as to size: "the act of Congress will not be construed to mean the universal disintegration of society into single men, each at war with all the rest, or even the prevention of all further combinations for a common end." [27] If in adopting the Sherman Anti-Trust Act Congress intended to break up America's economic system into smaller units, calling such a law a regulation of commerce would be a mere pretense: "It would be an attempt to reconstruct society. I am not concerned with the wisdom of such an attempt but I believe that Congress was not entrusted by the Constitution with the power to make it and I am deeply persuaded that it has not tried." [28]

It is impossible to read Holmes' vehement opinion in the *Northern Securities* Case without wondering as to just what accounted for the strength of his convictions. What made him so sure and untroubled about truly debatable matters? The puzzling thing is not that he was espousing a position which only the most conservative forces in

[27] *Ibid.*, at 407.
[28] *Ibid.*, at 411.

the country could applaud. The much more striking and significant fact is that his general attitude did violence to his own basic conception of judicial restraint. Even his reliance on common law is hardly the whole explanation. "By becoming the historian of the common law," it has been said, "Holmes goes beyond what any of the Congressional laymen who framed the Sherman Act or the people who accepted it could have known of the meaning and usage of the common-law concept." [29]

All of this is no doubt true, but it must also be recognized that there was an element of irresponsibility in the use which Holmes made of the common law. Nowhere in his highly repetitious opinion does he present any evidence to show that his reading of the Sherman Act was consistent with what Congress had in mind. There is good ground for believing, indeed, that he was so upset by the redirection of economic forces implicit in the Government's action against the Northern Securities Company that he convinced himself that Congress could never have intended such a policy. How else can one explain his unsupported generalizations and his glib statements in which he equates such re-direction with atomization of society and social anarchy.

The question has intrigued the commentators for many years. One of them has even ventured a purely psychological explanation. "He [Holmes] has an ascetic conception of the judicial process; and the very fact that he had reason to suspect that the man who had appointed him expected a certain decision from him in the case would have caused him to lean backward." [30] Even though his constitutional point of view in the case is at odds with the Holmesian tradition, his version of American capitalism cannot be regarded as an isolated aberration. Actually, the undisguised bias exhibited by him in the *Northern Securities* case was part of a coherent pattern of thought, his philosophy of a natural economic order.

The fact is that Holmes spoke out more than once against what his

---

[29] Lerner, *op. cit.*, p. 220.
[30] *Ibid.*, p. 219.

friend Pollock scornfully described as the Court's "anti-monopolist
zeal." [31] One of his most doctrinaire expositions is to be found in his
opinion in the *Dr. Miles Medical Company* case, decided in 1911.[32]
The only dissenter in the case, he took sharp issue with the ruling
of the majority, announced in an opinion by Justice Hughes, which
frustrated the effort of the Miles Medical Company to protect its
price maintenance contracts with the distributors of its medicines.
The Court's decision in the case came to be a leading precedent
on the subject of retail price-maintenance. It enunciated the doctrine
that "agreements or combinations between dealers, having for their
sole purpose the destruction of competition and the fixing of prices,
are injurious to the public interest and void."

With respect to Holmes' position in the case, it is not too much
to say that it would be hard to find a better example of a judicial
opinion which seems to have been shaped by preconceived economic dogmas. But characteristically enough, it was he who accused
the majority of indulging its economic preferences and of legislating
public policy:

There is no statute covering the case; there is no body of precedent that
by ineluctable logic requires the conclusion to which the Court has come.
The conclusion is reached by extending a certain conception of public
policy to a new sphere. On such matters we are in perilous country. I
think that . . . it is safe to say that the most enlightened judicial policy
is to let people manage their own business in their own way, unless the
ground for interference is very clear.[33]

Holmes assumed that the Court acted out of concern for the con-
suming public, but he thought that the motive was based on an
economic fallacy. "I think that we greatly exaggerate," he protests,
"the value and importance to the public of competition in the production or distribution of an article . . . as fixing a fair price. What
really fixes that is the competition of conflicting desires." Again it

[31] *Holmes-Pollock Letters,* II, 178.
[32] Dr. Miles Medical Company v. Park & Sons Company, 220 U.S. 373, 409
(1911).
[33] *Ibid.,* at 411.

is clear that it was no abstract theory of judicial abstinence, but his faith in the beneficent workings of economic forces, which controlled his position:

As soon as the price of something that we want goes above the point at which we are willing to give up other things to have that, we cease to buy it and buy something else . . . it seems to me that the point of most profitable returns marks the equilibrium of social desires and determines the fair price in the only sense in which I can find meaning in those words. The Dr. Miles Medical Company knows better than we do what will enable it to do the best business. . . . I see nothing to warrant my assuming that the public will not be served best by the company being allowed to carry out its plan. I cannot believe that in the long run the public will profit by this Court permitting knaves to cut reasonable prices for some ulterior purpose of their own and thus to impair, if not to destroy, the production and sale of articles which it is assumed to be desirable that the public should be able to get.[34]

IV

This brief glance at what Morris Raphael Cohen has called the "backwardness of his fundamental economic views"[35] should help to dispel some of the illusion concerning Holmes' liberalism. Indeed, his dissents in the *Northern Securities* and the *Dr. Miles* cases have been cited as evidence that he was not only illiberal but a downright reactionary. "Holmes's youth," Professor Cohen reminded us, "was spent in an atmosphere in which the abolition of the Corn Laws, the rise of the commercial classes, and the development of unrestrained competition were almost universally accepted as great liberal achievements. He continued, from force of habit, to use old phrases that assume a pre-established harmony between the individual desire for profit and the good of the whole community."[36]

Lawyer Boudin explains Holmes' adherence to old maxims some-

---

[34] *Ibid.*, at 412.
[35] Cohen, *The Faith of a Liberal*, p. 29.
[36] *Ibid.*, pp.28–29.

what differently but is in essential agreement with the Justice's
philosopher friend. "The notion that the world is now at peace," he
writes, "almost at rest,—is basic in Holmes' philosophy of life. . . .
He had completely matured by the time he was forty, and definitely
settled soon afterwards. Hence he could be jarred but not moved intellectually." [37] Mr. Boudin argues persuasively that the lack of
realism in Holmes' economic world was due largely to his failure to
perceive the true character of capitalist development in post-Civil
War America.

"Any general survey of Mr. Justice Holmes' work upon the Supreme Court," Laski had written in 1931, "must begin by noting the
realism of his approach." [38] Mr. Boudin would probably characterize
this view as "sheer nonsense." The label, he insists, can only hamper
understanding of the conflicts and methods within the courts on
which Holmes sat:

. . . the term "Realist" is most unsuited as a guide to Justice Holmes'
decisions. The term is used to imply a sense of economic realities as con-
trasted with adherence to legal theory. But such a distinction is wide of
the mark when applied to the divisions between "conservatives" and
"liberals" in our courts during the half-century that Holmes was on the
Bench; and if the distinction were rightly applied it would place Holmes
in the opposite camp from that in which his uncritical admirers would
like to place him. For Holmes was a scholarly lawyer, and he never
ceased to be such while on the bench. He was therefore much more
"legalistic" than the "conservative" judges who were his associates or contemporaries. Indeed, the notion that Justice Field, the most famous of his
"conservative" predecessors on the Supreme Court, or Justices McReynolds, Sutherland and Butler, among his associates on that Court, were
sticklers for legal theory is sheer nonsense. They were the true "realists"
on the Supreme Court, and not, the "liberals",—all of whom were much
more concerned that their decisions should square with legal theory than
were the "conservatives". And in this sense Holmes was a liberal of
liberals.[39]

[37] Boudin, *op. cit.*, p. 35.
[38] Laski, "The Political Philosophy of Mr. Justice Holmes," *40 Yale L. J.*,
683, 689 (1931).
[39] Boudin, *op. cit.*, pp. 26–27.

If by "realism" Mr. Boudin has in mind that stubborn refusal by some of Holmes' judicial contemporaries to make room for governmental melioration of the stark severities of the industrial system, he is of course right in saying that Holmes was not "a realist of the Field-Peckham school." He is guilty of a serious exaggeration, however, when he claims that Holmes "really never had the feel of the machine." Neither is it true, on the other hand, as another interpreter who has discovered Holmes' conservatism has said, that Holmes' "convictions stemmed from knowledge and cerebral mechanics rather than prejudice." [40] Holmes was capable of thinking in "stereotypes" as much as other judges. What Walton Hamilton has said—"The genius of the common law broods over Holmes's world" [41] —holds a far more reliable key to much of Holmes' conservatism. As one reads the opinions which have disappointed the Justice's liberal admirers, one is impressed with his inability to extricate himself from the pull of the common law tradition in which he was so deeply steeped. Unfortunately, a knowledge of history does not always set men free and enable "us to make up our minds dispassionately."[42]

Holmes' love for the common law was bound to affect his outlook and methods as a judge; so also was the fact that he came to intellectual maturity at a time when America was different in many fundamental ways from what it came to be in the present century. To recognize candidly these and other limitations of his judicial labors is no doubt a necessary and salutary corrective. No one need apologize for raising Holmes, in Hamilton's words, "from deity to mortality." [43] But any such effort to bring a great public figure to life-size must avoid the danger of the other extreme, which may be an even greater distortion.

It is simply not true that Holmes never had the "feel" of the issues

[40] Irving Bernstein, "The Conservative Mr. Justice Holmes," 23 *The New England Quar.* 435, 452 (Dec., 1950).
[41] Hamilton, "On Dating Mr. Justice Holmes," 9 *Univ. of Chicago L. Rev.* 1, 20 (1941).
[42] Holmes, *Collected Legal Papers*, p. 225.
[43] Hamilton, *op. cit.*, p. 1.

and problems of the new American society. Perhaps nothing in his early years on the Supreme Court refutes this sweeping condemnation as much as his discussion of "yellow dog" contracts, to mention just one illustration. In dissenting in the *Adair* case [44]—the case in which the Court had struck down the provision of the Erdman Act of 1898 making it illegal for railroads to discharge or otherwise discriminate against workers who joined unions—Holmes spoke of the connection between peaceful labor relations and the state of the transportation industry with an awareness of industrial realities that was not to come from the majority side of the Court until the 1930's.

Justice Harlan, in his opinion for the Court, found that the ban on yellow-dog contracts lay outside the commerce power because labor relations had no "real or substantial connection" with interstate commerce. The "connection" between railway labor and the railroad business, Holmes replied sardonically, "was at least as intimate and important as that of safety couplers." But the law was held invalid not only because it was regulating matters unrelated to interstate commerce but also because it unduly curtailed freedom to contract in violation of the Fifth Amendment.

It was Harlan's invocation of the liberty of contract concept which seems to have particularly annoyed Justice Holmes. He notes that this concept had been "stretched to its extreme"; that the notion of free choice is sometimes a "fiction" and that the law which the Court was condemning did no more than prohibit the "more powerful party" from discriminating against the weaker. When a particular limitation of contractual freedom is supported by considerations of public policy, the constitutional fate of the legislation ought not to depend on whether "this Court agrees or disagrees with the policy pursued." If prevention of strikes and the promotion of labor arbitration are legitimate objects of national policy, "Congress might reasonably think" that the outlawing of yellow-dog contracts would help effectuate such policies, even if it should lead to the complete unionization of railroad labor.

[44] Adair v. United States, 208 U.S. 161, 190 (1908).

I quite agree [Holmes concluded] that the question what and how much good labor unions do, is one on which intelligent people may differ,—I think that laboring men sometimes attribute to them advantages, as many attribute to combinations of capital disadvantages, that are really due to economic conditions of a far wider and deeper kind—but I could not pronounce it unwarranted if Congress should decide that to foster a strong union was for the best interests, not only of the men, but of the railroads and the country at large.[45]

Seven years later, the Supreme Court "stretched" its conception of liberty of contract even further, when it held that the due process clause of the Fourteenth Amendment forbade the States to pass laws prohibiting employers from exacting yellow-dog agreements from their employees. Again Justice Holmes dissented, renewing his plea for greater tolerance and realism in the discussion of the labor struggle.[46] The Kansas statute with which the case was concerned made it a crime for employers to insist on non-membership in a union as a condition of employment. In his opinion for the majority of six—an opinion which continues to serve as a classic example of the purely conceptual approach—Justice Pitney asked a question which phrases the basic issue in the case in such a way as to make the conclusion inescapable: "Granted the equal freedom of both parties to the contract of employment has not each party the right to stipulate upon what terms only he will consent to the inception, or the continuance, of that relationship?" Yet curiously, in answering this question, he actually refuted the premise that the parties to a labor contract enjoy "equal freedom." He was candid enough to acknowledge that inequality was an inevitable by-product under a system of private ownership of property. "No doubt, wherever the right of private property exists," Pitney declared, "there must and will be inequalities of fortune; and thus it naturally happens that parties negotiating about a contract are not equally unhampered by circumstances." [47]

---

[45] *Ibid.*, at 191–92.
[46] Coppage v. Kansas, 236 U.S. 1, 28 (1915).
[47] *Ibid.*, at 17.

As if in reply to Pitney's suspicion that the Kansas statute was aimed at "levelling the inequalities of fortune," Holmes said simply that it was entirely lawful for the legislature to concern itself with the unequal bargaining struggle between employers and employees. He urged the Court to overrule the *Lochner* and *Adair* cases and remarked that he still held the views he had expressed in Massachusetts. Those who fail to find in Holmes understanding of the modern labor problem might well pause to ponder the implications of the following sentences from his brief Coppage dissent:

In present conditions a workman not unnaturally may believe that only by belonging to a union can he secure a contract that shall be fair to him. . . . If that belief, whether right or wrong, may be held by a reasonable man, it seems to me that it may be enforced by law in order to establish the equality of position between the parties in which liberty of contract begins. Whether in the long run it is wise to enact legislation of this sort is not my concern, but I am strongly of opinion that there is nothing in the Constitution of the United States to prevent it, . . .[48]

V

This look at Holmes' work on the Supreme Court prior to the time Brandeis became his colleague reveals a striking contradiction in his thinking as well as the major paradox in his outlook as a judge. His "world of realities," even as probably that of most men, was not quite as free of illusion and fancy as he was inclined to believe. It was filled with a good many fallacies and superficial preconceptions which he assumed to be basic truths, such as the rigid economic laws on which he rested his social faith. But an exaggerated emphasis upon his conservatism may actually oversimplify the character of his constitutional philosophy, though, of course, his attachment to so-called conservative economics was not without its effect on his behavior as a judge. As it relates to his judicial labors, especially in the realm of constitutional law, it should serve to re-

[48] *Ibid.*, at 46–47.

mind us that Holmes' intellectual universe was marked by considerable inner conflict.

So persistent has been the tendency to picture Holmes as a completely "harmonious and integrated personality"—the words are those of a distinguished legal scholar—[49] that few have recognized the contradictions of his complex mind. In welcome contrast is Daniel J. Boorstin's remarkably perceptive effort to explore the "tantalizing elusiveness of Holmes' personal philosophy." [50] Professor Boorstin writes:

Mr. Justice Holmes, the product of a New England conservative tradition, clearly felt the tug of opposing forces. His family background drew him in the direction of respectability, elegance, and the genteel tradition. But the individuality of the Justice was intensely liberal; he was a man of extraordinary intelligence who was eager and happy to see a world of change. He was finally unable to reconcile these two aspects of his personality, although an apparent resolution took the form of a faith in conflict, in the process and struggle of life.[51]

In one of his most self-revealing utterances, Holmes himself spoke of his "long years of doubt, self-distrust, and solitude" but confessed that his "general point of view" came in time to be "confirmed and settled" in his mind.[52] While it is true, as Mr. Boorstin points out, that Holmes was "inclined to take refuge in mysticism"—and the theme of the "unknowable" and the "unexplainable" does indeed run through his letters and speeches—it is also clear that about some things the Justice was very sure. Perhaps his most inflexible bias concerned the nature of economic society. His deepest doubts had to do with the feasibility of changing the world by man-made intrusions. Still, when confronted with attempts to modify the social order, Holmes rarely succumbed to the fears which were leading other

[49] Walter Wheeler Cook, "Oliver Wendell Holmes: Scientist," *21 Amer. Bar Assoc. J. 211* (1935).

[50] Boorstin, "The Elusiveness of Mr. Justice Holmes," *14 The New England Quar. 478, 480* (Sept., 1941).

[51] *Ibid.,* pp. 480–81.

[52] Holmes, *Speeches,* pp. 86, 84.

judges who shared his general social views to try to halt the innovations.

When socialism first began to be talked about, [Holmes observed in 1897] the comfortable classes of the community were a good deal frightened. I suspect that this fear has influenced judicial action both here and in England, yet it is certain that it is not a conscious factor in the decisions to which I refer. I think that something similar has led people who no longer hope to control the legislatures to look to the courts as expounders of the Constitutions, and that in some courts new principles have been discovered outside the bodies of those instruments, which may be generalized into acceptance of the economic doctrines which prevailed about fifty years ago, and a wholesale prohibition of what a tribunal of lawyers does not think about right.[53]

What kept a genuine social conservative from becoming a reactionary on the Bench is thus the most important question that can be asked about Holmes. As another philosophically minded interpreter put it many years ago, "To be on the one hand above the battle, and on the other hand to have a conscious social philosophy is not an easy position." [54] In constitutional adjudication, moreover, a judge's opportunities for giving vent to social theory are obviously very great. The years following the advent of Justice Brandeis on the Supreme Court continued to afford further evidence of the way in which these contradictory impulses in Holmes' nature were harmonized to produce his unique conception of judicial objectivity. It therefore also helps to illumine the kinship between the two Justices.

[53] Holmes, *Collected Legal Papers*, p. 184.
[54] James H. Tufts, "The Legal and Social Philosophy of Mr. Justice Holmes," 7 *Amer. Bar Assoc. J.* 359, 362 (1921).

5

"The man of the future"

I

"For the rational study of the law the black-letter man may be the man of the present," Justice Holmes had observed in 1897, quickly adding, "but the man of the future is the man of statistics and the master of economics." [1] He went on to urge that "Every lawyer ought to seek an understanding of economics."

As one thinks of Louis D. Brandeis' special talents and the unique contribution he was destined to make to constitutional theory and practice, Holmes' prophetic words would almost appear to have been uttered with Brandeis in mind. At the time Holmes could not have been thinking about Brandeis. The two men, Brandeis' biographer informs us,[2] first met in 1879, and until Brandeis joined the Court their association was at most an intermittent one. In the days when both men were in Boston they would occasionally meet at the Parker House "for beer and talk." Later when Holmes moved to Washington, Brandeis would sometimes visit the Holmeses.

But Brandeis' mastery of the social disciplines was not the only respect in which he differed from the conventional practitioner. "He was one of the few in his profession who understood finance as well

[1] Holmes, "The Path of the Law," in *Collected Legal Papers,* p. 187.
[2] Mason, *Brandeis: A Free Man's Life,* p. 570.

as law" was the tribute of one adversary.[3] "I am but one among many," another highly informed observer wrote in 1914, "who look upon Mr. Brandeis as having, in the field of economics, the most inventive and sound mind of our time. . . . In the composition of his intellect, one of the most important elements is his comprehension of figures. As one of the leading financiers of the country said to me, 'Mr. Brandeis's greatness as a lawyer is part of his greatness as a mathematician.'"[4]

More significant than his methods, however, was Brandeis' diagnosis of America's social ills. The considerable fortune he had amassed out of his practice as an attorney for corporations did not prevent him from seeing and criticizing the evils of the very system in which he built his personal success. So disturbed had Brandeis become over the abuses of the new capitalism that by the turn of the century he had all but given up the private practice of law to be free to devote himself to the service of the community. Many a citizen came to think of him, in Woodrow Wilson's words, as "the people's advocate when public interests called for an effective champion."[5] His pre-occupation with public problems was never merely that of the technician or expert. The more he mastered the complexities of modern industry and finance, the more concerned did he become with their implications for the survival of the American democratic tradition. If his effort to apply social intelligence to the problems of a society undergoing revolutionary change struck some as coldly clinical, it was probably because his treatment of a public issue was always based on close study and careful prescription. "Nobody can form a judgment that is worth having," he had declared in 1915, "without a fairly detailed and intimate knowledge

[3] Homer Albers, Dean of the Boston University Law School, quoted in *Mr. Justice Brandeis, Great American*, edited by Irving Dilliard (St. Louis: The Modern View Press, 1941), p. 11.

[4] Norman Hapgood in his Preface to *Other People's Money and How the Bankers Use It* by Louis D. Brandeis (New York: Frederick A. Stokes Company, 1914), p. vi.

[5] Woodrow Wilson, *The New Democracy*, Presidential Messages, Addresses, and Other Papers, edited by Ray Stannard Baker and William E. Dodd (New York: Harper & Brothers, 1926), II, 160.

of the facts." [6] Whatever the problem—transportation, insurance, finance, trade-unionism, public utilities, the conservation of natural resources—his discussion of it was marked by a grasp of detail and breadth of perception that in time assumed the character of a distinctive philosophy. Viewed in this light, his legal techniques were but the necessary implements of a larger social purpose.

Of no early twentieth-century progressive was it more true than of Brandeis, that all of his intellectual powers and professional skills were put to use when he dealt with the basic issues of the age. "I have just written in the *N.R.*," Laski wrote to Holmes on November 3, 1917, "that we want somebody to do for this generation what John Stuart Mill did for the last—take the fundamental conceptions and re-examine them in the light of what has happened since his day." [7] Had Laski been familiar with the views of Louis D. Brandeis he might have been less regretful, unless, of course, the fact that Brandeis never wrote the type of formal treatise contributed by Mill would have led Laski to dismiss him anyway.

Even Edward Bellamy would have had to admit that Brandeis not only read the "signs of the times" aright,[8] but with an insight which was focused on "fundamental conceptions." Few Americans perceived as keenly as did Brandeis "the nature of the crisis" confronting the United States. "My observation leads me to believe," he told the United States Commission on Industrial Relations in 1915, "that while there are many contributing causes of unrest, that there is one cause which is fundamental. That is . . . the contrast between our political liberty and our industrial absolutism." [9]

[6] Testifying before the United States Commission on Industrial Relations, January 23, 1915; reprinted in *The Curse of Bigness, Miscellaneous Papers of Louis D. Brandeis,* edited by Osmond K. Fraenkel (New York: The Viking Press, 1934), p. 76.

[7] *Holmes-Laski Letters,* I, 107. See also *13 New Republic 6.*

[8] Dr. Leete to Mr. West: "The singular blindness of your contemporaries to the signs of the times is a phenomenon commented on by many of our historians." Bellamy, *Looking Backward* (New York: Houghton Mifflin Company, 1889), p. 49.

[9] Brandeis, *The Curse of Bigness,* p. 72.

All of Brandeis' efforts at social improvement were directed toward a fuller realization of the democratic way of life. Increase in material comforts was not his goal. "It is absolutely essential in order that men develop that they be properly fed and properly housed, and that they have proper opportunities of education and recreation. We cannot reach our goal without those things. But we may have all those things and have a nation of slaves." [10] The preservation of freedom and responsibility was his guiding star. Yet he was not one to invoke the shibboleths of the past because of their ritualistic or commemorative value. Nor was his use of the dogmas of the democratic faith the abstractions of a would-be philosopher. "He was not a philosopher in his leisure moments," one of his law secretaries has testified; adding, "His philosophy is found in his living." [11]

Each of his major public activities became the occasion for the articulation of democratic principles. The Brandeis approach was a curious mixture of anxiety and optimism. He feared that our failure to deal courageously and constructively with what he once characterized as the "baneful by-products" of the industrial system would lead to "the erosion of our political democracy." [12] The views he presented in 1911 before a Senate committee considering trust legislation epitomize his deep concern:

You cannot have true American citizenship, you cannot preserve political liberty, you cannot secure American standards of living unless some degree of industrial liberty accompanies it. . . .

The trust problem can never be settled right for the American people by looking at it through the spectacles of bonds and stocks. You must study it through the spectacles of people's rights and people's interests; you must consider the effect upon the development of the American democracy. When you do that you will realize the perils to our institutions which attend the trusts; you will realize the danger of letting the people

[10] *Ibid.*, p. 81.
[11] Paul A. Freund, as quoted in Dilliard, *op. cit.*, p. 11.
[12] Statement before Senate committee, December 14, 1911. Reprinted in Alfred Lief (ed.), *The Social and Economic Views of Mr. Justice Brandeis* (New York: The Vanguard Press, 1930), p. 374.

learn that our sacred Constitution protects not only vested rights but vested wrongs.[13]

II

To understand Brandeis' brand of reform it is necessary to look at his picture of America. The trouble with those who resisted change, he would say, was that they had not "thought out" the significance of the "revolution" ushered in by the age of big business:

Half a century ago nearly every American boy could look forward to becoming independent as a farmer or mechanic, in business or professional life; and nearly every American girl might expect to become the wife of such a man. To-day most American boys have reason to believe that throughout life they will work in some capacity as employees of others, either in private or public business; and a large percentage of the women occupy like positions. This revolutionary change has resulted from the great growth of manufacturing and mining as compared with farming; from the formation of trusts and other large business concerns; from the development of our transportation and other public utility corporations; from the marked increase in governmental functions; and, finally, from the invasion of women into industry.[14]

These fundamental transformations in American society, particularly the fact that we had become "a nation of employees," called for a careful appraisal of their impact upon our institutions. But Brandeis' outcries against the abuses of capitalism were never those of the sentimental humanitarian. Something Woodrow Wilson said of him in the course of the protracted battle over his appointment to the Supreme Court may well be the key to his motivations as social critic and crusader. "I cannot speak too highly," the President wrote to the Chairman of the Senate Judiciary Committee, "of his profound acquaintance with the historical roots of our institutions and insight into their spirit, or of the many evidences he has given

[13] *Ibid.*, pp. 373–74.
[14] Brandeis, "Our New Peonage: Discretionary Pensions," *The Independent,* vol. 73, p. 187 (July 25, 1912).

of being imbued to the very heart with our American ideals of
social justice and equality of opportunity."[15] Though he had, as
Wilson also said of him, "deep human sympathy," at times he
seemed to be moved less by the fact of individual misery and more
by its pervasive effect on the community.

We Americans are committed not only to social justice in the sense of
avoiding things which bring suffering and harm, like unjust distribution
of wealth, but we are committed primarily to democracy. The social justice for which we are striving is an incident of our democracy—not the
main end. It is rather the result of democracy—perhaps its finest expression—but it rests upon democracy, which implies the rule by the
people.[16]

Brandeis was convinced that bad economic conditions—excessive
hours of labor, irregular employment, low wages, oppressive use of
their power by employers, absentee ownership, monopolistic practices, bigness in business organization—were undermining the foundations of popular government. Such conditions lead to "demoralization" and "irresponsibility" and made "derelicts" out of the very
people who are presumed to be the ultimate rulers in a democracy.
One of the best examples of his habit of casting the denunciation of
a particular industrial abuse in the context of the democratic imperative is to be found in his testimony in 1912 before a House of Representatives committee investigating the United States Steel Corporation. While discussing the labor problem in the steel industry, he
took occasion to remind the Congressmen that more was at stake
than long hours for steel workers:

No matter what men are paid, no matter what the ordinary conditions
may be under which they work, the first question must be, How long
did this man work? Because not only does the excess of hours entail upon
the individual very serious consequences in respect to health and the
ability to endure labor in the future, but the effect upon the community
as a whole is of infinite importance; in the first place, in determining what

[15] Wilson, *op. cit.*, II, 160, 163.
[16] Testimony before United States Commission on Industrial Relations.
Senate Document #415, 64th Congress, First Session, Vol. VIII, p. 7659.

is the time that is left to the individual to devote himself to the needs of his own family, to aid in the education and the bringing up of his children; and in the second place, what is the time that is left to the individual to perform those duties which are incumbent upon him as a citizen of a free country.[17]

This profound student of our highly complex industrial society continued to believe that old American ideals were altogether applicable to the new conditions. The opinion of Professor Mason that at heart Brandeis was an "individualist democrat of the Jeffersonian type"[18] would seem to be entirely justified. In this almost obsessive emphasis on the virtues of the past, he revealed himself to be caught in the intellectual contradiction which more than one observer of our political traditions has seen as the chief dilemma of the whole Progressive movement. "Beginning with the time of Bryan," writes Richard Hofstadter, "the dominant American ideal has been steadily fixed on bygone institutions and conditions. In early twentieth-century progressivism this backward-looking vision reached the dimensions of a major paradox. Such heroes of the progressive revival as Bryan, La Follette, and Wilson proclaimed that they were trying to undo the mischief of the past forty years and re-create the old nation of limited and decentralized power, genuine competition, democratic opportunity, and enterprise."[19]

Unlike some of his fellow reformers of the era, however, Brandeis brought more than moral fervor to the cause of the new liberalism. "He knows more than how to talk about the right—he knows how to set it forward in the face of its enemies."[20] When President Wilson penned this testimonial, he was in fact summarizing Brandeis' career as the "people's counsel" as well as suggesting the underlying reason for the violent controversy over his selection for a place on the Supreme Court. Brandeis was not content merely to draw on

[17] Lief, *op. cit.*, p. 376.
[18] Mason, *Brandeis: Lawyer and Judge in the Modern State*, p. 74.
[19] Hofstadter, *The American Political Tradition* (New York: Alfred A. Knopf, 1948), p. vi (Introduction).
[20] Wilson, *op. cit.*, pp. 161–62.

his vast knowledge of modern economic forces and processes to analyze and expose the fruits of American capitalism. He fought for a better day by assailing the abuses and showing how they could be removed. This gift for translating ideas into practical results has been well summarized by Max Lerner in the course of indicating how greatly Brandeis differed from his fellow liberals in the Progressive years:

In two important respects he stands out from the group of turn-of-the-century liberals with whom his name is associated. He had a passion for detail and concreteness where most of them dealt in invective and generalities. And he had a capacity for constructive achievement in the field of social legislation and social invention. An exposure of insurance companies was accompanied by a plan for reorganizing the industry and by a new form of savings-bank insurance; an attack on the railroads gave him a chance to launch on its career the principle of scientific management; a call to arbitrate a labor dispute resulted in the "protocol" and the "preferential open shop." And he knew not only how to create and state these ideas and plans; he knew also the technique of publicity and persuasion without which in the apathy of modern life they would have been ignored. But perhaps most important of all was the will to "follow through" an idea until it was functioning, and the infinite capacity for pains which saw to the details of organization.[21]

But Brandeis' indictment of the business community was nevertheless fundamental and relentless. His major thesis was that business had become too big and socially irresponsible. While refraining from personal attacks—"We are dealing with a question, not of motive, but of condition"[22]—he frequently criticized the leaders of industry and finance for the ideas and policies which they sponsored. The more he grappled with the social problems arising from certain business practices, the more did he come to believe that largely because of their size the great corporations had become a menace to the nation. "Size may become such a danger in its results to the com-

[21] Lerner, "The Social Thought of Mr. Justice Brandeis," in *Ideas are Weapons* (New York: The Viking Press, 1943), p. 76.
[22] Brandeis, *The Curse of Bigness*, p. 72.

munity that the community may have to set limits." [23] By 1908, this belief had crystallized into a definite philosophy of business organization. Brandeis' aversion to bigness was grounded in economic theory as well as psychological realism:

> For every business concern there must be a limit of greatest efficiency. What that limit is differs under varying conditions; but it is clear that an organization may be too large for efficiency and economical management, as well as too small. The disadvantages attendant upon size may outweigh the advantages. Man's works have outgrown the capacity of the individual man. No matter what the organization, the capacity of the individual man must determine the success of a particular enterprise, not only financially to the owners, but in service to the community. Organization can do much to make possible larger efficient concerns; but organization can never be a substitute for initiative and judgment.[24]

But the fact that a business concern may become inefficient because it had grown to be too large was the least damning thing that could be said against bigness in business. It was the social consequences of the condition which Brandeis regarded as truly dangerous to the Republic. The "grave objection" to excessively large business units is that they inevitably lead to concentration of power, and absolutism, in whatever form, is dangerous: "There develops within the State a state so powerful that the ordinary social and industrial forces existing are insufficient to cope with it." [25] How strongly he felt about these matters and how seriously he applied his theories to concrete business problems is strikingly indicated by the answer he gave in 1908 to the call for greater railroad consolidation as the cure for the "wretched" transportation service New England was receiving:

> It has been suggested that we accept the proposed monopoly in transportation but provide safeguards.
> This would be like surrendering liberty and substituting despotism

[23] *Ibid.*, p. 80.
[24] Brandeis, "The New England Transportation Monopoly" (1908), an address reprinted in *Business—A Profession*, pp. 275–76.
[25] See above, note 16, p. 72.

with safeguards. There is no way in which to safeguard people from
despotism except to prevent despotism. There is no way to safeguard the
people from the evils of a private transportation monopoly except to prevent the monopoly. The objections to despotism and to monopoly are
fundamental in human nature. They rest upon the innate and ineradicable
selfishness of man. They rest upon the fact that absolute power inevitably
leads to abuse. They rest upon the fact that progress flows only from
struggle.[26]

Convinced that all of the major economic problems of the day—
trusts, monopolies, credit, labor—were traceable to the concentration
of power which the "curse of bigness"[27] made inevitable, Brandeis
used every suitable occasion to urge the need for limiting size and
power. This was the theme of his recurring attacks on the United
States Steel Corporation and other industrial trusts; his strictures on
the great insurance companies; his condemnation of inefficiency and
mismanagement in railway transportation; his exposé of the "money
trust"[28] and his denunciation of the mistreatment of the nation's

[26] Brandeis, *Business—A Profession*, p. 278.

[27] This phrase will be found in Brandeis' brief and argument before the
Interstate Commerce Commission in 1911 against a proposed advance in freight
rates. In the course of suggesting that many of the problems of the great railroad systems might be due to the fact that they had "exceeded . . . the limit
of greatest efficiency," he stressed the "incidents" of "This bigness, or, as I
would be inclined to call it, this curse of bigness." Lief, *op. cit.*, pp. 296–97.
The title of Chapter VIII of *Other People's Money* is "A Curse of Bigness." See
pp. 162–88.

[28] Brandeis' exposé of the "money trust" appeared first as a series of articles in
Harper's Weekly under the general title of "Our Financial Oligarchy" and later
as *Other People's Money and How Bankers Use It*. The essence of Brandeis'
attack on the influence which bankers were exerting through their use of
"other people's money" may be gleaned from the following passage: ". . . If
the bankers' power were commensurate only with their wealth, they would have
relatively little influence on American business. Vast fortunes like those of the
Astors are no doubt regrettable. They are inconsistent with democracy. They
are unsocial. And they seem peculiarly unjust when they represent largely un-
earned increment. But the wealth of the Astors does not endanger political or
industrial liberty. . . . It lacks significance largely because its owners have
only the income from their own wealth. The Astor wealth is static. The wealth
of the Morgan associates is dynamic. The power and the growth of power of
our financial oligarchs comes from wielding the savings and quick capital of
others. . . . The fetters which bind the people are forged from the people's
own gold." *Other People's Money*, pp. 18–19.

workers. His remedies and his goals were always basically the same —restoration of sound competition, efficiency through informed and responsible administration, and checks on the exercise of power. The fate of the nation's economy, Brandeis found, was being shaped by men who knew little about the affairs of the businesses they were directing and consolidating, men who, because of the enormous wealth they were accumulating, were able to wield inordinate power but without responsibility. Inefficiency, mismanagement and labor unrest were the unavoidable by-products.

So devastating and sustained an assault on the ways of big business and finance was bound to lead many a businessman to conclude that Brandeis was an enemy of capitalism. "The persecution of the business interests of America by Mr. Brandeis has worked a hardship on a vast number of people," a Boston paper angrily commented in 1913.[29] The blast was directed at Brandeis in the course of his work as special counsel to the Interstate Commerce Commission. Invited to assist the Commission in "seeing that all sides and angles" of a request by Eastern railroads for a freight-rate increase were presented, he prepared a questionnaire intended to reveal, in particular, whether interlocking directorates were responsible for the high costs of which the roads were complaining.

There is no evidence that Brandeis ever questioned the foundations of America's economic system. However much he sought to improve the conditions and to alter some of the power relations which monopoly capitalism had brought about, he did not seek the abolition of the institution of private property or the profit motive. Believing deeply that America was "after all, not a country of dollars, but of ballots," [30] he dedicated himself to the task of helping to make sure that it remained democratic, even though it was capitalist. To the "status quo" apologist for business, his talk of democratizing industry—"the problems of a trade should be no longer the prob-

[29] Quoted by Alfred Lief in *Brandeis: The Personal History of an American Ideal* (New York: Stackpole Sons, 1936), p. 305.

[30] Brandeis, "The Opportunity in the Law," an address before the Harvard Ethical Society, May 4, 1905; to be found in *Business—A Profession*, p. 334.

lems of the employer ˏalone"—was no doubt rank revolutionary heresy.[31] But it is one of the ironies of Brandeis' reputation as a radical that it was he who warned of the danger that the excesses of our "financial magnates" would lead to socialism. "The talk of the agitator alone does not advance socialism a step," he told the Commercial Club of Boston in 1905, going on to add, "but the formation of great trusts—the huge consolidations—the insurance 'racers' with the attendant rapacity or the dishonesty of their potent managers and their frequent corruption of councils and legislatures is hastening us almost irresistibly into socialistic measures. The great captains of industry and of finance, who profess the greatest horror of the extension of governmental functions, are the chief makers of socialism." [32]

III

The core of Brandeis' attitude toward capitalism was his belief, as he expressed it in a Commencement Day address at Brown University in 1912, that "the great industrial and social problems . . . will one by one find solution." [33] His penchant for practical results helps explain the unique character of his contribution to the Progressive movement. "The aid of a first-rate legal mind, when outstanding

---

[31] "The end for which we must strive is the attainment of rule by the people, and that involves industrial democracy as well as political democracy. That means that the problems of a trade should be no longer the problems of the employer alone. The problems of his business, and it is not the employer's business alone, are the problems of all in it. The union cannot shift upon the employer the responsibility for conditions, nor can the employer insist upon determining, according to his will, the conditions which shall exist. . . . But adequately to solve the trade problems there must be some machinery which will deal with these problems as they arise from day to day. You must create something akin to a government of the trade before you reach a real approach to democratization." Brandeis, testifying before the United States Commission on Industrial Relations, 1915. See *The Curse of Bigness*, pp. 73–74.

[32] Brandeis, "Life Insurance: The Abuses and the Remedies," reprinted in *Business—A Profession*, p. 112. This is the speech in which Brandeis urged that savings banks be authorized to issue life insurance policies.

[33] Brandeis, *Business—A Profession*, p. 12.

legal ability had become conventionally an adjunct of great corporate aggregates," Professor Mason has written, "was worth more to the cause of liberalism than the entire menagerie of publicists, politicos, muckrakers, and mob-rousers." [34] Indeed, Brandeis himself regarded it as one of the dangers of the times that the ablest lawyers were "ranged on the side of the corporations." His encounters with vested interests and his work as counsel for public causes served to impress him with the importance of the strategic role of the lawyer in a complex industrial society. He was distressed to see how often the public interest suffered because of the failures of inferior counsel, who were no match for the lawyers representing the corporations. His stinging indictment of his own profession deserves to be recalled:

> The leading lawyers of the United States have been engaged mainly in supporting the claims of the corporations; often in endeavoring to evade or nullify the extremely crude laws by which legislators sought to regulate the power or curb the excesses of corporations.
> Such questions as the regulation of trusts, the fixing of railway rates, the municipalization of public utilities, the relation between capital and labor, call for the exercise of legal ability of the highest order. Up to the present time the legal ability of a high order which has been expended on those questions has been almost wholly in opposition to the contentions of the people. The leaders of the Bar, without any preconceived intent on their part, and rather as an incident to their professional standing, have, with rare exceptions, been ranged on the side of the corporations, and the people have been represented, in the main, by men of very meagre legal ability.
> If these problems are to be settled right, this condition cannot continue. . . . There will come a revolt of the people against the capitalists, unless the aspirations of the people are given some adequate legal expression; and to this end cooperation of the abler lawyers is essential.[35]

Brandeis coupled these words of reproach with a warning and a challenge. Calling on lawyers to remove the "great unfairness to the public" which results from the fact that private interests are repre-

[34] Mason, *Brandeis: Lawyer and Judge in the Modern State*, p. 136.
[35] Brandeis, *Business—A Profession*, pp. 338–39.

sented by men of ability and that the public is represented inadequately or not at all, he beckoned them to see that they had an
opportunity to help determine how the impending social conflict
would be resolved:

> Here, consequently, is the great opportunity in the law. The next gen-
> eration must witness a continuing and ever-increasing contest between
> those who have and those who have not. The industrial world is in a
> state of ferment. . . . The people are beginning to doubt whether in
> the long run democracy and absolutism can co-exist in the same com-
> munity; beginning to doubt whether there is a justification for the great
> inequalities in the distribution of wealth, for the rapid creation of for-
> tunes, more mysterious than the deeds of Aladdin's lamp. . . . The
> people's thought will take shape in action; and it lies with us, . . . to say
> on what lines the action is to be expressed; whether it is to be expressed
> wisely and temperately, or wildly and intemperately; whether it is to be
> expressed on lines of evolution or on lines of revolution.[36]

As is so often true of one's image of the ideal, so Brandeis' conception of the social function of the able lawyer was no doubt a reflection of his own experience and motivations. He believed that
lawyers of large affairs owed the community the benefit of their
superior talents; they were lawyer-statesmen. That this was one of
his abiding convictions is confirmed by a rather revealing incident
which took place almost at the end of his service on the Supreme
Court. "When, on the approach of his eightieth birthday," Paul A.
Freund recalls, "the former secretaries of Mr. Justice Brandeis
planned a visit in his honor, word came that, more than the pil-
grimage, the Justice would welcome a message from each of the
group recounting the public services that he had of late been performing. The would-be pilgrims had known in their hearts that the
devotion the Justice cherished most from them was devotion to his
conception of the lawyer's calling." [37]

Brandeis' "conception of the lawyer's calling" was in fact an integral part of his whole philosophy of so-called "living law." Prob-

[36] *Ibid.*, pp. 342–43.
[37] 49 *Harv. L. Rev. 181,* 195 (1941).

ably his best statement of the inadequacies of the legal process is to be found in a speech which he delivered before the Chicago Bar Association in January, 1915.[38] Once again he coupled a severe attack with a constructive blueprint for the future. Both his criticism and the techniques he advocated have become so deeply embedded in American constitutional law that it may be difficult to appreciate the importance of his pioneering effort.

He began his address by reminding his audience of the way in which "the American ideal of government" had changed since the adoption of the Constitution. "At first our ideal was expressed as 'A government of laws and not of men.' Then it became, 'A government of the people, by the people, for the people.' Now it is, 'Democracy and social justice.' " [39] With the growth of democracy had come a change in our conception of justice—"a shifting of our longing from legal justice to social justice." Not only had the conditions of life been greatly altered as the result of invention and discovery, but the new institutions and relationships had brought "new dangers to liberty."

Large publicly owned corporations replaced privately owned concerns. Ownership of the instruments of production passed from the workman to the employer. Individual personal relations between the proprietor and his help ceased. The individual contract of service lost its character, because of the inequality of position between employer and employee. The group relation of employee to employer, with collective bargaining, became common; for it was essential to the workers' protection.[40]

The clamor for social justice, Brandeis pointed out, had been accompanied by a "waning respect" for law, particularly its administration. This was no accident; it was due in large measure, he suggested, to the failure of the law to keep pace with our political, economic and social ideals.

[38] Brandeis, "The Living Law," *10 Ill. L. Rev. 461* (1915); reprinted in *The Curse of Bigness*, pp. 316–26.
[39] *Ibid.*, p. 316.
[40] *Ibid.*, p. 318.

Political as well as economic and social science noted these revolutionary changes. But legal science—the unwritten or judge-made laws as distinguished from legislation—was largely deaf and blind to them. Courts continued to ignore newly arisen social needs. They applied complacently eighteenth-century conceptions of the liberty of the individual and of the sacredness of private property. Early nineteenth-century scientific half-truths, like "The survival of the fittest," which, translated into practice, meant "The devil take the hindmost," were erected by judicial sanction into a moral law. Where statutes giving expression to the new social spirit were clearly constitutional, judges, imbued with the relentless spirit of individualism, often construed them away . . . Constitutional limitations were invoked to stop the natural vent of legislation.[41]

Though acknowledging that there were good reasons for the widespread distrust of lawyers and courts, Brandeis did not agree that the remedy lay in the establishment of non-legal tribunals or resort to such schemes as the recall of judges or judicial decisions. These palliatives were no cure for the static state of the law. The trouble stemmed from the fact that too many lawyers and judges lacked an understanding of contemporary industrial conditions, a situation which Brandeis attributed to the growing specialization in the law brought on by the needs of urban life. He apparently shared the conviction which Brooks Adams voiced at about the same time—lawyers, like capitalists, "think with specialized minds."[42] As Brandeis saw it, the problem was mainly one of education: "What we need is not to displace the courts, but to make them efficient instruments of justice; not to displace the lawyer, but to fit him for his official or judicial task."[43] It was necessary to reckon with the "great change" wrought in the legal profession since the rise of large urban centers. When communities were small, every lawyer was apt to be a general practitioner, so that in addition to his legal education, his diversified practice and clientele were giving him "an economic and social education." As he said:

---

[41] *Ibid.*, pp. 318–19.
[42] Adams, *The Theory of Social Revolutions* (New York: The Macmillan Company, 1913), p. 215.
[43] Brandeis, *The Curse of Bigness*, p. 323.

The relative smallness of the communities tended to make his practice diversified not only in the character of the matters dealt with, but also in the character or standing of his clients. For the same lawyer was apt to serve at one time or another both rich and poor, both employer and employee. Furthermore—nearly every lawyer of ability took some part in political life. Our greatest judges, Marshall, Kent, Story, Shaw, had secured this training.[44]

The complexities of our industrial civilization had forced lawyers to specialize, but their highly technical knowledge, Brandeis complained, was "purchased at the cost of vast areas of ignorance." Intense specialization was developing at the very moment when what was needed was broad knowledge of economic and social problems. The resulting effect on the administration of justice was both serious and dangerous: "The judge came to the bench unequipped with the necessary knowledge of economic and social science, and his judgment suffered likewise through lack of equipment in the lawyers who presented the cases to him. For a judge rarely performs his functions adequately unless the case before him is adequately presented. Thus were the blind led by the blind." [45] Brandeis was not so unrealistic as to suppose that the trend toward specialization in the law could be reversed. He insisted, however, that if lawyer and judge were to be equipped for the task of "harmonizing law with life," a new type of education was required. The way to correct the "distorting effects" of excessive specialization was by means of "broader education—by study undertaken preparatory to practice—and continued by lawyer and judge throughout life: study of economics and sociology and politics which embody the facts and present the problems of to-day." Brandeis concluded his address before Chicago's lawyers by quoting with obvious approval the assertion of a contemporary scholar that "a lawyer who has not studied economics and sociology is very apt to become a public enemy." [46]

[44] *Ibid.*, p. 324.
[45] *Ibid.*, p. 325.
[46] *Ibid.*

IV

This quite elaborate statement of the requisites of a socially aware jurisprudence was, whether by intention or not, Brandeis' defense of the approach to constitutional problems with which his own name was already intimately identified. For years he had been striving to lessen what Thorstein Veblen once termed "the discrepancy between law and fact." [47] Long before his appointment to the Supreme Court, he sought to convince courts—and at times with considerable success—that economic and social data were as relevant as legal precedents in determining the validity of assailed social legislation. His now famous factual brief in Muller v. Oregon [48]—a case concerned with the constitutionality of a ten-hour law for women workers—became a model for all those interested in removing the legal barriers to the efforts of government to humanize industrial working conditions. "It marks an epoch in the disposition of cases presenting the most important present-day constitutional issues" [49] was the way Felix Frankfurter summarized its significance in 1932. His biographer has described Brandeis' achievement in the case as truly "epoch-making" and the brief itself as "revolutionary." [50]

Not only had Brandeis succeeded in perfecting a novel and persuasive instrument for the argument of constitutional cases, but in Muller v. Oregon he had the satisfaction of seeing the Supreme Court of the United States accord it its official blessing. The traditional approach was to argue the case for social legislation largely on the basis of legal precedents and abstract logic. Brandeis' brief in the *Muller* case devoted just two pages to the legal argument, merely summarizing the rules applicable to the case. The résumé of prevailing constitutional theory was legal craft at its best; a subtle use of a strategy designed to prepare the ground for the major

[47] Veblen, *The Theory of Business Enterprise* (New York: Charles Scribner's Sons, 1904), p. 278.
[48] 208 U.S. 412 (1908).
[49] Frankfurter (ed.), *Mr. Justice Brandeis*, p. 52.
[50] Mason, *Brandeis: A Free Man's Life*, pp. 245, 249.

thrust. Over and over again, Brandeis referred to the decision in
Lochner v. New York, only to draw from it, paradoxical as it may
seem, inferences supporting his contention that the States had ample
constitutional authority to regulate the hours of labor of adult
women. Indeed, one unfamiliar with the fact that the majority in the
Lochner case had held a maximum-hour law to be unconstitutional,
might easily have concluded from Brandeis' treatment of it that the
New York statute had been sustained. What was the nature of his
argument?

Brandeis began by accepting the fundamental premise of the
Lochner decision that "the right to purchase or sell labor," as he
phrased it, was part of the "liberty" guaranteed by the Fourteenth
Amendment. That case also stood for the proposition that in the
exercise of its police power, a State might limit an individual's freedom of action if that were necessary for the protection of health,
safety, morals, and the general welfare. Furthermore, Brandeis
agreed with the principle of the *Lochner* case that to be valid,
restriction of the hours of labor must have a "real or substantial relation" to public health and safety, and that courts must set it aside
as invalid if they deem it to be an "unreasonable, unnecessary and
arbitrary interference" with personal liberty. "If the end which the
Legislature seeks to accomplish be one to which its power extends,
and if the means employed to that end, although not the wisest or
best, are yet not plainly and palpably unauthorized by law, then the
Court cannot interfere. In other words, when the validity of a statute
is questioned, the burden of proof, so to speak, is upon those who
assail it." [51]

With the aid of these rules, Brandeis proceeded to present to the
Court what he regarded as the basic legal issue in the case: "The
validity of the Oregon statute must therefore be sustained unless the

[51] *Women in Industry.* Decision of the United States Supreme Court in Curt
Muller vs. State of Oregon, upholding the constitutionality of the Oregon ten-
hour law for women. Brief for the State of Oregon by Louis D. Brandeis.
Assisted by Josephine Goldmark. Reprinted for The National Consumers' League,
New York City (1908), pp. 9-10.

Court can find there is no 'fair ground, reasonable in and of itself, to say that there is material danger to the public health (or safety), or to the health (or safety) of the employees (or as to the general welfare), if the hours of labor are not curtailed.' " [52] It was for the purpose of convincing the Supreme Court that the legislature of Oregon had adopted the ten-hour law in order to safeguard the public health, safety and welfare, that Brandeis presented that mass of factual detail, comprising more than a hundred pages, which became the prototype for brief-making in all similar litigation. He invited the Court to take "judicial notice" of the "facts of common knowledge" which showed that the legislature was entirely justified in assuming that the employment of women in factories and other mechanical establishments for more than ten hours a day was dangerous for both the workers and the community. There then followed an orderly parade of expert opinions and statistics, culled from as diverse a collection of sources as any present-day social scientist would find it hard to improve upon. Among the items was a documented summary of the "world's experience" with similar legislation; the reports of numerous legislative inquiries and administrative agencies, and the views of medical and other specialists regarding the "evil effect" of long hours upon the health and morals of women and the benefits to be derived from shorter hours. All of this material was introduced by way of emphasizing the important considerations which led twenty other states and many foreign countries to limit the working day for women. "This legislation has not been the result of sudden impulse or passing humor,—it has followed deliberate consideration, and been adopted in the face of much opposition. . . . In no instance has any such law been repealed." [53]

In his speech at Chicago, Brandeis had complained that both lawyers and judges lacked knowledge of the "facts of business life." Much of his brief in the *Muller* case reads as if he wanted to make sure that the elderly Justices knew the facts of life itself;

[52] *Ibid.*, p. 10.
[53] *Ibid.*, p. 16.

perhaps he was unconsciously moved by Holmes' admonition that "judges too need education in the obvious." But of course his dominant motive was to impress the Court with the weight of scientific opinion establishing the special need for legislation protecting women against the hazards of long hours. A few brief paragraphs from this historic and human document may help convey the sweep and appeal of its argument:

Long hours of labor are dangerous for women primarily because of their special physical organization. In structure and function women are differentiated from men. Besides these anatomical and physiological differences, physicians are agreed that women are fundamentally weaker than men in all that makes for endurance; in muscular strength, in nervous energy, in the powers of persistent attention and application. Overwork, therefore, which strains endurance to the utmost, is more disastrous to the health of women than of men, and entails upon them more lasting injury.

    ✿   ✿   ✿

Such being their physical endowment, women are affected to a far greater degree than men by the growing strain of modern industry. Machinery is increasingly speeded up, the number of machines tended by individual workers grows larger, processes become more and more complex as more operations are performed simultaneously. All these changes involve correspondingly greater physical strain upon the worker.

    ✿   ✿   ✿

The fatigue which follows long hours of labor becomes chronic and results in general deterioration of health. Often ignored, since it does not result in immediate disease, this weakness and anaemia undermines the whole system; it destroys the nervous energy most necessary for steady work, and effectually predisposes to other illness. The long hours of standing which are required in many industries, are universally denounced by physicians as the cause of pelvic disorders.

    ✿   ✿   ✿

The evil effect of overwork before as well as after marriage upon childbirth is marked and disastrous.

    ✿   ✿   ✿

Accidents to working women occur most frequently at the close of the day, or after a long period of uninterrupted work. The coincidence of casualties and fatigue due to long hours is thus made manifest.

⁕   ⁕   ⁕

The effect of overwork on morals is closely related to the injury to health. Laxity of moral fibre follows physical debility. When the working day is so long that no time whatever is left for a minimum of leisure or home life, relief from the strain of work is sought in alcoholic stimulants and other excesses.

⁕   ⁕   ⁕

The experience of manufacturing countries has illustrated the evil effect of overwork upon the general welfare. Deterioration of any large proportion of the population inevitably lowers the entire community physically, mentally, and morally. When the health of women has been injured by long hours, not only is the working efficiency of the community impaired, but the deterioration is handed down to succeeding generations. Infant mortality rises, while the children of married working-women, who survive, are injured by inevitable neglect. The overwork of future mothers thus directly attacks the welfare of the nation.

⁕   ⁕   ⁕

History, which has illustrated the deterioration due to long hours, bears witness no less clearly to the regeneration due to the shorter working day. To the individual and to society alike, shorter hours have been a benefit wherever introduced. The married and unmarried working woman is enabled to obtain the decencies of life outside of working hours. With the improvement in home life, the tone of the entire community is raised. Wherever sufficient time has elapsed since the establishment of the shorter working day, the succeeding generation has shown extraordinary improvement in physique and morals.[54]

But Brandeis' triumph in Muller v. Oregon consisted of much more than success in arguing a case on the basis of the actual conditions of industrial life. One reason the case is considered to be a landmark in constitutional adjudication is that the Supreme Court accepted the brief filed by Brandeis as an entirely appropriate means for buttressing the legal argument in behalf of what would be called today welfare legislation. "The Muller case is epoch-making," Felix Frankfurter wrote in 1916, "not because of its decision, but be-

[54] Ibid., pp. 18, 24, 28, 36, 42, 44, 47, 57.

cause of the authoritative recognition by the Supreme Court that the way in which Mr. Brandeis presented the case . . . laid down a new technique for counsel charged with the responsibility of arguing such constitutional questions, and an obligation upon courts to insist upon such method of argument before deciding the issue." [55] Justice Brewer, a quite conservative judge but the author of the opinion sustaining the Oregon law, not only singled out the Brandeis brief for special mention, but took occasion to express the Court's approbation of the method it employed. He wrote:

It may not be amiss, in the present case, before examining the constitutional question, to notice the course of legislation as well as expressions of opinion from other judicial sources. In the brief filed by Mr. Louis D. Brandeis . . . is a very copious collection of all of these matters.

The legislation and opinions referred to in the margin may not be, technically speaking, authorities and in them is little or no discussion of the constitutional question presented to us for determination, yet they are significant of a widespread belief that woman's physical structure, and the functions she performs in consequence thereof, justify special legislation restricting or qualifying the conditions under which she should be permitted to toil.[56]

Of similar breadth and appeal were Brandeis' brief and argument in the case which challenged the constitutionality of the minimum wage law for women which the State of Oregon enacted in 1913.[57] In his oral presentation before the Supreme Court, on December 17, 1914, he first stressed the far-reaching significance of the decision the Justices were being asked to make. "This case," he told the Court, "involves . . . not only the constitutionality of the laws of these states which have already legislated on this subject, but upon the decision will depend also the action of the states which are in the process of preparing for legislation." [58] Nine States had passed

[55] Frankfurter, "Hours of Labor and Realism in Constitutional Law," (1916); reprinted in 2 *Selected Essays,* 699, 709.
[56] 208 U.S. 412, at 419–21.
[57] Stettler v. O'Hara, 243 U.S. 629 (1917).
[58] "The Constitution and the Minimum Wage," Argument before the Supreme Court of the United States in Stettler v. O'Hara, reprinted in *The Curse of Bigness,* pp. 52, 53.

minimum wage laws in 1913, a coincidence which Brandeis attributed to the ferment generated by several recent events. In 1909
England adopted its first minimum wage act; in 1910 the United
States Bureau of Labor published a nineteen-volume study concerned with the labor of women and children; and in 1912 the report
of the Massachusetts Commission on the Minimum Wage had been
followed by the enactment of a minimum wage measure in that
State.

Conceding that Oregon's Minimum Wage Law "restricts the liberty not only of the employer but also the liberty of the employee,"
Brandeis argued that the restriction was justified by the deplorable
condition of women in industry in the State. The situation in Oregon,
he emphasized, had been confirmed by the results of studies of conditions both in the United States and in foreign countries. "What
these results are," he said to the Justices, "I have endeavored to set
forth in my brief. In it you will find three hundred and sixty-nine
extracts which present the facts from various publications bearing
upon this subject." He then described for them the situation which
had induced the legislature of Oregon to enact the Minimum Wage
Law:

The first thing the people of Oregon did was to ascertain to what extent, as a matter of fact, women in industry in that state were working for
less than a minimum wage, for a wage less than the necessary cost of
decent living. That was the first subject of investigation; and it was found
that in the State of Oregon, whatever might be the case elsewhere, a
majority of the women to whom the investigation extended, were working for a wage smaller than that required for decent living.

The next inquiry was what happened to women who worked for wages
smaller than the minimum cost of decent living. It was found that in
Oregon a large number of such women were ruining their health because
they were not eating enough. That was the commonest result. They
scrimped themselves on eating, in order to live decently in other respects
or in order to dress and hold their jobs. Those that ate enough, roomed
under conditions that were unwholesome, or they were insufficiently
clothed. Besides those who lacked the ordinary necessities of life, the
investigators found another class of women whose wages were inade-

quate but who supplied themselves with the necessities by a sacrifice of
morality. They found that in a large number of cases, the insufficient
wage was supplemented by contributions from "gentlemen friends." [59]

Brandeis took the position that the constitutionality of minimum
wage legislation must rest on "facts or conclusions drawn from
facts" regarding the need for the legislation as seen by the law-
makers. But he went further. If this were so, it really did not matter
what data could be adduced in opposition to the experiment. The
passage in which Brandeis presented this view contains the core of
the attitude he was later to express as a member of the Court, and
for this reason it may be of interest to recall it:

> In answer to the question, whether this brief contains also all the data
> opposed to minimum-wage laws, I want to say this: I conceive it to be
> absolutely immaterial what may be said against such laws. Each one of
> these statements contained in the brief in support of the contention that
> this is wise legislation, might upon further investigation be found to be
> erroneous, each conclusion of fact may be found afterwards to be un-
> sound—and yet the constitutionality of the act would not be affected
> thereby. This court is not burdened with the duty of passing upon the
> disputed question whether the legislature of Oregon was wise or unwise,
> or probably wise or unwise, in enacting this law. The question is merely
> whether, . . . you can see that the legislators had no ground on which
> they could, as reasonable men, deem this legislation appropriate to
> abolish or mitigate the evils believed to exist or apprehended. If you can-
> not find that, the law must stand.[60]

And for those who are looking for clues to the affinity that developed between the two men soon after Brandeis became Holmes'
colleague, the following peroration from Brandeis' argument before
the Supreme Court in 1914 may not be without some illumination:

> In any or all of this legislation there may be economic and social error.
> But our social and industrial welfare demands that ample scope should
> be given for social as well as mechanical invention. It is a condition not
> only of progress but of conserving that which we have. Nothing could

[59] *Ibid.*, p. 54.
[60] *Ibid.*, pp. 65–66.

be more revolutionary than to close the door to social experimentation. The whole subject of woman's entry into industry is an experiment. And surely the federal constitution—itself perhaps the greatest of human experiments—does not prohibit such modest attempts as the woman's minimum-wage act to reconcile the existing industrial system with our striving for social justice and the preservation of the race.[61]

Something Roscoe Pound has said suggests a rather useful test for assessing the true significance of the Brandeis brief. "It is not one of the least problems of the sociological jurists," he wrote in 1911, "to discover a rational mode of advising the court of facts of which it is supposed to take judicial notice." [62] Pound's protest against the "mechanical" exercise of the judicial function was, of course, a criticism of courts generally and could be met only by a more "scientific" ascertainment of the "social facts" upon which court decisions were based. Yet the curious fact is that Pound did not recognize Brandeis for the leader of the new jurisprudence that he was. As one of Brandeis' law secretaries has suggested, Brandeis was "living proof" of the kind of jurist Pound was seeking.[63] In the constitutional sphere, Brandeis was the prophet of the new approach, an approach which was marked, in the colorful words of Judge Learned Hand, by "that insistence upon fact and reason which was at once his weapon and his shield." [64] To Judge Hand this was the quintessence of Brandeis' "style" as a Justice of the Supreme Court. But even if Louis D. Brandeis had not been afforded the opportunity to apply his methods and his ideas within the judicial laboratory, the social importance of the techniques he initiated would have assured him a lasting reputation as a master of sociological jurisprudence.

[61] Ibid., pp. 68–69. For a discussion of the outcome of Brandeis' effort in Stettler v. O'Hara, see below, pp. 143–44.
[62] Quoted by Felix Frankfurter, op. cit., 2 Selected Essays, 669, 716.
[63] Interview with James M. Landis, New York City, June 18, 1951.
[64] The Spirit of Liberty, Papers and Addresses of Learned Hand, collected with an introduction and notes by Irving Dilliard (New York: Alfred A. Knopf, 1952), p. 168.

6

"A system of living law"

Writing to Justice Holmes from Cambridge on January 13, 1918, Harold J. Laski registered a complaint about Brandeis. "Pound and I agreed yesterday that if you could hint to Brandeis that judicial opinions aren't to be written in the form of a brief it would be a great relief to the world. Pound spoke rather strongly as to the advocate in B. being over-prominent in his decisions just as in his general philosophy." [1]

Replying to Laski on January 18, Holmes wrote: "What you say about the form of Brandeis's opinions had been remarked on by me before you wrote, if you refer to the form in a strict sense—the putting in of headings and footnotes—and on one occasion I told him that I thought he was letting partisanship disturb his judicial attitude. I am frank with him because I value him and think he brings many admirable qualifications to his work." [2]

In the 1920's, the words "Justices Holmes and Brandeis dissented" had become a familiar refrain in discussions about the work of the Supreme Court. This affinity between two men so unlike each other in background and method naturally puzzled the observers, and the

[1] *Holmes-Laski Letters*, I, 127.
[2] *Ibid.*, I, 128.

effort to explain their relationship has produced two mutually contradictory theories. One view holds that though the two jurists ap-
proached problems differently, they usually arrived at the same
conclusion because they shared a common philosophy on all really
basic issues. "Oliver Wendell Holmes and Louis Dembitz Brandeis,"
a contemporary press comment read, "have achieved a spiritual kinship that marks them off as a separate liberal chamber of the Supreme Court. On the great issues that go down to the fundamental
differences in the philosophy of government these two are nearly
always together; often they are together against the rest of the
court." [3]

On the other hand, there were those who suspected that Holmes
was at heart a social conservative and that his "liberalism" was
largely the product of Brandeis' influence on him. "Holmes had his
education in the essential economic facts of life from Brandeis, and
he was sometimes a reluctant pupil. But when the immense mar-
shalling of facts by his younger colleague failed to interest him, the
character of Brandeis convinced him." [4] A much more plausible
theory has been advanced by one of Holmes' law secretaries. It
may well be, Mark DeWolfe Howe has suggested, that Brandeis'
influence in keeping Holmes on the liberal side in the 1920's was
exerted indirectly. The young secretaries who came to Holmes were
probably more sympathetic to the ideas for which Brandeis stood.
They no doubt helped to refresh the Justice's thinking and thus contributed to Brandeis' influence.[5]

Judging from Taft's private correspondence, it would seem that
the Chief Justice was partly responsible for nurturing the myth of
Holmes' complete dependence on Brandeis. In a letter to Henry L.
Stimson in May, 1928, Taft wrote about Holmes: "I am very fond
of the old gentleman, but he is so completely under the control of
Brother Brandeis that it gives to Brandeis two votes instead of one.

[3] Charles G. Ross in the *St. Louis Post-Dispatch*, June 19, 1927, quoted by
Irving Dilliard (ed.), *Mr. Justice Brandeis, Great American*, p. 14.
[4] Louis M. Lyons in the *Boston Daily Globe*, Oct. 6, 1941, *ibid.*, p. 18.
[5] Interview with Professor Howe, at Harvard, April 6, 1951.

He has more interest in, and gives more attention to his dissents than he does to the opinions he writes for the Court, which are very short and not very helpful." [6]

Granted that Taft's frustration over his failure to dominate the Court led him to exaggerate Brandeis' mischief, it nevertheless is becoming increasingly clear that the younger Justice's habit of urging his "elder brother to speak out in dissent" had its intended effect. Nor did Holmes hesitate to acknowledge Brandeis' pressure on him, especially in the early years, as the following comments in his letters to Laski show:

Unless I let Brandeis egg me on to writing a dissent in advance.

On that day came down an opinion that stirred the innards of Brandeis and me and he spurred me to write a dissent.

When I can get calm I am catspawed by Brandeis to do another dissent on burning themes.

Brandeis, . . . reminded me of a case argued last term in which he said I should have to write a dissent.

But meantime a dissent that the ever active Brandeis put upon my conscience waits untouched. [7]

Taft thought that he discerned the chief factor in Brandeis' effect on Holmes when he commented in 1923: "I think perhaps his age makes him a little more subordinate or yielding to Brandeis, who is his constant companion, than he would have been in his prime." [8]

Yet when one stops to consider the fact that by the time Brandeis became his colleague, Justice Holmes had already been sitting in judgment on the "burning themes" for more than thirty years and had developed a distinct and mature philosophy of his own, it is hard to accept the picture of Holmes being led astray by a younger even if respected and persuasive associate. After all, we have Taft's

[6] Henry F. Pringle, *The Life and Times of William Howard Taft* (New York: Farrar & Rinehart, 1939), II, 969–70.

[7] *Holmes-Laski Letters,* I, 148, 157, 176; II, 1192, 1347.

[8] Pringle, *op. cit.,* II, 969.

own word as to the undiminished vigor of Holmes' intellectual powers at age eighty-two. "Association with Justice Holmes," Taft wrote to Learned Hand on March 3, 1923, "is a delight. He is feebler physically, but I cannot see that the acuteness of his mind has been affected at all. . . . In many ways he is the life of the court." [9]

Brandeis' presence on the Court may have been of decisive importance in getting Holmes to appreciate the extent to which their conservative colleagues were unaware of the conditions and issues of the day. However, it must not be forgotten that there was much in Holmes' own prior record to explain the general direction of his constitutional philosophy in the 1920's. The basic presuppositions— "aperçus" Holmes liked to call them—of the two men may have diverged and their thought processes may have been different, but a close look at their behavior as judges during this period will demonstrate that the affinity between them is neither mysterious nor the product of personal ascendancy.

II

As the exchange between Holmes and Laski reprinted at the beginning of this chapter suggests, Brandeis revealed at the very outset of his judicial career that his handling of constitutional cases was going to be different, if not unique. Though he found himself disagreeing with the majority in five cases during his first term on the Court,[10] he submitted formal dissents in only two, prefacing each opinion with the apology that it was the "importance of the question involved" which had induced him "to state the reasons" for dissenting. The first of these dissents—in New York Central Railroad Company v. Winfield,[11] decided May 21, 1917—is the one

[9] *Ibid.*

[10] During his first year on the Bench, Brandeis was the Court's spokesman in twenty-two cases. He dissented for the first time when he concurred in the opinion of Justice Pitney in Louisville and Nashville RR. v. United States, 242 U.S. 60, 75 (1916).

[11] 244 U.S. 147, 154 (1917).

Holmes had in mind when he agreed with Laski as to the form of Brandeis' opinions: "In one case when he [Brandeis] wrote a long essay on the development of employers' liability, I told him that I thought it out of place and irrelevant." [12] Holmes was with the majority in this case, and Brandeis had the support only of Justice Clarke.

The *Winfield* case involved a rather knotty question of legislative intent, more specifically, the effect of the Federal Employers' Liability Act upon state workmen's compensation systems. Justice Van Devanter's opinion for the Court held that when Congress in 1908 made interstate railroads liable for their negligence resulting in personal injuries to their employees, it intended to keep the States from dealing with the legal liability of interstate railroads for injuries suffered by their employees. As applied in the circumstances of the particular case—and this is the aspect which evoked Brandeis' sharp dissent—the ruling meant that a state might not require compensation for railway employees engaged in interstate commerce for injuries which were not the fault of the railroad. The Federal law provided no remedy for injuries not attributable to the negligence of the railroad.

Brandeis came to the opposite conclusion, namely, that the limited effect of the Employers' Liability Act was to impose liability for negligence, and that the States were left free to regulate the obligation of interstate carriers for accidents arising from other causes. The final sentence of his opinion sums up his position: "I find no justification for imputing to Congress the will to deny to a large class of persons engaged in a necessarily hazardous occupation and otherwise unprovided for the protection afforded by beneficent statutes enacted in the long-deferred performance of an insistent duty and in a field peculiarly appropriate for state action." [13] Examination of the ground he traversed in arriving at this conclusion suggests that Holmes may have misjudged his junior colleague's purpose.

[12] *Holmes-Laski Letters*, I, 128.
[13] 244 U.S. 147, 154, at 169–70.

It is obvious that Brandeis did not share Holmes' view that "the only question" was "whether Congress had dealt with the matter so far as to exclude state action." [14] To him the more important consideration—and the one which he thought the majority was ignoring —was the impact of the decision upon state workmen compensation laws and the ends they were meant to serve. He examined the "world's experience" with industrial accidents in order to indicate the considerations which led to the development of employer liability. One cannot read his searching survey of the origin, purposes and methods of employer liability laws without appreciating that this was no idle display of erudition; nor was it merely the product of the impulse of the "advocate." It was his way of showing the Court that the issue before it could not be adjudicated without regard to social consequences. After summarizing the common law precepts respecting liability,[15] he went on to speak of the injustice which the traditional approaches to the question of liability in industrial employment had produced. His blunt language deserves to be recalled:

In an effort to remove abuses, a study had been made of facts; and of the world's experience in dealing with industrial accidents. That study uncovered as fiction many an assumption upon which American judges and lawyers had rested comfortably. The conviction became widespread, that our individualistic conception of rights and liability no longer fur-

[14] *Holmes-Laski Letters*, I, 128.

[15] "By the common law as administered in the several States, the employee, like every other member of the community, was expected to bear the risks necessarily attendant upon life and work; subject only to the right to be indemnified for any loss inflicted by wrongdoers. The employer, like every other member of the community, was in theory liable to all others for loss resulting from his wrongs; the scope of his liability for wrongs being amplified by the doctrine of *respondeat superior*. The legal liability, which in theory applied between employer and employee as well as between others, came, in course of time, to be seriously impaired in practice. The protection it provided employees seemed to wane as the need for it grew. Three defenses—the doctrines of fellow servant's negligence, of assumption of risk and of contributory negligence—rose and flourished. When applied to huge organizations and hazardous occupations, as in railroading, they practically abolished liability of employers to employees; and in so doing they worked great hardship and apparent injustice." 244 U.S. 147, 154, at 159–60.

nished an adequate basis for dealing with accidents in industry. It was
seen that no system of indemnity dependent upon fault on the employers'
part could meet the situation; even if the law were perfected and its
administration made exemplary. For in probably a majority of cases of
injury there was no assignable fault; and in many it must be impossible
of proof.[16]

With his attention fixed on the need for protecting workers against
the hazards of modern industry, it is not surprising that Brandeis
should have construed the federal Employers' Liability Act as leav-
ing the States entirely free to provide relief for injuries not covered
by Federal legislation. Not the technicalities as to the employer's
fault but the social effects of the "employee's misfortune" must be
of primary interest to government. Expressing concern over the
impact of industrial accidents upon the community as a whole, he
stressed the fact that under the American federal system it is the
States which have the responsibility for alleviating individual
misery:

It is the State which is both primarily and ultimately concerned with
the care of the injured and of those dependent upon him; even though
the accident may occur while the employee is engaged directly in interstate commerce. Upon the State falls the far heavier burden of the
demoralization of its citizenry, and of the social unrest, which attend
destitution and the denial of opportunity. Upon the State also rests under
our dual system of government the duty owed to the individual to avert
misery and promote happiness so far as possible.[17]

Brandeis finished his first year on the Court by writing a dissenting opinion with which even Justice Holmes was able to agree.
In his dissent in Adams v. Tanner [18] may be seen, perhaps more so
than in the *Winfield* case, both the attitude and techniques which
were to become the hallmarks of the Brandeis opinions in cases concerned with the constitutional validity of social legislation. He was
taking exception to the decision of the Court, arrived at by a vote

[16] *Ibid.*, at 164–65.
[17] *Ibid.*, at 166.
[18] 244 U.S. 590, 597 (1917).

of five-to-four, setting aside a measure which the voters of the State of Washington had adopted by means of an Initiative Petition prohibiting employment agencies from taking fees from workers for placing them in jobs.

The glaring contrast between Brandeis' discussion of the problem posed by the case and Justice McReynolds' treatment of it was symptomatic of the great schism within the Court which was only to be intensified in the coming years. Defending the reasonableness of the law, the lawyers for the State of Washington had argued that the business of private employment agencies was "economically . . . non-useful, if not vicious, because it compels the needy and unfortunate to pay for that which they are entitled to without fee or price, that is, the right to work." Justice McReynolds, who spoke for the Court, rejected this sweeping condemnation of private employment agencies. If there were abuses in the business, he said, they might justify regulation, whereas the prohibition of fees would bring about its destruction. To forbid the agencies to collect fees for a legitimate service was, therefore, both "arbitrary and oppressive."

Brandeis thought that the majority had rested its decision on a false distinction. He began his elaborate dissent by speaking of the "seriousness" of the power to invalidate a State's laws and by borrowing from Holmes' first Supreme Court opinion. He recalled Holmes' observation that courts were not to interfere with a State's exercise of its police power unless they were convinced that it was "a clear, unmistakable infringement of rights secured by the fundamental law." [19] Tested by this yardstick—judicial presumption of constitutionality—it did not matter whether the method for protecting the public was one of regulating or prohibiting altogether the calling or activity sought to be curbed. Brandeis' statement of the factors to be taken into account by courts when they are passing on the constitutionality of social legislation helps explain why the rest of his opinion reads like a brief. He wrote:

[19] Quoted by Brandeis from Otis v. Parker, 187 U.S. 606, at 609 (1903).

Whether a measure relating to the public welfare is arbitrary or unreasonable, whether it has no substantial relation to the end proposed is
obviously not to be determined by assumptions or by *a priori* reasoning.
The judgment should be based upon a consideration of relevant facts,
actual or possible—*ex facto jus oritur.* That ancient rule must prevail in
order that we may have a system of living law.[20]

He then asked a series of questions: "What was the evil which the
people of Washington sought to correct? Why was the particular
remedy embodied in the statute adopted? And, incidentally, what
has been the experience, if any, of other States or countries in this
connection?" [21]

Before turning to the materials which he thought ought to govern the answer to these inquiries, Brandeis made it clear that his object was not to determine whether the legislation under attack was
"wise" or even to ascertain what the facts were. The wisdom of public policy "lies with the legislative branch of Government," he observed. His "sole purpose" was to determine whether in view of the
known facts of the situation, the action of the State of Washington
was so "arbitrary or unreasonable" as to violate fundamental
rights.

What were the facts? They indicated that the evils with which
the State was dealing were serious and widespread. Quoting from
numerous publications of Federal and State agencies in the labor
field and the findings of official as well as private investigations,
Brandeis pointed out that the experience with private employment
agencies had revealed the existence of such grave abuses as exorbitant fees, discrimination, "fee-splitting" with foremen who discharged men in order to hire others, and misrepresentation of terms
and conditions of employment. Following extensive public hearings,
the United States Commission on Industrial Relations had concluded in 1914 that even the properly conducted private agencies
only congest the labor market, increase irregularity of employment,

[20] 244 U.S. 590, 597, at 600.
[21] *Ibid.*

and make the poorest class of wage earners pay "the largest share for a service rendered to employers, to workers, and to the public as well."

Washington was not the first State to attempt to regulate the private employment agencies. As many as twenty-four States had sought to cope with the problem either by statute or municipal ordinances, and in nineteen of them municipal employment offices were established to compete with private agencies. These various experiments proved to be unsatisfactory, so that the conviction grew, Justice Brandeis stated, that "the evils of private agencies were inherent and ineradicable, so long as they were permitted to charge fees to the workers seeking employment." In Washington, as in the other Pacific States, the situation was accentuated by the lack of staple industries and the frequent shifting from job to job due to the seasonal nature of much of the work. Moreover, the low cost of the municipally-operated labor offices in several of Washington's cities had only served to show that the way to protect those seeking jobs was to prohibit fees for the service. In view of these facts and circumstances, it was not unreasonable for the people of Washington to believe that the collection of fees from employees was a "social injustice" and that its prohibition might lessen chronic unemployment—"perhaps the gravest and most difficult problem of modern industry."

III

We learn from his biographer that Brandeis' early dissents were soon recognized as launching an innovation in judicial technique. Brandeis was using the dissenting opinion, writes Professor Mason, "as an educational device to explore and illumine not only the law but also the relations which law governs, . . . in a persuasive demonstration of what the law ought to be in terms of social justice." [22] He adds that since the Supreme Court was at the time

[22] Mason, *Brandeis: A Free Man's Life*, p. 518.

"reactionary" in both outlook and temperament, Brandeis "was fated to write his most notable opinions in dissent." [23]

To what extent did this situation on the Court also help to cast Justice Holmes in the role of "the great dissenter"? The more one observes the pervasive strain of skepticism in his thought, the more convinced one must become that the intransigence and dogmatism of many of his colleagues may well have been the principal force moving Holmes to protest, as it may also account for his coming ever closer to Brandeis. Certainly any suggestion that the two Justices found themselves at war with their colleagues most of the time would completely misrepresent their position on the Court. As the late George W. Kirchwey said of Holmes in 1929, "He is not a voice crying in the wilderness. While he has not hesitated on occasion to stand alone, this has rarely been his fate . . . the opinions in which he has given expression to the judgment of the Court or in which he has concurred in its judgment far out-number, in the ratio of eight or ten to one, those in which he has felt it necessary to record his dissent." [24]

The same is true of Justice Brandeis. Moreover, some of the most significant decisions from which they dissented had been reached by a bare majority of the Court, and increasingly their dissents came to be shared by one or two other Justices. Nevertheless, there is intellectual peril in using dissenting opinions as a vehicle for assessing the distinctive thought and methods of men who were members of an institution whose chief importance in the polity is as a collective body. The dissenter, too, must bend his utterance to the requisites of his office and even to the vagaries of the majority's pronouncement. Especially in the case of Justice Holmes, there is considerable evidence that he strove rather conscientiously to adjust his criticisms to the views of his colleagues. "When I am going to dissent," he wrote to Laski in 1920, "I almost always prepare my opinion at once

[23] *Ibid.*
[24] Foreword to *The Dissenting Opinions of Mr. Justice Holmes,* edited by Alfred Lief (New York: Vanguard Press, 1929), p. x.

—and then when the majority speaks, simply make such adjustments as to bring our discussion *ad idem*—which I think is the decent way, but which is not practiced." [25]

Yet as compared with the necessity for subordinating individuality when speaking for the Court, the dissenting opinion is a far more reliable guide to the distinctive thought of the judge than is "the opinion of the Court." In the very nature of things, the dissent, since it is the product of conflict and has been occasioned by disagreement which makes silence intolerable, is obviously useful in revealing fundamental differences among men whose dominant professional impulse should be to speak with one voice. It is an excellent vehicle through which the combatants may register, deliberately or unwittingly, the ideas and values motivating the struggle and at the same time appeal to the judgment of posterity. "I wish a lawyer would measure the development of law by dissents," a learned and experienced judge once wrote, and he added: "In a court not subject to sudden change, able and continued dissent delimits and accentuates decisions; it reveals far more than does the majority opinion the intellectual differences of the council table." [26]

If it is true, as Holmes himself has said, that "the place for a man who is complete in all his powers is in the fight," [27] then surely the dissenting opinions of two such powerful intellects as Holmes and Brandeis may be assumed to embody their most deeply felt precepts about the American constitutional system. What Felix Frankfurter wrote about Holmes in 1927 is equally true of Brandeis, "some of his weightiest utterances are dissenting opinions—but they are dissents that record prophecy and shape history." [28]

But many a commentator has insisted that the reputation of

[25] *Holmes-Laski Letters*, I, 240.
[26] Charles M. Hough, "Due Process of Law—Today," *32 Harv. L. Rev. 218* (1919); reprinted in *1 Selected Essays 302, 313.* Hough was a United States District Judge for the Southern District of New York between 1906 and 1916 and Judge of the United States Circuit Court of Appeals, Second Circuit, 1916–1926.
[27] Holmes, *Collected Legal Papers*, p. 224.
[28] Frankfurter (ed.), *Mr. Justice Holmes*, p. 116.

Holmes and Brandeis as dissenters has been greatly exaggerated, because their dissents were few compared with the number of times they concurred in the actions of the Court. This is a misleading criterion. Evaluation of a phenomenon of profound intellectual and historical significance ought not to be made on the basis of mere statistics. The quantitative sticklers, that is to say, are not reckoning sufficiently with the fact that the dissents by Holmes and Brandeis were directed to a condition on the Supreme Court which was not only, as future events proved, socially explosive, but one which afforded dramatic demonstration of the major paradox in America's experiment with democratic government. Robert H. Jackson was not guilty of special pleading, but was merely recording accurate history, when he pointed out in 1941 that President Roosevelt's 1937 plan for reorganizing the Supreme Court "was the political manifestation of a long smouldering intellectual revolt" against the Court's constitutional philosophy.[29] Long before political leaders made the Court's conservatism an issue of public debate, Justice Holmes and Brandeis had come to be looked upon as spokesmen for the growing protest against the abuse of judicial power.

Ever since our earliest constitutional debates, the relation of a non-elective judiciary—possessing the power to negate the policies of the other branches—to the processes of representative government has been the fundamental but unresolved issue in American constitutionalism. The fear of unbridled majority rule and the search for political stability largely explain the ease with which the Constitutional Convention of 1787 adopted the provisions establishing an appointive judiciary, whose members were to serve for life. One

---

[29] "The Court Reorganization Message of President Roosevelt was the political manifestation of a long smouldering intellectual revolt against the philosophy of many of the Supreme Court's decisions on constitutional questions. This protest was led by outspoken and respected members of the Court itself. Among its most influential spokesmen were those in our universities distinguished for disinterested legal scholarship. It counted among its followers many thoughtful conservatives and practically all liberal and labor leadership." Jackson, *The Struggle for Judicial Supremacy*, p. 1 (Preface).

need only follow the forthright discussion in the *Federalist Papers* of the elaborate scheme of checks and balances embodied in the Constitution to appreciate that judicial supremacy was probably the inevitable by-product of the grand design of republican government. "This very system of checks and balances, which is undeniably the essential element of the Constitution," Charles A. Beard has written, "is built upon the doctrine that the popular branch of the government cannot be allowed full sway, and least of all in the enactment of laws touching the rights of property." [30]

Alexander Hamilton—whose ideas proved to be too extreme for most of the delegates—urged the Convention to establish an "hereditary" chief magistrate, representing the "permanent will" of society and capable of curbing the "turbulent and uncontrouling disposition" of democracy. But seeing no chance for the adoption of his proposals, he soon became a convert to constitutional checks as the most practicable means for giving effect to his conviction that "there ought to be a principle in government capable of resisting the popular current." [31] It is not surprising, therefore, that Hamilton should have become a vigorous supporter of judicial supremacy long before John Marshall succeeded in making it an accomplished fact. No more enlightening revelation of the purposes ultimately to be served by judicial review is to be found than in his "Examination of the Judiciary Department." [32]

Hamilton candidly acknowledged that the courts "were designed to be an intermediate body between the people and the legislature" and that they were meant to be "the bulwarks" of the Constitution "against legislative encroachments." His defense of judicial authority is accompanied by repeated invocation of the need for protecting society against "legislative invasions" of the Constitution "instigated by the major voice of the community." By way of bolster-

[30] Beard, *The Supreme Court and the Constitution* (New York: The Macmillan Company, 1912; 1938 ed.), p. 95.

[31] Max Farrand (ed.), *The Records of the Federal Convention of 1787* (New Haven: Yale University Press, 1937), I, 299, 309, 310.

[32] *The Federalist, No. LXXVIII* (The Heritage Press, 1945), p. 519.

ing his argument for permanent tenure of judicial offices, he maintained that the independence of judges was an "essential safeguard"
against those "ill-humors in society" which may injure "the private
rights of particular classes of citizens, by unjust and partial laws."
He expected the judiciary to be a force "in mitigating the severity
and confining the operation of such laws." Yet he denied that the
authority to control the legislative department made the judiciary
superior to the legislature, and thereby he furnished Marshall with
the chief rationalization for reconciling the power assumed by the
Supreme Court "to say what the law is" [33] with the traditional notion
of popular sovereignty. Hamilton wrote:

Nor does this conclusion [the authority of courts "to ascertain" the
"meaning" of the Constitution] by any means suppose a superiority of the
judicial to the legislative power. It only supposes that the power of the
people is superior to both; and that where the will of the legislature,
declared in its statutes, stands in opposition to that of the people, declared
in the Constitution, the judges ought to be governed by the latter rather
than the former. They ought to regulate their decisions by the fundamental laws, rather than by those which are not fundamental.[34]

[33] "It is emphatically the province and duty of the judicial department to
say what the law is." Chief Justice Marshall, in Marbury v. Madison, 1 Cranch
137, at 177 (1803).
[34] *The Federalist*, p. 523. Marshall's logic on the same matter went as follows:
"That the people have an original right to establish, for their future government, such principles, as, in their opinion, shall most conduce to their own
happiness is the basis on which the whole American fabric has been erected.
. . . The principles, therefore, so established, are deemed fundamental. And
as the authority from which they proceed is supreme, and can seldom act, they
are designed to be permanent.
"This original and supreme will organizes the government, and assigns to
different departments their respective powers. . . .
". . . The powers of the legislature are defined and limited; and that those
limits may not be mistaken, or forgotten, the Constitution is written. To what
purpose are powers limited, and to what purpose is that limitation committed
to writing, if these limits may, at any time, be passed by those intended to be
restrained? . . .
"Certainly all those who have framed written constitutions contemplate them
as forming the fundamental and paramount law of the nation, and, consequently,
the theory of every such government must be, that an act of the legislature,
repugnant to the constitution, is void." 1 Cranch 137, at 175–76.

Before concluding his case for judicial control of legislative action, Hamilton remarked that this function "was calculated to have more influence upon the character of our governments than but few may be aware of." [35] This is but one of Hamilton's many prophetic judgments which justified Parrington in calling him "the most modern— and the most American of our eighteenth century leaders." [36] While Hamilton might have been baffled by the intense aversion to vigorous government shared by men who considered themselves to be his intellectual heirs, he would have understood the behavior of a George Sutherland or a Pierce Butler in their special roles as judges. Their use of the judicial veto to restrain legislative majorities from tampering with rights they deemed to be fundamental was, after all, within his conception of the courts as "faithful guardians of the Constitution." [37]

In the face of overwhelming evidence that certain basic transformations in the character of American society were precipitating governmental regulation in the public interest, members of the Supreme Court were clinging to presuppositions which no longer corresponded to the realities of life in the twentieth century. Their stubborn adherence to old dogmas led them to espouse legal doctrines which were convincing more and more people that the Constitution was a barrier to social progress. It was this unabashed use of judicial power to frustrate necessary experiments with considered remedies for pressing economic and social problems which induced Holmes and Brandeis to speak out in dissent so often.

One of the factors which stimulated resentment against the trend of the Court's thinking in the post-war years was the fact that it actually represented a step backward. No amount of summoning of ineluctable constitutional mandates could hide the fact that the Court itself was changing its own prior meanings of the Constitution. The reversion has been sketched by Felix Frankfurter in a few telling sentences:

[35] *The Federalist*, p. 526.
[36] Vernon Louis Parrington, *Main Currents in American Thought* (New York: Harcourt, Brace and Company, 1927), I, 306–307.
[37] *The Federalist*, p. 525.

His [Holmes'] influence was powerful in arresting the tide which reached its crest in the *Lochner* case. There followed a period of judicial recession, of greater tolerance towards the exercise of legislative discretion. Between 1908 and the World War, the Court allowed legislation to prevail which in various aspects curbed freedom of enterprise and withdrew phases of industrial relations from the area of individual bargaining. In the period between Muller v. Oregon,[38] in 1908, and Bunting v. Oregon,[39] in 1917, Mr. Justice Holmes' views prevailed. But those who had assumed a permanent change in the Court's outlook were to be disappointed. . . . Change in the Court's personnel, and pressure of post-war economic and social views soon reflected themselves in decisions.[40]

Although this resurgence of judicial conservatism was manifest in the Court's attitude toward almost all constitutional questions, it was felt most acutely in the cases concerned with the constitutionality of social legislation. On this major battleground of constitutional controversy in the years following World War I, Holmes and Brandeis were together in resisting what they regarded as too aggressive an exercise of judicial power. Building on Holmes' own theory that "A great man represents . . . a strategic point in the campaign of history" and that "part of his greatness consists in his being there," [41] it might well be argued that one reason for the importance of Holmes and Brandeis as dissenters is that they were on the scene at a fateful moment in the life of the Court as a coordinate institution of government. They were destined to play a vital role in evolving attitudes and doctrines the ultimate effect of which was to rescue the Court from self-destruction.

And yet one of the really complex—some would say mystifying—facets of that period of sharp judicial conflict is the kinship between two such diverse temperaments as Holmes and Brandeis. How can one account for the fact that most of the time they agreed with each other when they were disagreeing with the rest of their colleagues?

[38] 208 U.S. 412 (1908).
[39] 243 U.S. 426 (1917). The decision in this case sustained Oregon's ten-hour law for industrial establishments. No doubt because of his previous association with the litigation, Justice Brandeis disqualified himself from participating in the case.
[40] Frankfurter (ed.), *Mr. Justice Holmes*, pp. 80–81.
[41] Holmes, "John Marshall," in *Collected Legal Papers*, p. 267.

"A judge will be estimated," Judge Learned Hand has suggested, "in terms of his outlook and his nature." [42] No two men then serving on the Supreme Court were more different in outlook and nature than were Holmes and Brandeis.

Holmes—by instinct a scholar and philosopher, whose cynicism about man and society made him contemptuous of the "upward and onward" impulse of the reformer—was found, in crucial divisions of the Court, in the company of the colleague whose moral fervor and scheme of values had given him the reputation of a social crusader. Brandeis—by nature a fighter for causes, whose faith in the possibilities of social regeneration stemmed from his belief that through the use of intelligence men can learn to control their fate— was at home with the Justice whose detachment and skepticism at times bordered on social apathy. "In him the lawyer's genius was dedicated to the prophet's vision," one of his law secretaries has said of Brandeis, adding, "and the fusion produced a magnificent weapon for righteousness." [43] Though they differed radically in their conceptions of the good society and employed radically different methods as judges, skeptic and crusader usually arrived at the same conclusions in matters of constitutional law.

One student of Brandeis' judicial approach has found that he used the "technique of the advocate" in order to serve "the ends of social justice"; [44] another has frankly stated that Justice Brandeis did not make "too ascetic a dissociation between his views of public policy and his opinions." [45] The opposite, of course, has been said of Justice Holmes. Thus, just a few years before the end of Holmes' service on the Supreme Court, Judge Learned Hand placed him in that school of constitutional interpretation which demands of the

[42] Hand, "Mr. Justice Holmes at Eighty-Five," in Frankfurter (ed.), *Mr. Justice Holmes*, pp. 122–23.

[43] Paul A. Freund, at Proceedings in Memory of Mr. Justice Brandeis, 317 U.S. IX, at XVI (Dec. 21, 1942).

[44] Walton Hamilton, "The Jurist's Art," *XXXI Col. L. Rev. 1073*, reprinted in Frankfurter (ed.), *Mr. Justice Brandeis*, p. 188.

[45] Lerner, "The Social Thought of Mr. Justice Brandeis," reprinted in *Ideas are Weapons*, p. 83.

judge a "temper of detachment" and "counsel of scepticism." We were cautioned not to read Holmes' opinions as "indicating his own views on public matters," but rather as signifying the Justice's "settled belief that in such matters the judges cannot safely intervene." [46] The question is, it may be repeated, what explains the affinity between two jurists as dissimilar in outlook and approach as were Holmes and Brandeis? This is the crucial problem, but the answer must rest, in the end, on a close analysis of the occasions when they concurred in each other's conclusions though dissenting from the position of the majority.

IV

Shortly after Brandeis became a member of the Supreme Court, Justice Holmes wrote a dissent, concurred in by Brandeis, which may be seen as presaging the kinship between the two jurists on constitutional questions. His opinions in the *Child Labor* case [47] contains ideas which help explain why he and Brandeis so often reached the same results though not sharing each other's social philosophy. When the Supreme Court overruled the decision almost a quarter of a century later, Justice Stone, spokesman for a unanimous Court, in effect adopted Holmes' dissent, which he characterized as "powerful and now classic." [48] Nor were these words a mere expression of homage; they quite accurately described both the force and effect of the dissent. Not only did Holmes explode the entire basis for the majority's ruling in Hammer v. Dagenhart, but he set down a view of the judicial function which, by sheer reiteration, was itself to become both a tradition and a school. No finer example of the conscious effort to be guided by the self-denying inhibition of the constitutional judge is to be found among his dissents.

In Hammer v. Dagenhart a bare majority of the Court, led by

[46] Hand, *op. cit.*, p. 124.
[47] Hammer v. Dagenhart, 247 U.S. 251, 277 (1918).
[48] United States v. Darby, 312 U.S. 100, at 115 (1941).

Justice Day, held that Congress had overstepped its constitutional bounds when it passed in 1916 a law prohibiting the interstate shipment of goods produced with the aid of child labor. Relying on the formula which classified the conditions existing within the industrial plant as necessarily local, it found that under the pretext of regulating interstate commerce, Congress was attempting to control a matter which was within the exclusive domain of the States. "The production of articles, intended for interstate commerce, is a matter of local regulation." If the child labor law were sustained, the majority concluded, the American system of dual governmental powers might be "practically destroyed." [49] However, this note of impending doom was somewhat premature, to say the least. It struck the minority—Holmes, McKenna, Clarke and Brandeis—as entirely inconsistent with the Court's quite recent rulings upholding the right of Congress to bar from interstate channels lottery tickets,[50] impure food and drugs,[51] women being transported for immoral purposes,[52] and intoxicating liquors.[53]

It was these applications of the settled doctrine that regulation by Congress may take the form of outright prohibition which gave the majority in the *Child Labor* case its chief trouble. Justice Day sought to reconcile the decision with the earlier cases by creating a quite artificial distinction. The Child Labor Law, he argued, was designed to exclude from interstate commerce articles in themselves harmless and incapable of spreading any evil to the "state of destination." The evil, if any, was in the "state of origin," where the children were employed. Justice Day wrote:

> In each of these instances [the earlier cases] the use of interstate transportation was necessary to the accomplishment of harmful results. In other words, although the power of interstate transportation was to regulate, that could only be accomplished by prohibiting the use of the facilities of

[49] 247 U.S. 251, at 276.
[50] Champion v. Ames, 188 U.S. 321 (1903).
[51] Hipolite Egg Co. v. United States, 220 U.S. 45 (1910).
[52] Hoke v. United States, 227 U.S. 308 (1913).
[53] Clark Distilling Co. v. Western Maryland Ry. Co., 242 U.S. 311 (1917).

interstate commerce to effect the evil intended. This element is wanting in the present case. . . . The Act in its effect does not regulate transportation among the States but aims to standardize the ages at which children may be employed in mining and manufacturing within the States. The goods shipped are of themselves harmless. . . . When offered for shipment, and before transportation begins, the labor of their production is over, and the mere fact that they were intended for interstate commerce transportation does not make their production subject to federal control under the commerce power.[54]

Justice Holmes found this view of the limits of Congress's powers altogether without foundation. Through a close examination of the precedents, he showed that Congress's authority to deal with an evil never depended on whether it existed before or after interstate transportation had been resorted to. "I should have thought that the most conspicuous decisions of this Court," he summarized, "had made it clear that the power to regulate commerce and other constitutional powers could not be cut down or qualified by the fact that it might interfere with the carrying out of the domestic policy of any State."[55] Though he preserved the customary politeness of his differences with colleagues, there is no mistaking the inference that a majority of them in this case had been unduly influenced by their disapproval of the ultimate purpose of the Child Labor Law. After all, Justice Day's suspicion that the Child Labor Law was designed to "standardize" or equalize industrial conditions is in a class with Justice Pitney's condemnation in Coppage v. Kansas of the use of the police power to achieve a more equitable distribution of wealth.

Holmes' dissent in Hammer v. Dagenhart is primarily an argument against the injection into judicial decisions of such personal views of social policy. Significantly, he quoted the assertion by Chief Justice Chase from a fifty-year-old decision that "The Judicial cannot prescribe to the legislative department of the Government limitations upon the exercise of its acknowledged powers."[56] Was

[54] 247 U.S. 251, at 271–72.   [55] *Ibid.*, at 278.
[56] Veazie Bank v. Fenno, 8 Wall. 525, at 584 (1869).

Holmes not implying that in order to vindicate the constitutional powers of a coordinate branch of the government, the judiciary must curb its own will to power?

"The first step in my argument," he wrote, "is to make plain what no one is likely to dispute—that the statute in question is within the power expressly given to Congress if considered only as to its immediate effects and that if invalid it is so only upon some collateral ground." [57] The "collateral ground" for the invalidation of the Child Labor Law was, of course, its alleged impact on the internal economy of the States. To Holmes this was an irrelevant consideration, since it was agreed that Congress's commerce power was broad enough to permit it to prohibit shipments in interstate and foreign commerce. The integrity and scope of national power were to him the decisive issues:

The Act does not meddle with anything belonging to the States. They may regulate their internal affairs and their domestic commerce as they like. But when they seek to send their products across the state line they are no longer within their rights. If there were no Constitution and no Congress their power to cross the line would depend upon their neighbors. Under the Constitution such commerce belongs not to the States but to Congress to regulate. It may carry out its views of public policy whatever indirect effect they have upon the activities of the States. Instead of being encountered by a prohibitive tariff at her boundaries the State encounters the public policy of the United States which it is for Congress to express. The public policy of the United States is shaped with a view to the benefit of the nation as a whole. . . . The national welfare as understood by Congress may require a different attitude within its sphere from that of some self-seeking State. It seems to me entirely constitutional for Congress to enforce its understanding by all means at its command.[58]

This vision of the Constitution as an organic instrument of effective government Holmes was to express even more majestically two years later in his opinion for the Court in Missouri v. Holland, an opinion which has grown in stature and importance with the

[57] 247 U.S. 251, 277.
[58] *Ibid.*, at 281.

passage of time.[59] Characterized by one legal historian as "a paragraph which has become a classic in constitutional law," [60] the sentences in which this view is delineated reveal Holmes at his best as an exponent of constitutional interpretation imbued with a sense of history:

. . . when we are dealing with words that are a constituent act, like the Constitution of the United States, we must realize that they have called into life a being the development of which could not have been foreseen completely by the most gifted of its begetters. It was enough for them to realize or to hope that they had created an organism; it has taken a century and has cost their successors much sweat and blood to prove that they created a nation. The case before us must be considered in the light of our whole experience and not merely in that of what was said a hundred years ago. . . . We must consider what this country has become in deciding what that Amendment [the Tenth] has reserved.[61]

[59] Missouri v. Holland, 252 U.S. 416 (1920). This is the opinion in which Holmes suggested that it may be constitutional for the Federal Government to enter fields as the result of its adherence to a treaty on which it would not be permitted to legislate in the absence of a treaty. He stated this possibility in these words: "It is obvious that there may be matters of the sharpest exigency for the national well-being that an act of Congress could not deal with but that a treaty followed by such an act could, and it is not lightly to be assumed that, in matters requiring national action, 'a power which must belong to and somewhere reside in every civilized government' is not to be found." (At 433.) America's greatly increased international obligations have obviously enhanced the implications of Holmes' dictum. Thus, in its search for constitutional bases for federal protection of civil rights, the committee named by President Truman in 1946 to survey civil rights had this to say:
"In its decision in Missouri v. Holland in 1920, the Supreme Court ruled that Congress may enact statutes to carry out treaty obligations, even where, in the absence of a treaty, it has no other power to pass such a statute. This doctrine has an obvious importance as a possible basis for civil rights legislation.
"The United Nations Charter, approved by the United States Senate as a treaty, makes several references to human Rights. Articles 55 and 56 are of particular importance." *To Secure these Rights*, Report of the President's Committee on Civil Rights (Washington: United States Government Printing Office, 1947), pp. 110–11. It is perhaps no exaggeration to say that the principle enunciated by Holmes in Missouri v. Holland is a major source of anxiety for the proponents of the so-called "Bricker Amendment," but they have overlooked some reassuring words by Holmes himself: "We do not mean to imply that there are no qualifications to the treaty-making power." 252 U.S. 416, at 433.
[60] Willard Hurst, "The Role of History," in *Supreme Court and Supreme Law*, edited by Edmond Cahn (Bloomington: Indiana Univ. Press, 1954), p. 56.
[61] 252 U.S. 416, at 433–34.

In the *Child Labor* case, Holmes insisted that the Justices were not "at liberty" to concern themselves with the motives of legislation. His call for judicial objectivity was stern and even sardonic:

The notion that prohibition is any less prohibition when applied to things now thought evil I do not understand. But if there is any matter upon which civilized countries have agreed—far more unanimously than they have with regard to intoxicants and some other matters over which this country is now emotionally aroused—it is the evil of premature and excessive child labor. I should have thought that if we were to introduce our own moral conceptions where in my opinion they do not belong, this was preeminently a case for upholding the exercise of all its powers by the United States.

But I had thought that the propriety of the exercise of a power admitted to exist in some cases was for the consideration of Congress alone and that this Court always had disavowed the right to intrude its judgment upon questions of policy or morals. It is not for this Court to pronounce when prohibition is necessary to regulation if it ever may be necessary— to say that it is permissible as against strong drink but not so against the product of ruined lives.[62]

The emotion-packed words just quoted are obviously the utterance of a man who had been deeply stirred by the controversy, and it is easy to understand why to some they prove that Holmes was a great humanitarian. He himself would have disclaimed any such motivations. It is likely that he would have accepted the judgment of a fellow Bostonian as nearer to the truth: "No deep perception of the great pain and pathos of life nor strong compassion for the lot of the average man ever took any powerful hold on his mind."[63] In any case, we do know that Holmes was "mighty sceptical of hours of labor and minimum wages regulation,"[64] a sentiment he voiced just a year before writing his *Child Labor* opinion. As a judge, however, he tried to free himself of any such subjective considerations. Esoteric though it may appear, the view of Holmes' approach pro-

[62] 247 U.S. 251, 277, at 280.
[63] George R. Farnum (Assistant United States Attorney General, 1927–30), "Holmes—The Soldier-Philosopher," 2 *American Lawyer* 9 (1939).
[64] *Holmes-Laski Letters*, I, 51.

pounded by one who had observed him for many years from the other side of the Supreme Court lectern is essentially correct—"He seemed to be without prejudice or fear as to the consequence of a decision, and the one question of concern to him was: 'What is the law?' Whether he liked it or not, he so declared it." [65]

Thus did the social conservative become the liberal judge. This happened, it has been remarked, because he had "the detachment to refuse to substitute his judgment for that of the legislature." [66] Holmes' judicial liberalism stemmed from a willingness to give constitutional sanction to the developing forces of society, and it was this attitude of forbearance which was bound to produce the common ground between him and Justice Brandeis. While Holmes may have doubted the utility or wisdom of the schemes of social control to which he saw no legal objection, Brandeis was in many instances deeply convinced of the necessity of the legislation. Holmes was no champion of the underdog; but neither was Brandeis, in any sentimental sense. As Paul A. Freund has noted—after examining some of the evidence showing that Brandeis was an "unsentimental" judge —"Brandeis was prepared to reject the claims, almost literally, of a workman, a widow and an orphan in pursuance of what seemed to him to be a more harmonious federalism." [67] But it is also true that his general social philosophy rested on a genuine desire to strengthen the democratic community by improving the conditions under which the great mass of ordinary men and women lived and worked. Holmes was not so sure of the goal or of the means for reaching it, but he joined Brandeis in deploring the action of courts in aborting the efforts of legislators to further the public good.

[65] James M. Beck (Solicitor General of the United States, 1921–25), "Justice Holmes and the Supreme Court," *1 Fed. Bar J. 36, 38* (1932).

[66] Karl N. Llewellyn, "Holmes," *35 Col. L. Rev. 485* (1935).

[67] Freund, *On Understanding the Supreme Court* (Boston: Little, Brown and Company, 1950), p. 67.

7

"Trial by combat"

That it was their common approach to the judicial task which brought about the harmonious relationship between Justices Holmes and Brandeis is strikingly illustrated in the labor cases which found them together in dissent. Both men acknowledged that the exercise of judicial power is in its results essentially legislative in character. "I recognize without hesitation," Holmes declared in one of his best known dissents, "that judges do and must legislate, but they can do so only interstitially; they are confined from molar to molecular motions." [1] A few years later, while speaking of the divergent judicial attitudes toward labor's weapons of self-defense, Brandeis had this to say: "Judges being thus called upon to exercise a *quasi* legislative function and weigh relative social values, naturally differed in their conclusions on such questions." [2]

Such candid discussion of the role of judges raises a troublesome question: How is the power they exercise to be "confined"? More simply, when are judges exercising their authority properly and when are they guilty of the abuse of their power? The dissents by Holmes and Brandeis develop at least a partial answer to this ques-

[1] Southern Pacific Co. v. Jensen, 244 U.S. 205, 218, at 221 (1917).
[2] Dissenting in Truax v. Corrigan, 257 U.S. 312, 354, at 365 (1921).

tion. Regardless of the nature of the case—whether they were differing with their colleagues over the pertinence of common law principles, the meaning of statutes, or the effect of constitutional limitations— these two Justices usually put into their opinions some animadversions on the judicial process itself.

It was to be supposed that Brandeis' understanding of the labor struggle would bring him into conflict with colleagues with a less sympathetic view. The expected began to happen very soon. It ought to be remembered, however, that many of the cases concerned with the legal rights of labor involved issues toward which Holmes had revealed a progressive and enlightened view as long ago as his days in Massachusetts. Thus, impressive as is Brandeis' first opinion directed against yellow dog contracts and court injunctions in labor disputes,[3] it rested on a philosophy which Holmes had done much to crystallize.

I

The employees of the Hitchman Coal Company had signed individual agreements promising not to join any union. When the United Mine Workers of America launched a drive to unionize the company's West Virginia mine and thus force it to end these contracts, the company obtained a court order restraining the union's agents from continuing their organizing activities. In sustaining the lower court's decree, Justice Pitney's opinion for a majority of the Supreme Court held that the company had a right to operate a non-union shop and that the organizers were seeking by illegal means to compel the company to change its system of labor relations. The fact that the Union organizers did not resort to violence did not make their activities legal. "In our opinion," Pitney wrote, "any violation of plaintiff's legal rights contrived by defendants for the purpose of inflicting damage, or having that as its necessary effect, is as plainly inhibited by the law as if it involved a breach of the peace. A com-

[3] Hitchman Coal and Coke Co. v. Mitchell, 245 U.S. 229, 263 (1917).

bination to procure concerted breaches of contract by plantiff's employees constitutes such a violation." [4]

Brandeis argued in dissent that this conclusion was basically at variance with the legally recognized right of workingmen to form unions, to invite others to join their ranks, and to safeguard the power of their associations. Since the United Mine Workers union was a lawful organization and not in itself a conspiracy, the issues in the case reduced themselves to the question as to how far it might go in strengthening its position in the bargaining struggle. Brandeis pointed out that the non-union mines of West Virginia were competing with the union mines of the adjoining States and that the union was merely seeking to protect itself. Hence, whatever "coercive" effect the activities of the organizers might have was justified by a legitimate aim. In other words, granted that the efforts of the U.M.W. to persuade the Hitchman workers to become members of the Union, if successful, would interfere with the company's methods for dealing with its employees, the interference was legal since it was "for justifiable cause." Brandeis pleaded for greater equality in the labor-management contest for power:

Coercion in a legal sense, is not exerted when a union merely endeavors to induce employees to join a union with the intention thereafter to order a strike unless the employer consents to unionize his shop. . . . The employer is free either to accept the agreement or the disadvantage. Indeed, the plaintiff's whole case is rested upon agreements secured under similar pressure of economic necessity or disadvantage. If it is coercion to threaten to strike unless plaintiff consents to a closed union shop, it is coercion also to threaten not to give one employment unless the applicant will consent to a closed non-union shop.[5]

The dissenter in Vegelahn v. Guntner and Plant v. Woods had no hesitation, it may be assumed, in supporting Brandeis' position in the *Hitchman* case, as did also Justice Clarke. Both of them joined Brandeis four years later in dissenting against another decision of the Court inimical to the interests of organized labor.[6] For

[4] *Ibid.*, at 237.
[5] *Ibid.*, at 271.
[6] Duplex Printing Press Co. v. Deering, 254 U.S. 443, 479 (1921).

Holmes, however, the issue in the *Duplex* case must have been more perplexing than for Brandeis, and for the reason that it put to the test his conception of consistency in the judicial process. In the well known *Danbury Hatters'* case,[7] decided in 1908, Holmes had joined in the unanimous opinion of the Court holding that a secondary boycott, conducted for the purpose of compelling a manufacturer of hats sold in other states to unionize his plant, was an illegal restraint of interstate commerce in violation of the Sherman Act. And seven years later, he wrote the Court's decision holding the officers of the United Hatters responsible for the acts done in the name of the union.[8] "It requires more than the blindness of justice," he had there observed, "not to see that many branches of the United Hatters and the Federation of Labor, to both of which the defendants belonged, in pursuance of a plan emanating from headquarters made use of such lists [lists of 'unfair dealers'], and of the primary and secondary boycott in their effort to subdue the plaintiffs to their demands." [9]

Unless it be that Holmes was ultimately persuaded—possibly as

[7] Loewe v. Lawlor, 208 U.S. 274 (1908).

[8] Lawlor v. Loewe, 235 U.S. 522 (1915). Holmes summarized the controversy as follows: "The substance of the charge is that the plaintiffs were hat manufacturers who employed non-union labor; that the defendants were members of the United Hatters of North America and also of the American Federation of Labor; that in pursuance of a general scheme to unionize the labor employed by manufacturers of fur hats (a purpose previously made effective against all but a few manufacturers), the defendants and other members of the United Hatters caused the American Federation of Labor to declare a boycott against the plaintiffs and against all hats sold by the plaintiffs to dealers in other States and against dealers who should deal in them; and that they carried out their plan with such success that they restrained or destroyed the plaintiff's commerce with other States." (At 533.) Relying on a case in which he himself had written the Court's decision—Eastern States Retail Lumber Dealers' Association v. United States, 234 U.S. 600 (1914)—he stated the governing principle in one sentence: "Whatever may be the law otherwise, that case establishes that, irrespective of compulsion or even agreement to observe its intimation, the circulation of a list of 'unfair dealers', manifestly intended to put the ban upon those whose names appear therein, among an important body of possible customers combined with a view to joint action and in anticipation of such reports, is within the prohibitions of the Sherman Act if it is intended to restrain and restrains commerce among the States." (At 534.)

[9] 235 U.S. 522, at 534.

the result of Brandeis' prodding—that the Clayton Act, which had been adopted by Congress in the intervening years, deprived the federal courts of jurisdiction over the controversy, it would be difficult to reconcile the part he played in the *Danbury Hatters* cases with his concurrence in the dissent by Justice Brandeis in the *Duplex* case.[10] The Duplex Printing Press Company, a manufacturer of newspaper printing presses in Michigan, applied to a United States District Court for an injunction to restrain the New York local of the International Association of Machinists from interfering with its business in violation of the Sherman Anti-Trust Act. It complained that the union was waging a campaign intended to keep the company's customers from buying its presses and the employees of the customers from handling and installing them. But before the District Court could hear the case, the Clayton Act was adopted by Congress. Section 20 of the new law forbade federal courts to grant injunctions in cases "between an employer and employee . . . involving or growing out of, a dispute concerning terms or conditions of employment." On the basis of this provision, the two lower courts declined to issue the injunction. However, a majority of the Supreme Court, again speaking through Justice Pitney, held that Section 20 of the Clayton Act did not bar the granting of such an injunction. "Congress had in mind particular controversies, not general class war," Pitney declared. Section 20 of the Clayton Act merely removed the taint of illegality from certain of labor's acts,[11] but the permitted activities had to do with the

[10] In an effort to explain the "seeming inconsistency" between Holmes' position in the Danbury Hatters' cases and the later interstate boycott cases in which he dissented, it has been suggested that the fact that the boycott inspired by the hatters was prosecuted by a national labor organization may have led Holmes to conclude that there was "a clear and present danger of tyrannous labor domination." Walter Nelles and Samuel Mermin, "Holmes and Labor Law," *XIII N.Y. Univ. L. Quar. Rev. 517, 546* (1936). The authors of this article did an excellent job in tracing and assessing the "impressive recognition" accorded to what they call "Holmes' theory of justification" as applied to the industrial struggle.

[11] 254 U.S. 433 at 472. Section 20 of the Clayton Act provides that no restraining order or injunction granted by any federal court or judge "shall prohibit any

relation between an employer and his own employees and not with a controversy between an employer and workingmen not in his employ. Pitney thought that it would distort the meaning of the exemption embodied in Section 20 were it to be extended beyond "the parties affected in a proximate and substantial, not merely a sentimental or sympathetic, sense by the cause of the dispute." By organizing sympathetic strikes and boycotts against the companies which used Duplex presses, the machinists' union was guilty of conspiring to restrain interstate trade.[12]

Without bluntly saying so, Justice Brandeis clearly implied in his dissent that he attributed the Court's decision to the failure of the majority to reckon with the facts of the situation which had led to the trouble. His simple summary of the circumstances culminating in the strike and boycott set the stage for his argument that there are times when economic coercion may be justified by self-interest:

There are in the United States only four manufacturers of such presses; and they are in active competition. Between 1909 and 1913 the machinists' union induced three of them to recognize and deal with the union, to grant the eight-hour day, to establish a minimum wage scale and to comply with other union requirements. The fourth, the Duplex Company, refused to recognize the union; insisted upon conducting its factory on the open shop principle; refused to introduce the eight-hour day and operated for the most part, ten hours a day; refused to establish a mini-

person or persons, whether singly or in concert, from terminating any relation of employment, or from ceasing to perform any work or labor, or from recommending, advising, or persuading others by peaceful means so to do; or from attending at any place where any such person or persons may lawfully be, for the purpose of peacefully obtaining or communicating information, or from peacefully persuading any person to work or to abstain from working; or from ceasing to patronize or to employ any party to such dispute, or from recommending, advising, or persuading others by peaceful and lawful means so to do; or from paying or giving to, or withholding from, any person engaged in such dispute, any strike, benefits or other moneys or things of value; or from peaceably assembling in a lawful manner, and for lawful purposes; or from doing any act or thing which might lawfully be done in the absence of such dispute by any party thereto; nor shall any of the acts specified in this paragraph be considered or held to be violations of any law of the United States."

[12] 254 U.S. 443, at 472.

mum wage scale; and disregarded other union standards. Thereupon two
of the three manufacturers who had assented to union conditions, notified
the union that they should be obliged to terminate their agreements with
it unless their competitor, the Duplex Company, also entered into the
agreement with the union, which, in giving more favorable terms to
labor, imposed correspondingly greater burdens upon the employer. Because the Duplex Company refused to enter into such an agreement and
in order to induce it to do so, the machinists' union declared a strike
at its factory, and in aid of that strike instructed its members and the
members of affiliated unions not to work on the installation of presses
which plaintiff had delivered in New York.[13]

Brandeis accepted the union's contention that the refusal of the
Michigan firm to deal with the machinists threatened not only their
own continued existence but the interest and standards of the union
members employed by the company's competitors. Hence, whatever
damage was suffered by the Michigan employer as the result of the
boycott against its product had been inflicted not "maliciously" but
in self-defense. Brandeis' basic attitude would seem to have been
revealed by a rhetorical question asked by him: "May not all
with a common interest join in refusing to expend their labor upon
articles whose very production constitutes an attack upon their
standard of living and the institution which they are convinced
supports it?" [14]

From beginning to end, Brandeis' thesis in the *Duplex* case has as
its "major premise" the complaint that the rights of labor have depended too much upon the private prejudices of judges. It was because of a "better realization of the facts of industrial life" that
courts came to view strikes as legal though they were illegal at
common law. At first, strikes were deemed to be lawful only when
called for the purpose of raising wages or reducing hours, but in
time some judges "because they viewed the facts differently" began
to see that the same sort of "self-interest" justifying such strikes also
made lawful the injury inflicted on an employer by a strike to union-

[13] *Ibid.*, at 479–80.
[14] *Ibid.*, at 481.

ize his shop. Everything depended on how judges appraised the economic system of the country:

> When centralization in the control of business brought its corresponding centralization in the organization of workingmen, new facts had to be appraised. A single employer might, as in this case, threaten the standing of the whole organization and the standards of all its members; and when he did so the union, in order to protect itself would naturally refuse to work on his materials wherever found. When such a situation was first presented to the courts, judges concluded that the intervention of the purchaser of the materials established an insulation through which the direct relationship of the employer and the workmen did not penetrate; and the strike against the material was considered a strike against the purchaser by unaffected third parties. . . . But other courts, with better appreciation of the facts of industry, recognized the unity of interest throughout the union, and that, in refusing to work on materials which threatened it, the union was only refusing to aid in destroying itself.[15]

The machinists and those from whom they sought cooperation had a common interest which the Duplex Printing Press Company threatened. Brandeis argued that unlike the boycott condemned in the *Danbury Hatters* cases, the cooperation sought by the machinists was from unions which were united with them by common interest rather than merely sympathy. "It is lawful for all members of a union by whomsoever employed to refuse to handle materials whose production weakens the union."

Taking sharp issue with the majority over Congress's purpose in adopting the Clayton Act, Brandeis insisted that it was meant to assure greater equality in the relations between employers and employees by keeping the federal courts from injecting themselves prematurely into the struggle. Reminding his colleagues that the statute was "the fruit of unceasing agitation" lasting more than twenty years, he undertook to show that it was "designed to equalize before the law the position of workingmen and employer as industrial combatants." One sentence from his summary of the discontent which led to the legislation adopted in 1914 gives the crux of the

[15] *Ibid.*, at 482.

matter as he saw it: "Aside from the use of the injunction, the chief source of dissatisfaction with the existing law lay in the doctrine of malicious combination, and, in many parts of the country, in the judicial declarations of the illegality at common law of picketing and persuading others to leave work." The state of the law was both confused and uncertain, since some concerted activities by labor organizations were held to be lawful—as phases of "trade competition"—and others were condemned as "malicious" and therefore illegal. Those who sought remedial legislation believed that the outcome in labor struggles depended entirely on whether or not judges considered the purposes of the particular recourse by labor to be "socially or economically harmful." Brandeis put it this way: "It was objected that, due largely to environment, the social and economic ideas of judges, which thus became translated into law, were prejudicial to a position of equality between workingman and employer; that due to this dependence upon the individual opinion of judges great confusion existed as to what purposes were lawful and what unlawful; and that in any event Congress, not the judges, was the body which should declare what public policy in regard to the industrial struggle demands." [16]

His study of the background of the Clayton Act convinced Brandeis that it was the intention of Congress to immunize certain of labor's activities, regardless of their effect on others, against "judicial declarations" of illegality.[17] Judges were no longer to be free to determine "according to their economic and social views" whether the harm inflicted on the employer in an industrial dispute

[16] *Ibid.*, at 485.
[17] "The resulting law set out certain acts which had previously been held unlawful, whenever courts had disapproved of the ends for which they were performed; it then declared that, when these acts were committed in the course of an industrial dispute, they should not be held to violate any law of the United States. In other words the Clayton Act substituted the opinion of Congress as to the propriety of the purpose for that of differing judges; and thereby it declared that the relations between employers of labor and workingmen were competitive relations, that organized competition was not harmful and that it justified injuries necessarily inflicted in its course." 254 U.S. 443, 479, at 486.

was lawful because an incident in trade competition or an illegal injury. Yet before concluding his opinion Brandeis made it clear that he had no desire to endow his own views with any kind of higher moral or constitutional authority. This disclaimer, combining as it does a theory of political obligation with an insistence upon judicial restraint, is in the best tradition of the precepts we associate with Justice Holmes:

> Because I have come to the conclusion that both the common law of a State and the statute of the United States declare the right of industrial combatants to push their struggle to the limits of the justification of self-interest, I do not wish to be understood as attaching any constitutional or moral sanction to that right. All rights are derived from the purposes of the society in which they exist; above all rights rises duty to the community. The conditions developed in industry may be such that those engaged in it cannot continue their struggle without danger to the community. But it is not for judges to determine whether such conditions exist, nor is it their function to set the limits of permissible contest and to declare the duties which the new situation demands. This is the function of the legislature which, while limiting individual and group rights of aggression and defense, may substitute processes of justice for the more primitive method of trial by combat.[18]

An even sharper note of bitterness and irony was struck by Justice Brandeis when he dissented, along with Holmes, six years later in a similar case.[19] To Sutherland, who wrote the Court's decision in this case, it appeared that the ruling in the *Duplex* case "might serve as an opinion in this case." Brandeis, on the other hand, tried to distinguish the earlier case in order to show that it did not apply to the struggle between the Journeymen Stone Cutters' Association and the Bedford Cut Stone Company.

In its drive to organize the Bedford Cut Stone Company and twenty-three other producers of Indiana limestone, the Association called on the members of all its local unions not to handle stone on

[18] *Ibid.,* at 488.
[19] Bedford Cut Stone Co. v. Journeymen Stone Cutters' Association, 274 U.S. 37, 56 (1927).

which work had been done by non-union labor. These companies had had contracts with the Association, but after the contracts lapsed they began to employ men not affiliated with the Journey-men. All efforts to renegotiate the working agreements had proved fruitless.

Though the Journeymen Stone Cutters' Association and its general purposes were lawful, said Sutherland, its action in organizing strikes against the limestone companies threatened "to destroy or narrow petitioners' interstate trade." Brandeis thought that the restraint on interstate trade was entirely reasonable, because it sprang from the Journeymen Association's use of a perfectly legitimate instrument of "self protection." Observing that "the propriety of the unions' conduct can hardly be doubted by one who believes in the organization of labor," he stressed that in their "struggle for existence" workingmen may cooperate even if in doing so "the interstate trade of another is thereby affected." This was also the position of the two lower federal courts, which had declined to issue the injunction sought by the employers. Brandeis maintained that the only "serious question" on which the Supreme Court was divided in the *Duplex* case was whether the Clayton Act had forbidden Federal courts to issue injunctions in the type of controversy involved in that case. And so he proceeded to enumerate the respects in which the conduct of the Stone Cutters differed from that of the machinists: "There was no attempt to seek the aid of members of any other craft, by a sympathetic strike or otherwise. The contest was not a class struggle. It was a struggle between particular employers and their employees." [20]

Despite his painstaking effort to differentiate the two cases, it was apparent that Justice Brandeis was primarily interested in safeguarding the rights and weapons of workers as combatants in industrial conflict. He spoke of the power and great financial resources of the employers, organized in a trade association and together controlling seventy per cent of all the cut stone in the United States, and

[20] *Ibid.*, at 60.

of the relatively weak position of each of the one hundred and fifty union locals, which could easily be destroyed by "scabs" brought in from other cities. Justice Brandeis ended his dissent by calling on the Court to be consistent and allow labor the right to combine and cooperate even as it had permitted business so to do:

If, on the undisputed facts of this case, refusal to work can be enjoined, Congress created by the Sherman Law and the Clayton Act an instrument for imposing restraints upon labor which reminds one of involuntary servitude. The Sherman Law was held in *United States v. United States Steel Corporation*, 251 U.S. 417, to permit capitalists to combine in a single corporation 50 per cent of the steel industry of the United States dominating the trade throughout its vast resources. The Sherman Law was held in *United States v. United Shoe Machinery Co.*, 247 U.S. 32, to permit capitalists to combine in another corporation practically the whole shoe machinery industry of the country, necessarily giving it a position of dominance over shoe-manufacturing in America. It would, indeed, be strange if Congress had by the same Act willed to deny to members of a small craft of workingmen the right to cooperate in simply refraining from work, when that course was the only means of self-protection against a combination of militant and powerful employers. I cannot believe that Congress did so.[21]

II

The growing resistance to "government by injunction" summarized by Justice Brandeis in the *Duplex* case was not confined to the halls of Congress. But state statutes outlawing labor injunctions fared no better before the Supreme Court than did Section 20 of the Clayton Act. Indeed, less than a year following the *Duplex* decision, an almost identical measure adopted by the first legislature of Arizona in 1913 was set aside.[22] It prohibited the State's courts from

[21] *Ibid.*, at 65. It may be of interest to recall that Justice Brandeis had refrained from participating in both United States v. United States Steel Corp. and United States v. United Shoe Machinery Co. Thus did the foe of bigness in business keep himself from discussing the issue whether mere size is an offense under the Sherman Act.
[22] Truax v. Corrigan, 257 U.S. 312, 342, 344, 354 (1921).

issuing injunctions in cases growing out of labor disputes unless
necessary to protect property against violence. It was obviously intended to keep the courts from interfering with peaceful picketing
and boycotts. Claiming that the statute was unconstitutional, Truax,
the owner of a restaurant in Bisbee, sought an injunction to restrain
the strikers from continuing the activities that had resulted in a
drastic decline of his business. The strikers had proclaimed their
grievances in the usual ways—by handbills, pickets, and banners informing the public that the restaurant was "unfair" to union labor.

William Howard Taft, who but recently had been named to the
Chief Justiceship on the death of Edward D. White, led the Court
in holding the Arizona law to be an infringement of the Fourteenth
Amendment. For Taft the fundamental consideration appeared to be
that the business of the restaurateur was a property right and that
"free access" to the restaurant was an "incident" of that constitutionally protected right. Under the compulsion of this premise, the
final judgment naturally depended on the evaluation of the conduct
of the strikers. Once again the fate of public policy was apparently
determined by judicial distaste for an isolated set of facts. Taft's
conclusion that the activities of the strikers constituted "moral coercion by illegal annoyance and obstruction" followed logically from
his view that the methods used to bring the employer to terms were
unlawful. "The real question," he said, was: "Were the means used
here illegal?" The continuous patrolling of the premises, the loud
appeals of the pickets at the entrance to the restaurant, the abusive
epithets, threats, and libelous attacks—these things convinced him
that the union had set out to win its demands not by peaceful persuasion but by a campaign of force. So a majority of the Supreme
Court found that by legalizing acts intrinsically unlawful, the
Arizona statute violated due process of law. It also held that by
barring relief by injunction only in cases arising from controversies
over terms or conditions of employment, Arizona was resorting to a
discriminatory classification and was therefore denying to employers
equal protection guaranteed by the Fourteenth Amendment.

This five-to-four decision of the Supreme Court was described by

Felix Frankfurter in a contemporary editorial comment as "fraught with more evil than any which it has rendered in a generation." [23] Professor Frankfurter was particularly critical of the Chief Justice for his failure to reckon with the realities of modern industrial conflict, all the more surprising, he thought, in view of Taft's service on the War Labor Board. The Chief Justice's approval of the court injunction in labor controversies was so firm, it was suggested, that he was led by a "process of self-delusion" to sanctify it with constitutional authority, forgetting that the use of injunctions in such cases was at the time only thirty years old. For Chief Justice Taft "there never was a time," Professor Frankfurter wrote, "when injunctive relief was not the law of nature. For him the world never was without it, and therefore the foundations of the world are involved in its withdrawal." [24]

Curiously enough, even conservative Mahlon Pitney—who dissented in this case, along with Justices Holmes, Brandeis and Clarke —found Taft's position too reactionary. "I cannot believe," he observed, "that the use of the injunction in such cases—however important—is so essential to the right of acquiring, possessing and enjoying property that its restriction or elimination amounts to a deprivation of liberty or property without due process of law, within the meaning of the Fourteenth Amendment." Since there was always the redress of the criminal law and suits for damages, it could not be said that property was left unprotected. Nor was it arbitrary for the legislature to deny to a particular class of litigants the injunctive remedy in the courts, not so long as all employers "similarly circumstanced" were treated alike. The majority's view of equal protection, Pitney continued, would "transform the provision of the Fourteenth Amendment from a guaranty of the 'protection of equal laws' into an insistence upon laws complete, perfect, symmetrical." [25]

[23] "The Same Mr. Taft," *New Republic* (Jan. 18, 1922); reprinted in *Law and Politics: Occasional Papers of Felix Frankfurter,* edited by Archibald MacLeish and E. F. Prichard (New York: Harcourt, Brace and Company, 1939), p. 44.
[24] *Ibid.,* p. 47.
[25] 257 U.S. 312, 344, at 351.

At one point in his elaborate refutation, Justice Pitney strongly implied that a majority of his colleagues were disregarding the principle that within certain limits, it was for the States themselves to determine "their respective conditions of law and order, and what kind of civilization they shall have as a result." [26] This criticism, along with comments on related themes in the opinions by Taft, Holmes and Brandeis, only served to substantiate the inference that the Justices were not unaware that the deeper issue in Truax v. Corrigan was the effect of the judicial veto upon necessary social adjustments. "The Constitution was intended, its very purpose was, to prevent experimentation with the fundamental rights of the individual"—Chief Justice Taft stated categorically.[27]

Both Holmes and Brandeis reacted rather vigorously against the use of such absolutes in the discussion of practical constitutional problems. Holmes might well have been tempted to quote one of his own aphorisms to describe the hazard inherent in the Chief Justice's intellectual process in this case: "To rest upon a formula is a slumber that, prolonged, means death." [28] For he politely suggested in his short dissent that the Court had been led into error by too rigid a conception of property rights. Once again he deplored "delusive exactness" in the application of constitutional provisions, insisting that it was "a source of fallacy throughout the law." He thought that the case in hand illustrated both the confusion and the dangers inherent in a too easy reliance on abstract formulas.

By calling a business "property" you make it seem like land, and lead up to the conclusion that a statute cannot substantially cut down the advantages of ownership existing before the statute was passed. An established business no doubt may have pecuniary value and commonly is protected by law against various unjustified injuries. But you cannot give it definiteness of contour by calling it a thing. It is a course of conduct and like other conduct is subject to substantial modification according to time and circumstances both in itself and in regard to what shall justify doing it a harm.[29]

[26] *Ibid.*, at 349.   [27] *Ibid.*, at 338.
[28] Holmes, "Ideals and Doubts," in *Collected Legal Papers,* p. 306.
[29] 257 U.S. 312, 342, at 342–43.

Taft's objection to the Arizona law as discriminatory because it restricted the power of courts to grant injunctions in employer-employee controversies only struck Holmes as equally unreal. "Legislation may begin where an evil begins," he remarked, adding, "If, as many intelligent people believe, there is more danger that the injunction will be abused in labor cases than elsewhere I can feel no doubt of the power of the legislature to deny it in such cases." [30] Holmes ended his opinion with what he called a "general consideration" but it is in the nature of a quite specific rejoinder to Taft's sweeping shibboleth about experimentation. It has become one of the most widely quoted clues to the core of Holmes' constitutional philosophy. "There is nothing I more deprecate," the Justice wrote, "than the use of the Fourteenth Amendment beyond the absolute compulsion of its words to prevent the making of social experiments that an important part of the community desires, in the insulated chambers afforded by the several States, even though the experiments may seem futile or even noxious to me and to those whose judgment I most respect." [31]

The wisdom of not using the Constitution to stifle social experiments may be said to have been fully documented by Justice Brandeis in his massive dissent. His opinion in this case is fundamentally a plea for recognizing the essentially tentative character of governmental efforts to deal with social problems. Particularly in the difficult field of labor relations, it would only aggravate the struggle among the contending parties if government were stopped from trying out new methods for dealing with it. "The rules governing the contest necessarily change from time to time. For conditions change; and, furthermore, the rules evolved, being merely experiments in government, must be discarded when they prove to be failures." [32] Judged by existing rules, practically every change in the legal relation between employers and employees necessarily curtails to some degree the liberty or property of one of the parties, but that fact in itself does not make the modification unconstitutional.

[30] *Ibid.,* at 343.   [31] *Ibid.,* at 344.
[32] *Ibid.,* at 354–55.

The basic question is whether such changes in the law are arbitrary
or unreasonable, and it can be answered satisfactorily only if the
Court would take a close look at the nature and history of the problem with which the legislature was concerned. Justice Brandeis
therefore proceeded once again to summarize the guides to informed decision:

Whether a law enacted in the exercise of the police power is justly
subject to the charge of being unreasonable or arbitrary, can ordinarily
be determined only by a consideration of the contemporary conditions,
social, industrial and political, of the community to be affected thereby.
Resort to such facts is necessary, among other things, in order to appreciate the evils sought to be remedied and the possible effects of the
remedy proposed. Nearly all legislation involves a weighing of public
needs as against private desires; and likewise a weighing of relative social
values. Since government is not an exact science, prevailing public opinion
concerning the evils and the remedy is among the important facts deserving consideration; particularly, when the public conviction is both
deep-seated and widespread and has been reached after deliberation.[33]

In the context of such an inquiry, the elaborate historical survey
that followed seems almost unavoidable. The experience with both
the judicial and legislative treatment of conflicts between employers and employees in Great Britain, its Dominions and the
United States is sketched and the reasons for the opposition to
the labor injunction are sympathetically set forth. To Brandeis the
fluctuations in the conceptions of liberty and property which this
history revealed were the best of reasons for not declaring a particular law to be arbitrary and unreasonable "merely because we
are convinced that it is fraught with danger to the public weal, and
thus to close the door to experiment within the law." This is one of
those occasions when, as Walton Hamilton has said of Brandeis'
dissents generally, after reading "the opinion of the Court" and
turning to the Brandeis dissent, one "finds himself in another intellectual world." [34]

[33] *Ibid.*, at 356–57.
[34] Hamilton, "The Jurist's Art," in Frankfurter (ed.), *Mr. Justice Brandeis*,
p. 178.

To meet the objection that the ban on injunctions invaded property rights, Justice Brandeis pointed out that "the real motive" in seeking an injunction was ordinarily not to protect property but "to endow property with active, militant power which would make it dominant over men." [35] Moreover, the labor injunction gives to the employer the benefits deriving from criminal penalties while curtailing the personal liberty of the employee without affording him the protection of the Bill of Rights.[36] Under the guise of protecting property, a single judge by means of the injunction is putting the "sovereign power" of the community on the side of the employer; the prohibition on injunctions would merely equalize the industrial struggle. Again and again, Brandeis referred to the great diversity of opinion to be found in both legislation and judicial decisions concerned with labor disputes, thus underscoring his conviction that "pending the ascertainment of new principles to govern industry, it was wiser for the state not to interfere in industrial struggles by the issuance of an injunction." [37] He saw the Arizona law as being simply an exercise of the legislature's prerogative to control the equity

[35] 257 U.S. 312, 354, at 368.
[36] "In America the injunction did not secure recognition as a possible remedy until 1888. When a few years later its use became extensive and conspicuous, the controversy over the remedy overshadowed in bitterness the question of the relative substantive rights of the parties. . . . The equitable remedy, although applied in accordance with established practice, involved incidents, which, it was asserted, endangered the personal liberty of wage-earners. The acts enjoined were frequently, perhaps usually, acts which were already crimes at common law or had been made so by statutes. The issues in litigation arising out of trade disputes related largely to questions of fact. But in equity issues of fact as of law were tried by a single judge, sitting without a jury. Charges of violating an injunction were often heard on affidavits merely, without the opportunity of confronting or cross-examining witnesses. Men found guilty of contempt were committed in the judge's discretion, without either a statutory limit upon the length of the imprisonment, or the opportunity of effective review on appeal, or the right to release on bail pending possible revisory proceedings. The effect of the proceeding upon the individual was substantially the same as if he had been successfully prosecuted for a crime; but he was denied, in the course of the equity proceedings, those rights which by the Constitution are commonly secured to persons charged with a crime." 257 U.S. 312, 354, at 366–67.
[37] *Ibid.*, at 368.

jurisdiction of courts. One of his concluding remarks is in itself a key to the difference between Brandeis and his more conservative colleagues: "Rights of property and the liberty of the individual must be remoulded, from time to time, to meet the changing needs of society." [38]

III

Even while he was still on the Court, Brandeis had had the satisfaction of seeing some of his views on the labor question embodied in prevailing judgments. Thus in a case decided two years prior to his retirement, he led the Court—though still over the protest of Justices Butler, Van Devanter, McReynolds and Sutherland—in sustaining a state law permitting peaceful picketing as a means of publicizing a labor dispute.[39] "If the end sought by the unions is not forbidden by the Federal Constitution," his opinion held, "the State may authorize working men to seek to attain it by combining as pickets, just as it permits capitalists and employers to combine in other ways to attain their desired economic ends." Whether it was "wise" for Wisconsin to permit labor unions to picket for such purposes, the Justice added, was "a question of its public policy—not our concern." [40]

One comment by Justice Brandeis in the *Senn* case was soon to be converted by the Roosevelt Court into an explicit doctrine of constitutional law. He had there observed: "Members of a union might, without special statutory authorization by a State, make known the facts of a labor dispute, for freedom of speech is guaranteed by the Federal Constitution." [41] Three years later, this statement was cited as authority by Justice Murphy when he spoke for all members of the Court except Justice McReynolds in holding that "In the circumstances of our times the dissemination of information concern-

[38] *Ibid.*, at 376.
[39] Senn v. Tile Layers Union, 301 U.S. 468, 483 (1937).
[40] *Ibid.*, at 478, 481.
[41] *Ibid.*, at 478.

ing the facts of a labor dispute must be regarded as within that area of free discussion that is guaranteed by the Constitution." [42]

The following year, Justice Frankfurter was able to deliver an opinion for the Court—supported by the three other "New Deal" Justices participating in the case—which for all practical purposes overruled the decisions in the *Duplex* and *Bedford Cut Stone Co.* cases.[43] Only Hughes and Roberts dissented. Justice Frankfurter first discussed the "powerful judicial dissents and informed lay opinion" which had been arrayed against the ruling in the *Duplex* case that Section 20 of the Clayton Act applied only to disputes between an employer and his own employees. He then pointed out that the agitation against the decision culminated in the adoption by Congress of the Norris–LaGuardia Act in 1932. That legislation withdrew from the Federal courts the power to grant injunctions in labor disputes.

The main issue dividing the Court in the *Hutcheson* case was whether the officials of labor unions could be prosecuted under the Sherman Act for organizing a secondary boycott. In this case, the leaders of the United Brotherhood of Carpenters had been indicted as the result of their action in instituting a campaign to get union members and their families and friends not to patronize an employer who had given to a rival union jobs demanded by the carpenters. The prosecution was in line with the determination of Thurman Arnold—then head of the Anti-Trust Division in the Justice Department—to bring "big labor" under the Sherman Act.

The opinions in the *Hutcheson* case illustrate the great power exercised by judges in the process of construing statutes. Relying on the decisions holding that secondary boycotts violate the Sherman Act, Chief Justice Hughes and Justice Roberts emphasized in their dis-

[42] Thornhill v. Alabama, 310 U.S. 88, at 102 (1940). In later years, both Murphy and the Court came to be criticized for distorting Brandeis' opinion in the *Senn* case by failing to quote the sentence which follows the one cited. Brandeis had also stated: "The State may, in the exercise of its police power, regulate the methods and means of publicity as well as the use of public streets." 301 U.S. 468, at 478.

[43] United States v. Hutcheson, 312 U.S. 219, 237, 243 (1941).

sent that if the criminal penalties of the law were not to apply to labor, the exemption should be granted by Congress and not the Court. Their position was, that is to say, that the Clayton and Norris–LaGuardia Acts merely barred court injunctions in labor disputes and not criminal prosecutions of illegal restraints of trade initiated by labor unions. Unconvinced that there was a conspiracy to violate the Sherman Act, Justice Stone concurred in the result, but saw "no occasion to consider the impact of the Norris–LaGuardia Act."

For Justice Frankfurter, the situation called for a much broader inquiry. As he said, "But to argue, as it was urged before us, that the *Duplex* case still governs for purposes of a criminal prosecution is to say that that which on the equity side of the court is allowable conduct may in a criminal proceeding become the road to prison." [44] His opinion held that the prosecution of the carpenters under the Sherman Act was foreclosed by Section 20 of the Clayton Act when construed in the light of the definition of a "labor dispute" in the Norris–LaGuardia Act. Justice Frankfurter's final summary of the effect of the Norris–LaGuardia Act reveals how far the dissents by Justice Brandeis had become the law of the land:

The underlying aim of the Norris-LaGuardia Act was to restore the broad purpose which Congress thought it had formulated in the Clayton Act but which was frustrated, so Congress believed, by unduly restrictive judicial construction. . . . The Norris-LaGuardia Act was a disapproval of *Duplex Printing Press Co. v. Deering* . . . and *Bedford Cut Stone Co. v. Journeymen Stone Cutters' Association,* . . . as the authoritative interpretation of Section 20 of the Clayton Act, for Congress now placed its own meaning upon that section.[45]

[44] *Ibid.,* at 234–35.
[45] *Ibid.,* at 235–36.

8

"If we would guide by the light of reason"

"A cherished American myth is that Oliver Wendell Holmes, Jr., was a liberal. This notion, as baseless as the tale of Washington and the cherry tree, was born during the great jurist's life and persists in the national folk lore since his death. . . . The time has come to lay the ghost of 'Holmes and Brandeis dissenting.'"[1]

In an age of iconoclasm, the debunking of so-called myths may sometimes result in the creation of other myths, especially if the object is merely to disturb prior conceptions. The smashing of gods may have an intellectual as well as a social utility; but if the new image is also a distortion, one might well ponder the price for the new enlightenment. Without undertaking to define terms and clarify the correct picture, those out to demolish the myth of "Holmes the Liberal" are not likely to do much more than exchange labels. Furthermore, a too cavalier indulgence in the fashion to paint Holmes as a "conservative" may even obscure the most significant question of all: What is liberalism and what is conservatism in a constitutional judge?

What, for instance, is implied in the statement "the time has come

[1] Irving Bernstein, "The Conservative Mr. Justice Holmes," 23 *New Eng. Quarterly* 435 (Dec., 1950).

to lay the ghost of 'Holmes and Brandeis dissenting.'" Whether the purpose is to deflate the impression that Holmes was more advanced than his Court, or to dissociate him from Brandeis, the new look must be rejected on both counts, at least as applied to the judicial record. Holmes himself, to be sure, disliked the popular picture of him as a dissenter. "I regret being called a dissenting Judge in the papers for I don't like to dissent," he complained shortly after his eighty-ninth birthday.[2] Yet the fact remains that during the fifteen and one-half years that Justices Holmes and Brandeis served together on the Supreme Court, they were united in their opposition to prevailing attitudes in several significant fields, most conspicuously to prevailing conceptions of the judicial function itself.

In the effort to erase superficial impressions, some of those who have essayed reappraisals have ignored the large area of agreement between the two Justices. Notwithstanding differences in method and motivation, they stood together firmly against judicial reaction. There is no denying, of course, that as a judge, in the words of Felix Frankfurter, Holmes not infrequently enforced "statutes based upon economic and political theories which he does not share and of whose efficacy in action he is sceptical."[3] Brandeis' sympathies, on the other hand, were deeply engaged in many of the causes argued before him; no one can attribute to him such impartiality or lack of concern over social policy and its consequences. Unlike Holmes, he personally believed in the "economic and political theories" implicit in many of the laws whose validity he sought to save.

[2] Holmes to Laski, June 8, 1930. *Holmes-Laski Letters*, II, 1258–59.
[3] Frankfurter (ed.), *Mr. Justice Holmes*, p. 100. For an interesting discussion taking exception to this view—in which the writer undertakes to show that some of Holmes' judicial opinions coincided with his own deep conviction that the way to improve society was to build a better race—see Martin B. Hickman, "Mr. Justice Holmes: A Reappraisal," V *Western Pol. Quart. 66*, particularly pp. 70–72 (March, 1952). Mr. Hickman finds support for his thesis in Holmes' opinion for the Court upholding a Virginia statute providing for the sterilization of feeble-minded persons in public institutions. Buck v. Bell, 274 U.S. 200 (1927).

This paradox was illustrated with almost unbroken consistency in the response of the two jurists in the major fields of judicial conflict. In the years when Taft presided over the Court, all the really significant issues dividing the Justices seemed to turn on their clashing views as to their function under the American constitutional system. Almost without exception, Holmes contented himself with short statements as to why in his judgment the governmental action complained of was not "unconstitutional." Brandeis invariably undertook the more arduous task of seeking to persuade that the measure was entirely necessary and "constitutional." So completely did Brandeis indulge his passion for facts that many lawmakers must have marveled, as one commentator has phrased it, "at the unsuspected depth of their own thinking." [4] Holmes believed in the right to experiment; but because Brandeis believed in the importance of experimentation, he strove to supply a rational as well as a constitutional basis for it.

The contrast between what has been called "the factual method of Brandeis and the philosophical approach of Holmes" [5] stands out in practically every instance in which the two had occasion to discuss the issues before the Court. This contrast is indicative, however, of something more fundamental than a difference in judicial craft. It helps us to understand not only the manner of the man but also the basic reason for his characteristic behavior as a judge. Brandeis was looking to the future to vindicate the positions he was voicing in dissent; hence the highly didactic character of many of his utterances. No such sense of mission is discernible in Holmes' opinions, unless it was to bring his Court back to "first principles" of the law.

Yet there is also good ground for believing that it was the attitude and methods of some of their more conservative colleagues which helped to forge the unique responses of both Holmes and Brandeis. The tendency of the Court's conservatives to think in

[4] Paul A. Freund, *On Understanding the Supreme Court*, pp. 73–4.
[5] Hamilton, "The Jurist's Art," in Frankfurter (ed.), *Mr. Justice Brandeis*, p. 219, n. 45.

absolute terms and to exalt legal concepts as ends in themselves, it is fairly obvious, served to release Holmes' deeply ingrained skepticism and propelled him to espouse a legal relativism. Similarly, the treatment of great public questions on the basis of inadequate information may very well have stirred Brandeis to undertake to fill the vacuum. By nature an empiricist, he was appalled by the failure of some of his colleagues to heed the lessons of social experience; hence his repeated admonition that "underlying questions of fact may condition the constitutionality of legislation." [6]

II

One of the most dramatic episodes illustrative of the forces within the Court which were generating this counter-current is the case concerned with the constitutionality of the District of Columbia Minimum Wage Law.[7] Though Justice Brandeis remained silent in this case—having disqualified himself from sitting because his daughter Elizabeth was Secretary to the Minimum Wage Board— it is not mere idle speculation to surmise that he would have supported Holmes' protest and that he would probably have filed one of his typically informative minority reports. In a sense, the formidable factual brief presented by Felix Frankfurter [8] made it unnecessary for Brandeis to dissent. Citing the findings of economists, sociologists and physicians, the eleven-hundred-page document analyzed the social effects of "poor wages" for women and sought to demonstrate that there was urgent need for the legislation adopted by Congress in 1918. This statute authorized the Minimum Wage Board to prescribe wages sufficient "to supply the necessary cost of living . . . to women workers to maintain them in good health and to protect their morals."

[6] O'Gorman and Young v. Hartford Insurance Co., 282 *U.S. 251*, at 257 (1931).
[7] Adkins v. Children's Hospital, 261 U.S. 525, 562, 567 (1923).
[8] *District of Columbia Wage Cases*, Brief for Appellants, 2 vols. (New York: National Consumers' League, 1923).

Five of the Court's members—Sutherland, McKenna, McReynolds, Van Devanter and Butler—remained unconvinced. The many authorities in favor of the minimum wage which were quoted in the Frankfurter brief "are proper enough for the consideration of lawmaking bodies," declared Justice Sutherland, spokesman for the majority; but he added, opinions regarding the desirability or undesirability of minimum wage legislation "reflect no legitimate light" upon its validity. "The elucidation of that question," we were told, "cannot be aided by counting heads."

Justice Sutherland's "Spencerian edict," as his biographer has aptly characterized the majority opinion in the *Adkins* case,[9] was unacceptable even to Chief Justice Taft, though he could not agree with some of the observations in the "forcible opinion" of Justice Holmes. "It is not the function of this Court," Taft remarked, "to hold congressional acts invalid simply because they are passed to carry out economic views which the Court believes to be unwise or unsound."[10] Max Lerner is indeed justified in suggesting that this pronouncement is but "an echo of earlier Holmesian opinion."[11] Such sometimes is the ironic fate of subtle influence.

The fact is that the result in the *Adkins* case affords striking proof of the great risk run by him who would predict the future course of judicial performance. Surely no one familiar with the extent to which the principle of the *Lochner* case had been departed from during the decade following its decision could have questioned the soundness of the conclusion confidently stated by Professor Frankfurter in 1916: "The groundwork of the *Lochner* case has by this time been cut from under."[12] Cases such as Muller v. Oregon and Bunting v. Oregon, it was generally assumed, had vindicated the right of the states to regulate hours of labor, and even a minimum wage law for women had been left undisturbed in 1917, though by

[9] Joel Francis Paschal, *Mr. Justice Sutherland: A Man Against the State* (Princeton: Princeton Univ. Press, 1951), p. 122.
[10] 261 U.S. 525, at 562.
[11] Lerner, *The Mind and Faith of Justice Holmes*, p. 174.
[12] 2 *Selected Essays on Constitutional Law* 699, 713.

an equally divided Court.[13] But in the judicial universe, too, new battles are fought from time to time over old ground. For not only does Sutherland's opinion in the *Adkins* case review sympathetically the decisions in the *Lochner, Adair* and *Coppage* cases, but the Justice actually resurrected the principle of the *Lochner* case. Both Taft and Holmes simply assumed that a decision which had been discredited as greatly as the ruling in the *Lochner* case was no longer controlling. "I have always supposed that the *Lochner case* had been overruled *sub silentio*," [14] said the Chief Justice. Holmes remarked, somewhat more elegantly, that he had assumed that "Lochner v. New York would be allowed a deserved repose." [15]

Rufus W. Peckham could not have wished for a truer disciple of his intense laissez-faire outlook than George Sutherland revealed himself to be in the *Adkins* case. Peckham's insistence in the *Lochner* case that laws "limiting the hours in which grown and intelligent men may labor" were "mere meddlesome interferences with the rights of the individual" [16] was more than matched by Sutherland's concern for preserving the equal rights of women. Through a fantastic disregard of economic and social facts, he was able to spell out a constitutional hypothesis which made the minimum wage law appear to be a veritable conspiracy against basic human freedom. But his conclusion that the statute transgressed "the right to contract about one's affairs" guaranteed by the Fifth Amendment flowed logically from his conception of liberty. There was no such thing as "absolute freedom of contract," he admitted, but he made it quite clear at the very start of his opinion that freedom of contract was "the general rule and restraint the exception; and the exercise of legislative authority to abridge it can be justified only by the existence of exceptional circumstances." [17] That an employee should have entered the case to plead for the right to work at the wage her em-

[13] Stettler v. O'Hara, 243 U.S. 269 (1917).
[14] 261 U.S. 525, 562, at 564.
[15] *Ibid.*, at 570.
[16] 198 U.S. 45, at 61.
[17] 261 U.S. 525, at 546.

ployer thought her services were worth may well have served to confirm the Justice's conviction, at least so it has been suggested by his
perceptive biographer:

The fact that the statute was assailed by one of its supposed bene-
ficiaries has a significance which, although generally overlooked, is of the
highest importance. For whatever suspicions are generated by Willie
Lyons' plea that she be allowed to work for $35 a month and two meals a
day, there could have been no shrewder appeal to the sympathy of
George Sutherland. The express pronouncement of the statute was that
women were treated differently by the law than men. Such discrimination
had been denounced by both John Stuart Mill and Herbert Spencer as an
anomalous survival from a barbarous past. And Sutherland, doubtless
moved by their words, had battled against it throughout his political
career.[18]

Since the District of Columbia Minimum Wage Law applied only
to women and children, the dissenters assumed that Muller v.
Oregon would be the controlling case. To Sutherland the statute
was "simply and exclusively a price-fixing law confined to adult
women . . . who are legally as capable of contracting for themselves as men." [19] While conceding that there were physical differences between men and women, he insisted that the Woman Suffrage Amendment had "emancipated women from the old doctrine
of special protection and restraints." His repudiation of "the ancient
inequality of the sexes" is a rather striking example of the use of
legal sophistry as a mask for social obtuseness, and for that reason
ought to be recalled:

In view of the great—not to say revolutionary—changes which have taken
place . . . in the contractual, political, and civil status of women, culminating in the Nineteenth Amendment, it is not unreasonable to say that
these differences have come now almost, if not quite, to the vanishing
point. In this aspect of the matter, while the physical differences must
be recognized in appropriate cases, and legislation fixing hours or conditions of work may properly take them into account, we can not accept
the doctrine that women of mature age, *sui juris*, require or may be sub-

[18] Paschal, *op. cit.*, p. 119.
[19] 261 U.S. 525, at 554.

jected to restrictions upon their liberty of contract which could not lawfully be imposed in the case of men under similar circumstances. To do so would be to ignore all the implications to be drawn from the present day trend of legislation, as well as that of common thought and usage, by which woman is accorded emancipation from the old doctrine that she must be given special protection or be subjected to special restraint in her contractual and civil relationship.[20]

To all of which Justice Holmes retorted, "It would need more than the Nineteenth Amendment to convince me that there are no differences between men and women, or that legislation cannot take those differences into account." [21] Believing that Muller v. Oregon was "as good law to-day as it was in 1908," he could not understand on what basis the right to fix a minimum wage for women was denied by those who recognized the power to limit their hours of work. "The bargain is equally affected whichever half you regulate," he asserted. As was his familiar practice, he merely listed some outstanding instances in which the legislation sustained by the Court had curtailed "liberty" as greatly as does a minimum wage law. How best to protect women against ill health and immorality and how to prevent the deterioration of the race were problems for the legislature, and the sole matter of concern to the Court was whether the legislative remedy was "reasonably" calculated to achieve the desired result.

At a first glance, Holmes' dissent in the *Adkins* case would seem to be a mere reiteration of old themes. In its general disavowal of personal preferences and in its attack on dogmatic interpretation of the Constitution, it reminds one, of course, of Lochner v. New York. Yet something has been added. His discussion of the statute [22] and of the way to test its constitutionality has about it the kind of practical

[20] *Ibid.*, at 553.

[21] *Ibid.*, at 569–70.

[22] "This statute does not compel anybody to pay anything. It simply forbids employment at rates below those fixed as the minimum requirement of health and right living. It is safe to assume that women will not be employed at even the lowest wages allowed unless they earn them, or unless the employer's business can sustain the burden." *Ibid.*, at 570.

or concrete touch which is rather rare in his opinions. Instead of
dismissing the need for research, as he had done in the *Lochner*
case, he actually acknowledges the relevance of the Brandeis type of
brief in such matters. Characterizing the compilation submitted by
Professor Frankfurter as a "very remarkable collection of documents," he found it "material" in showing that the belief manifested
by Congress in the Minimum Wage Law could be held by "reasonable men." [23]

Holmes' treatment of what he called "the criterion of constitutionality" is probably the best and most persuasive part of his
opinion; "The criterion of constitutionality is not whether we believe
the law to be for the public good." Confessing that he had "doubts"
about the ultimate wisdom of minimum wage legislation—whether
the "interstitial detriments" may not outweigh in the long run
the social gain—he nevertheless went on to maintain that as a judge
he must refrain from translating his doubts into law. In no other
of his opinions is the essence of his judicial philosophy stated with
greater clarity or force:

The question in this case is the broad one, Whether Congress can establish minimum rates of wages for women in the District of Columbia with
due provision for special circumstances, or whether we must say that
Congress has no power to meddle with the matter at all. To me, notwithstanding the deference due to the prevailing judgment of the Court, the
power of Congress seems absolutely free from doubt. The end, to remove
conditions leading to ill health, immorality and the deterioration of the
race, no one would deny to be within the scope of constitutional legislation. The means are means that have the approval of Congress, of many
States, and of those governments from which we have learned our greatest
lessons. When so many intelligent persons, who have studied the matter
more than any of us can, have thought that the means are effective and
are worth the price, it seems to me impossible to deny that the belief
reasonably may be held by reasonable men . . . the only objection that
can be urged is found within the vague contours of the Fifth Amendment,
prohibiting the depriving of any person of liberty or property without due
process of law. To that I turn.

[23] *Ibid.*

The earlier decisions upon the same words in the Fourteenth Amendment began within our memory and went no farther than an unpretentious assertion of the liberty to follow the ordinary callings. Later that innocuous generality was expanded into the dogma, Liberty of Contract. Contract is not specially mentioned in the text that we have to construe. It is merely an example of doing what you want to do, embodied in the word liberty. But pretty much all law consists in forbidding men to do some things that they want to do, and contract is no more exempt from law than other acts.[24]

Probably the most devastating contemporary evisceration of Justice Sutherland's logic in the *Adkins* case is to be found in the article discussing the decision which Thomas Reed Powell wrote for the *Harvard Law Review* in 1924.[25] Not only did Professor Powell expose what he rightly called the "crass legalistic formalism" by which the majority dealt with a problem of great practical importance, but in his relentless analysis of the basic constitutional question he illuminated the general line of judicial cleavage itself. The essay is, indeed, a superb clinical study of the whole process of constitutional adjudication in the period when the apostles of laissez-faire were in the ascendancy, even though the *Adkins* case found the conservative Chief Justice siding with the liberals. One of Professor Powell's closing observations is particularly acute in delineating the fundamental issue:

Is it not clear that the difference between Congress and Mr. Justice Sutherland is a difference of opinion as to the desirability or undesirability of minimum-wage legislation? Congress thought it so desirable that it enacted it. Thirty-five of forty-five judges who have been called upon to consider it thought it at least not so undesirable as to warrant the interposition of a judicial veto. Mr. Justice Sutherland and four of his colleagues on the Supreme Court are of different opinion. The importance of their opinion is that under our system of government it has, for a time, at least, the casting vote. This vote was determined by the capacity of economic analysis and the views of public policy of five individuals. It is

[24] *Ibid.,* at 567–68.
[25] Powell, "The Judiciality of Minimum Wage Legislation," 37 *Harv. L. Rev.* 545 (1924); reprinted in two parts in *Selected Essays on Constitutional Law,* vol. 1, 553–60, vol. 2, 716–32.

their preference which has rendered minimum-wage legislation invalid. It is not wholly true that the elucidation of the question of its validity cannot be aided by counting heads. Only because in the final vote some heads rather than others are the ones to be counted is minimum-wage legislation invalid.[26]

The statement of implications by Sutherland's biographer is even more sweeping. "Taken at its face value," writes Mr. Paschal, "Sutherland's opinion [in the *Adkins* case] could only be interpreted as asserting that under the Constitution it was impossible to attempt the solution of certain modern social problems by legislation." [27] This is not too extreme a view of the constitutional impasse precipitated by the Court's conservatives in the 1920's, only to be exacerbated in the thirties. On the contrary, it comes pretty close to describing the diagnosis of the situation made by some of the Court's own members, notably Justices Holmes and Brandeis, soon to be supported with increasing frequency and vigor by Harlan Fiske Stone.

At the time the *Adkins* case was decided, the impression was created that the chief reason which compelled the majority to invalidate the District of Columbia Minimum Wage Law was the failure of Congress to relate the minimum wage to the value of the service rendered by the employee. Justice Sutherland had observed that this feature of the statute "perhaps more than any other" put upon it "the stamp of invalidity." He even seemed to suggest a model law when he remarked that "a statute requiring an employer to pay . . . the value of services rendered, even to pay with fair relation to the extent of the benefit obtained from the service, would be understandable." [28]

In subsequent years, several States sought to meet this objection by adopting laws embodying formulas for taking into account the value of services rendered. Thus, the law which the legislature of New York enacted in 1933 provided that a "fair minimum wage"

[26] *2 Selected Essays 716, 732.*
[27] Paschal, *op. cit.*, p. 302.
[28] 261 U.S. 525, at 558, 559.

was to be one "fairly and reasonably commensurate with the value of the service or class of services rendered." When the Supreme Court, voting five to four, invalidated this statute on June 1, 1936,[29] it made it quite clear that the particular standard for fixing minimum wages was not the determining factor. "The State is without power," wrote Justice Butler in the *New York Minimum Wage* case, "by any form of legislation to prohibit, change or nullify contracts between employers and adult women workers as to the amount of wages paid." Butler was joined in this opinion by Van Devanter, McReynolds, Sutherland and Roberts, the vote cast by Justice Roberts no doubt being the decisive one. Chief Justice Hughes, in a dissenting opinion which had the support of Justices Brandeis, Stone and Cardozo, argued that since the New York statute required a "fair equivalence of wages and service" it was distinguishable from the legislation set aside in the *Adkins* case.[30]

Justice Stone's separate dissent, concurred in by Brandeis and Cardozo, advanced a more uncompromising attack on the Court's position. Much of his opinion is an echo of Holmes' dissents in the *Lochner* and *Adkins* cases. His fundamental point was that in the exercise of their power to promote the public interest, the States were free to select the particular forms of regulation for dealing with economic maladjustments. "The vague and general pronouncement of the Fourteenth Amendment against deprivation of liberty without due process of law," Justice Stone maintained, "is a limitation of legislative power, not a formula for its exercise."[31] The "liberty" guaranteed by that Amendment did not secure to anyone freedom from the restraints of a law which "reasonable men" deemed to be an "appropriate means" for coping with the particular problem. The experience of the United States and numerous foreign countries afforded all the proof one needed to show that the control of wages was "an appropriate corrective for serious social

---

[29] Morehead v. New York ex rel. Tipaldo, 298 U.S. 587, 618, 631 (1936).
[30] *Ibid.,* at 623.
[31] *Ibid.,* at 631.

and economic maladjustments growing out of inequality in bargaining power." Since the general purpose of minimum wage legislation is to prevent the deterioration of the race and impairment of health and morals, its interference with freedom of contract was but a necessary means for realizing a perfectly valid governmental purpose. Irked by the Court's disregard of the conditions which minimum wage laws were intended to remedy,[32] Stone could not refrain from voicing the suspicion that the Justices constituting the majority allowed their private views of social policy to dictate their decision:

It is not for the courts to resolve doubts whether the remedy by wage regulation is as efficacious as many believe, or is better than some other, or is better even than the blind operation of uncontrolled economic forces. The legislature must be free to choose unless government is to be rendered impotent. The Fourteenth Amendment has no more embedded in the Constitution our preference for some particular set of economic beliefs than it has adopted, in the name of liberty, the system of theology which we may happen to approve.[33]

Thanks to the vote of Justice Roberts, the minority in the *Tipaldo* case was transformed into a majority when the Supreme Court upheld less than a year later the Minimum Wage Law of the State of

[32] Justice Stone felt that the Court's action in invalidating the New York Minimum Wage Law was inconsistent with its 1934 decision upholding New York's Milk Control Act. Nebbia v. New York, 291 U.S. 502, 539 (1934). In the *Nebbia* case, Justice Roberts, spokesman for the majority, had stressed that the important consideration was the need for regulation (as revealed by prevailing circumstances) and not the particular remedy. In as much as this was the more recent ruling, Stone saw no reason for not using it as a basis for reconsidering the *Adkins* decision. He knew of no principle or practice which limited the Court's "choice between conflicting precedents in deciding a question of constitutional law." Just how significant he regarded the Nebbia decision to have been may be gleaned from the fact that he saved the final summarizing sentence of his dissent for repeating that the point of view for which he was pleading had been accepted in the *Nebbia* case: "We should follow our decision in the *Nebbia* case and leave the selection and the method of the solution of the problems to which the statute is addressed where it seems to me the Constitution has left them, to the legislative branch of the government." 298 U.S. 587, 631, at 636.
[33] 298 U.S. 587, 631, at 636.

Washington.[34] In an opinion by Chief Justice Hughes which drew heavily upon the "sound" views of Taft and Holmes in the *Adkins* case,[35] the Court at last overruled the decision in that case. Reacting sharply to the Chief Justice's argument that "recent economic experience" had demonstrated the need for protecting women against exploitation lest the burden of their support be thrown upon the community, Justice Sutherland, now speaking in dissent, replied that "the meaning of the Constitution does not change with the ebb and flow of economic events." [36]

III

One of the more paradoxical aspects of this continuing debate over the scope of judicial power to annul legislation is that conservatives and liberals alike regarded themselves as adherents of what Professor Powell has spoken of as "the professed traditions of judicial tolerance." [37] Justice Sutherland invoked the ritual even in the *Adkins* case: "This Court, by an unbroken line of decisions from Chief Justice Marshall to the present day, has steadily adhered to the rule that every possible presumption is in favor of the validity of an act of Congress until overcome beyond rational doubt." [38] It is clear that this innocuous formula has been of no great value in assuring agreement in its application; a public policy of whose validity one judge may be absolutely certain will strike another as beyond the pale of both reason and law. Part of Justice Brandeis' contribution to the practice of the judicial art was to perfect the means for sustaining the case for legislative action by a convincing demonstration of the social situation which had induced it. "The chief significance of Brandeis' influence," Professor Mason noted in his first book on the Justice, "is that he has forced a consideration of the

[34] West Coast Hotel Co. v. Parrish, 300 U.S. 379, 400 (1937).
[35] *Ibid.*, at 397.
[36] *Ibid.*, at 402.
[37] 1 *Selected Essays* 553, 559.
[38] 261 U.S. 525, at 544 (1923).

facts and has greatly weakened, even in professional esteem, purely abstract and conceptualist arguments and opinions." [39]

Exactly a year following the decision in the *Adkins* case, Brandeis gave dramatic emphasis to the importance of the fullest information in the rational and responsible resolution of modern social and economic problems. This occurred in the heavily footnoted dissent which he filed in Burns Baking Co. v. Bryan,[40] wherein he made it known that he had done research in order to learn even more about the history and scientific phases of bread-making than was revealed by the record. "Much evidence referred to by me," he disclosed, "is not in the record. Nor could it have been included. It is the history of the experience gained under similar legislation, and the results of scientific experiments made, since the entry of the judgment below." [41] It may be of interest to note that following these observations Brandeis invited comparison with the decision in Muller v. Oregon, citing the pages containing Justice Brewer's commendation of his own brief in that case. Brandeis supplied the rationale for his unorthodox methods when he declared: "Knowledge is essential to understanding; and understanding should precede judging. Sometimes, if we would guide by the light of reason, we must let our minds be bold." [42]

The decision to which Justice Brandeis, with whom Holmes agreed, was taking exception overturned a Nebraska law which attempted to prevent deception in the sale of bread. Under the statute, every loaf of bread made or sold in the State had to be of a standard weight. It prohibited the sale of loaves which were below the standard as well as those which exceeded the standard weight by more than the permitted "tolerance" of two ounces. Speaking through Justice Butler, the Supreme Court held that these provisions violated the due process clause of the Fourteenth Amendment by subjecting "bakers and sellers of bread to restrictions which are essentially unreasonable and arbitrary." All the members of the Court agreed

[39] Mason, *Brandeis: Lawyer and Judge in the Modern State*, p. 129.
[40] 264 U.S. 504, 517 (1924).
[41] *Ibid.*, at 533.   [42] *Ibid.*, at 520.

that there was ample governmental power to forbid the sale of loaves below standard weights, as had indeed been held on a previous occasion.[43] According to the majority, however, the provision against excess weights imposed unreasonable burdens on the trade and was not necessary in order to prevent fraud.

In his attack on these conclusions, Justice Brandeis undertook to show that they were reached in utter disregard of the facts of the situation with which the legislation was concerned. Everybody understands why the sale of bread less than the standard weight is a "handy instrument" of fraud, but it is not so obvious as to why the sale of a loaf in excess of the standard also could lead to deception.[44] If the Court were not to act on the superficial impression that the regulation was unreasonable, it had a duty to inform itself of the practicalities of the problem with which it was dealing. The test of due process made this task unavoidable:

With the wisdom of the legislation we have, of course, no concern. But, under the due process clause as construed, we must determine whether the prohibition of excess weights can reasonably be deemed necessary; whether the prohibition can reasonably be deemed an appropriate means of preventing short weights and incidental unfair practices; and whether compliance with the limitation prescribed can reasonably be deemed practicable. The determination of these questions involves an enquiry into facts. . . .

Why did legislators, bent only on preventing short weights, prohibit, also, excessive weights? It was not from caprice or love of symmetry. It was because experience had taught consumers, honest dealers and public officials charged with the duty of enforcing laws concerning weights and

[43] Schmidinger v. Chicago, 226 U.S. 578 (1913).
[44] "In order that the buyer may be afforded protection, the difference between the standard sizes must be so large as to be evident and conspicuous. The buyer has usually in mind the difference in appearance between a one-pound loaf and a pound-and-a-half loaf, so that it is difficult for the dealer to palm off the former for the latter. But a loaf weighing one pound and five ounces may look so much like the buyer's memory of the pound-and-a-half loaf that the dealer may effectuate the fraud by delivering the former. The prohibition of excess weight is imposed in order to prevent a loaf of one standard size from being increased so much that it can readily be sold for a loaf of a larger standard size." 264 U.S. 504, 517, at 519.

measures that, if short weights were to be prevented, the prohibition of excessive weights was an administrative necessity.[45]

Brandeis' summary of prior experience, going back to 1858, stressed in particular the fact that the action of the United States Food Administration in limiting excess weights for bread as a means of preventing short weights was so successful that when the controls ended at the close of World War I, twelve states hastened to adopt similar regulations. The same was done for the District of Columbia and by the legislatures of Hawaii and Puerto Rico.

Acknowledging that there was evidence in the record in contradiction to the inference that a limitation on excess weights was essential to the protection of the public against short weights, Justice Brandeis simply insisted that it was not the "province" of the Court to weigh conflicting evidence. Before concluding, he once again defended the vital role of facts in the review of legislation enacted in the exercise of a State's police power and spoke out against the abuse of judicial power. The Justice admonished the Court to refrain from acting as a "super-legislature," a phrase destined to become the stock of the critics of judicial conservatism. He wrote:

Put at its highest, our function is to determine, in the light of all facts which may enrich our knowledge and enlarge our understanding, whether the measure, enacted in the exercise of an unquestioned police power and of a character inherently unobjectionable, transcends the bounds of reason. That is, whether the provision as applied is so clearly arbitrary or capricious that legislators acting reasonably could not have believed it to be necessary or appropriate for the public welfare.

To decide, as a fact, that the prohibition of excess weights "is not necessary for the protection of the purchasers against imposition and fraud by short weights"; that it "is not calculated to effectuate that purpose"; and that it "subjects bakers and sellers of bread" to heavy burdens, is, in my opinion, an exercise of the powers of a super-legislature—not the performance of the constitutional function of judicial review.[46]

[45] *Ibid.*, at 519–20.
[46] *Ibid.*, at 534. The phrases quoted by Justice Brandeis in the final sentences are from Justice Butler's opinion for the Court.

IV

Justice Brandeis maintained, especially in his dissents, a ceaseless effort to make the lessons of social experience part of the living tissue of constitutional adjudication. Keenly aware of the danger that slavish adherence to legal formulas may becloud fundamental issues, he was constantly preaching, in a variety of ways, that "the logic of words should yield to the logic of realities." [47] His aim was to prevent the Constitution from being used to justify judicial determinations having no basis in reason or the actualities of modern life. No wonder so many of his opinions give the impression that he was less concerned with his role as a judge and far more with the cause of effective government. As Felix Frankfurter wrote after the Justice had completed fifteen years of service on the Court, "His wide experience, his appetite for fact, his instinct for the concrete and his distrust of generalities, equip Mr. Justice Brandeis with unique gifts for the discharge of the Court's most difficult and delicate tasks." [48]

Holmes, on the other hand, lacked experience outside the legal domain, had an acute distaste for profusion of details and was rather fond of philosophic generalizations. At the same time that Brandeis was presenting his elaborately scaffolded critiques of prevailing attitudes, Holmes, while usually agreeing with Brandeis on results, contented himself with making some general, even if pungent, observations as to what was wrong with current judicial thinking. His dissent in Tyson v. Banton [49] is about as good an illustration as one can find.

With Justice Sutherland as its spokesman, a majority of the Court declared unconstitutional a New York law which made it illegal to sell theatre tickets at an advance of more than fifty cents above the printed box-office price. Obviously intended to protect theatre-

[47] Dissenting in DiSanto v. Pennsylvania, 273 U.S. 24, 33, at 43 (1927).
[48] Frankfurter (ed.), *Mr. Justice Brandeis,* p. 75.
[49] 273 U.S. 418, 445, 447 (1927).

goers against "scalping" by brokers who had bought up the best tickets, the legislation was a remedy for serious abuses which had been apparent for some years. The mere fact that the statute declared the price of admission to theatres to be "affected with a public interest" did not make it so, Sutherland's opinion held. The regulation was a price-fixing measure, but to be subject to price controls a business must be such as "to justify the conclusion" that it has been "devoted to a public use and its use thereby in effect granted to the public." [50]

Thus did the Court seal the fate of an effort to deal with a problem of modern urban life by invoking a concept borrowed from seventeenth century England. Walton Hamilton has traced its curious origin for us in these vivid words:

> If, towards the close of a life which ended in 1676, Sir Matthew Hale scribbled into a treatise on the ports of the sea the words "affected with a public interest" with an intent of making a great contribution to American constitutional law, the records make no mention of it. But whatever his meaning and purpose, events have conspired to accord to Britain's Chief Justice of the Restoration period a share in the authorship of the supreme law of the land; for a phrase which hails from a Merry England of a quarter-millennium ago has come to be the "established test by which the legislative power to fix the prices of commodities, use of property, and services, must be measured." [51]

More directly, the notion of business "affected with a public interest" was introduced into American constitutional law by Chief Justice Waite in the famous case of Munn v. Illinois, decided in 1876. [52] Waite converted Lord Chief Justice Hale's ambiguous phrase into a formula for upholding the right of government to regulate business; in the particular instance, an Illinois law fixing maximum rates for

[50] *Ibid.*, at 434.

[51] Hamilton, "Affectation with Public Interest," *39 Yale L. J. 1089* (1930); reprinted in *2 Selected Essays 494*. The words quoted by Professor Hamilton which speak of the so-called "established test" are from the decision which Justice Sutherland had written in a case decided in 1929, Williams v. Standard Oil Company, 278 U.S. 235, at 239.

[52] 94 U.S. 113 (1876).

grain elevators. Property becomes "clothed with a public interest," Waite had written, "when used in a manner to make it of public consequence, and affect the community at large. When, therefore, one devotes his property to a use in which the public has an interest, he, in effect, grants to the public an interest in that use, and must submit to be controlled by the public for the common good, to the extent of the interest he has thus created. He may withdraw his grant by discontinuing the use; but, so long as he maintains the use, he must submit to the control." [53]

In Tyson v. Banton, Sutherland accepted the argument of the ticket brokers that tickets were property and that the regulation invaded their property rights. In answer to the State's contention that shorter working days and the greater need for leisure and recreation had made theatres more essential to the people of large urban centers, Sutherland replied: "It may be true, as asserted, that among the Greeks, amusement and instruction of the people through the drama was one of the duties of government. But certainly no such duty devolves upon any American government." [54]

It is in the dissenting opinion of Justice Stone that one will find a point by point dissection of the Court's decision in Tyson v. Banton. He argued, in the first place, that strictly speaking the New York law was not even a price-fixing measure. As he said:

Although the statute in question declares that the price of tickets of admission to places of amusement is affected with a public interest, it does not purport to fix prices of admission. The producer or theatre proprietor is free to charge any prices he chooses. The statute requires only that the sales price, whatever it is, be printed on the face of the ticket, and prohibits the licensed broker, an intermediary in the marketing process, from reselling the ticket at an advance of more than fifty cents above the printed price. Nor is it contended that this limit on the profit is unreasonable.[55]

When he turned to the merits of the controversy, Justice Stone directed his main attack against the Court's use of the "affected with

[53] *Ibid.*, at 126.   [54] 273 U.S. 418, at 441.
[55] *Ibid.*, at 448–49.

a public interest" standard. Describing it as "vague and illusory," he maintained that it inevitably led the Court to ignore the basic issue. If it did not wish to continue "begging the question to be decided" —namely, when is a business subject to price control—the Court must stop using artificial tests and examine the circumstances which called forth the regulation. When free competition between buyer and seller has collapsed, it is obvious that the only way to prevent abuse is to control their relationship. Since the facts showed that the theatre ticket speculators had usually acquired the most desirable seats in the theatre, it was clear that "the regulative force of competition" could not be depended on to protect the public. Conceding that there might be differences of opinion as to the economic wisdom of the policy adopted by New York, Justice Stone insisted that for the Court to side with one of the conflicting views would take it from the "judicial to the legislative field." The Court's function is over, he stated, "when it is determined that there is basis for legislative action in a field not withheld from legislative power by the Constitution." [56]

Holmes' much shorter opinion is in the nature of a gentle lecture on the demands of political power in the modern state. "To the technical constitutional lawyer," a contemporary commentator observed, "the dissenting opinion of Mr. Justice Holmes in the *Tyson* Case will perhaps appear to have been without usefulness; it might be regarded as an attempt to destroy that which has been laboriously built up by the court." [57] The allusion is, of course, to Holmes' strictures on the "affected with a public interest" formula. More fundamental and more reflective of the Justice's whole political philosophy, however, was his objection to the apologetic attitude toward the exercise of power.

Holmes opened his opinion with a general complaint that would seem to have been meant as a criticism of the American political

[56] *Ibid.,* at 454.
[57] Maurice Finkelstein, "From Munn v. Illinois to Tyson v. Banton: A Study in the Judicial Process," *27 Col. L. Rev.* 769 (1927); reprinted in *2 Selected Essays 516, 530.*

character: "We fear to grant power and are unwilling to recognize it when it exists." [58] Impatient with the habit of discussing governmental activities designed to promote the public welfare by resort to such "apologetic phrases" as "police power" and "public use," he argued for a more sophisticated approach. What is the "police power" but a convenient expression with which "to conciliate the mind to . . . the fact that the constitutional requirement of compensation when property is taken cannot be pressed to its grammatical extreme; that property rights may be taken for public purposes without pay if you do not take too much; some play must be allowed to the joints if the machine is to work." [59] He did not believe in making apologies for "the general power of the legislature to make a part of the community uncomfortable by a change" and thought that the principle could be reduced to one simple proposition: "Subject to compensation when compensation is due, the legislature may forbid or restrict any business when it has a sufficient force of public opinion behind it." Holmes illustrated the effect of changing public opinion upon legislative policy by some rather striking examples:

Lotteries were thought useful adjuncts of the State a century ago; now they are believed to be immoral and they have been stopped. Wine has been thought good for man from the time of the Apostles until recent years. But when public opinion changed it did not need the Eighteenth Amendment, notwithstanding the Fourteenth, to enable a State to say that the business should end. . . . What has happened to lotteries and wine might happen to theatres in some moral storm of the future, not because theatres were devoted to a public use, but because people had come to think that way.

But if we are to yield to fashionable conventions, it seems to me that theatres are as much devoted to public use as anything well can be. We have not that respect for art that is one of the glories of France. But to many people the superfluous is the necessary, and it seems to me that Government does not go beyond its sphere in attempting to make life livable for them.[60]

[58] 273 U.S. 418, at 445.
[59] *Ibid.*, at 445–46.
[60] *Ibid.*, at 446–47.

As for the concept of a business affected with a public interest, Holmes found the whole idea "little more than a fiction intended to beautify what is disagreeable to the sufferers." Again he pleaded for restraint on the part of judges when dealing with the demands of legislation. "I think the proper course is to recognize," he commented, "that a State legislature can do whatever it sees fit to do unless it is restrained by some express prohibition in the Constitution of the United States or of the State, and that Courts should be careful not to extend such prohibitions beyond their obvious meaning by reading into them conceptions of public policy that the particular Court may happen to entertain." [61] And then, as if to demonstrate his own disinterestedness, he emphasized that his vote to sustain the New York law did not signify that he approved of its wisdom. Holmes concluded his opinion with these words:

I am far from saying that I think this particular law a wise and rational provision. That is not my affair. But if the people of the State of New York speaking by their authorized voice say they want it, I see nothing in the Constitution of the United States to prevent their having their will.[62]

In one of those curious inversions of the original intent of constitutional doctrines, Chief Justice Waite's famous distinction in Munn v. Illinois between business "clothed with a public interest" and property not so "affected" was later turned against the very purpose which the principle was meant to serve.[63] Venturing to specu-

[61] *Ibid.*, at 446.
[62] *Ibid.*, at 447.
[63] The extent of this process of historical distortion has been briefly sketched by Felix Frankfurter as follows: "In the light of his whole opinion [in Munn v. Illinois] and of the undogmatic temper of his mind, Waite's reference to property 'clothed with a public interest,' and 'devoted to a public use,' surely meant no more than that the Court must be able to attribute to the legislature the fulfillment of a public interest, and thereby relieve it of the imputation of sheer arbitrariness. To give this simple idea the cast of legal thought, he employs one of those sanctifying phrases with which the law reports are full. His philosophy for regulation became at the hands of others an imprisoning definition of the allowable scope of legislation. Waite's quotation of Taney's sweeping conception of the 'police power,' his explicit rejection of the idea that prices were removed from the fields of regulation, and especially his emphasis that only 'if

late about the ultimate effect of Justice Holmes' resistance to the use of such mechanical formulas in the discussion of constitutional questions, Maurice Finkelstein expressed the opinion that his dissent in the *Tyson* case—an outstanding example of this opposition—was "destined to cause a realignment of decisions on the basis of sound . . . constitutional interpretation." [64] The Justice's viewpoint in the case was said to be just one more application of his "oft reiterated test—the importance of the ends and reasonableness of the means adopted to reach the ends." [65] And yet, on a closer look, it would seem that the suggested "test" is a better description of Justice Brandeis' approach to the problems of governmental regulation than it is of Holmes'. It was Brandeis whose opinions conveyed the definite impression that he personally attached the same "importance" to the "ends" as did the legislators who were seeking to implement them. Though he voted to uphold the right to pursue those ends, Holmes did not hide his doubts about their wisdom or efficacy. For him it was enough that there was reasonable basis for the belief on which the experimenters had acted.

V

In retrospect, it can be seen that it is this difference between the two men which furnishes the key to the special significance of each jurist's work for future generations. One can derive from Brandeis' opinions real understanding of the great social and economic problems which had given rise to the controversies. Holmes is more helpful to those who wish to acquire a clearer perception of the judicial function in the American scheme of government. So effec-

---

no state of circumstances could exist to justify such a statute' was it to be invalidated—all indicate how alien to his own outlook was any attempt to confine legislative power by a mechanical formula." Frankfurter, *The Commerce Clause Under Marshall, Taney and Waite* (Chapel Hill: Univ. of North Carolina Press, 1937), pp. 86–87.

[64] Finkelstein, *op. cit.*, in 2 *Selected Essays* 516, 530.

[65] *Ibid.*, p. 531.

tively did Holmes and Brandeis complement each other that many were bound to mistake their judicial consensus for a common social philosophy.

To Brandeis, the social scientist with a conscience, what mattered most was continued progress toward a better society. Whatever the issue—differentiation in the tax structure, the growth of chain stores and cooperatives, the basis for determining public utility rates—to all of these problems he brought the creative approach of one who cared deeply about the results of social arrangements. "The very conception of the instrumental character of the mechanism of justice," Walton H. Hamilton has rightly said, "makes the intellectual views of the man dominant in the opinions of Mr. Justice Brandeis." [66] This is the judgment of a friendly observer interested in finding a psychological clue to the character of Brandeis' inclinations as a judge.

It also has been suggested, however, that the Justice employed his judicial opinions as a vehicle for broadcasting economic and social ideas which he wished to see advanced. Those who take this view have even intimated that Brandeis was much more like a McReynolds or a Sutherland than a Holmes. His main concern was with the strategy for effectuating his pet theories, a fact said to explain why so many of his opinions are really ingenious briefs. The "open-mindedness" of the man was in his "manner" but did not disturb the "substance" of his beliefs. [67]

Admittedly, one can point to numerous opinions in which Brandeis seemingly used the occasion to voice beliefs reflective of his purely personal philosophy. But does this fact in itself necessarily establish that in common with his conservative brethren, he was lost to all sense of judicial objectivity?

Brandeis' dissenting opinion in the *Quaker City Cab* case [68] cer-

[66] Hamilton, "The Jurist's Art," in Frankfurter (ed.), *Mr. Justice Brandeis,* p. 183.
[67] Interview with David Riesman, at Brattleboro, Vt., Sept. 12, 1951. Professor Riesman served as law secretary to Justice Brandeis for a year, 1935–36.
[68] Quaker City Cab Company v. Pennsylvania, 277 U.S. 389, 403, 412 (1928).

tainly may be cited as an example of a judicial utterance mirroring the private notions of the man who wrote it. An 1889 Pennsylvania statute imposed on transportation companies organized as corporations a tax on their gross receipts from passenger and freight traffic within the State. Because its competitors engaged in business as individuals and partnerships were not subject to the tax, the Quaker City Cab Company objected to paying the tax, contending that the exemption resulted in a denial of the equal protection of the laws guaranteed by the Fourteenth Amendment. Justice Butler spoke for the Supreme Court when in a six-to-three decision it held the Pennsylvania law to be unconstitutional. The majority found the discrimination between corporations and concerns operating under other forms of organization to be an arbitrary classification since it was predicated entirely on the character of the owner of the business. Its principal objection to the statute was that it failed "to meet the requirement that a classification to be consistent with the equal protection clause must be based on a real and substantial difference having reasonable relation to the subject of the legislation." [69]

Justices Holmes, Brandeis and Stone all wrote dissents in this case, Holmes confining himself to one paragraph. "If usually there is an important difference of degree between business done by corporations and that done by individuals," Holmes observed, "I see no reason why the larger business may not be taxed and the small ones disregarded." Characteristically, he merely noted that distinctions in the law "may be determined by differences of degree" and that the Fourteenth Amendment did not prevent a State from enforcing its desire to discourage the conduct of the transportation business in corporate form.[70]

After showing that the Pennsylvania law met the test that there must be a rational basis for a legislative classification,[71] Brandeis

[69] *Ibid.*, at 402.
[70] *Ibid.*, at 403.
[71] ". . . the equality clause requires merely that the classification shall be reasonable. We call that action reasonable which an informed, intelligent, just-minded, civilized man could rationally favor. In passing upon legislation assailed

concerned himself mainly with the considerations which might have
induced the State to adopt the particular tax policy. While his account may be seen as just another example of his penchant for setting straight the historical record, it is impossible to escape the
feeling that it is also the presentation of one with a vigorous personal predilection for small business. Justice Brandeis wrote:

> In Pennsylvania the practice of imposing heavier burdens upon corpo-
> rations dates from a time when there, as elsewhere in America, the fear
> of growing corporate power was common. The present heavier imposi-
> tion may be a survival of an early effort to discourage the resort to that
> form of organization. The apprehension is now less common. But there
> are still intelligent, informed, just-minded and civilized persons who be-
> lieve that the rapidly growing aggregation of capital through corporations
> constitutes an insidious menace to the liberty of the citizen; that, it tends
> to increase the subjection of labor to capital; that, because of the guidance
> and control necessarily exercised by great corporations upon those engaged
> in business, individual initiative is being impaired and creative power will
> be lessened; that the absorption of capital by corporations, and their per-
> petual life, may bring evils similar to those which attended mortmain;
> that the evils incident to the accelerating absorption of business by cor-
> porations outweigh the benefits thereby secured; and that the process of
> absorption should be retarded. The Court may think such views unsound.
> But, obviously, the requirement that a classification must be reasonable
> does not imply that the policy embodied in the classification made by the
> legislature of a State shall seem to this Court a wise one.[72]

Brandeis' economic philosophy also comes through with unmistakable clarity in his dissenting opinion in the case in which an important section of Florida's 1931 Chain Stores Law was held to

---

under the equality clause we have declared that the classification must rest
upon a difference which is real, as distinguished from one which is seeming,
specious, or fanciful, so that all actually situated similarly will be treated alike,
that the object of the classification must be the accomplishment of a purpose or
the promotion of a policy which is within the permissible functions of the
State, and that the difference must bear a relation to the object of the legislation which is substantial, as distinguished from one which is speculative, remote, or negligible. Subject to this limitation of reasonableness, the equality
clause has left unimpaired, both in range and in flexibility, the State's power to
classify for purposes of taxation." 277 U.S. 389, 403, at 406.
[72] *Ibid.*, at 410–11.

violate the equal protection clause of the Fourteenth Amendment.[73] The provision in question laid a heavier privilege tax per store on the owner whose stores were located in different counties than on the owner whose stores were in the same county. "We are unable to discover any reasonable basis for this classification," Justice Roberts announced for the majority in justifying the Court's action holding this particular method of graduating the tax to be arbitrary and void. The Justice drew a sharp distinction between those parts of the law which made the tax rise in accordance with the number of stores owned by a chain and the use of the county line as a yard-stick:

. . . gradation of the tax according to the number of units operated cannot be said to be so unreasonable as to transcend the constitutional power of the legislature. The addition of a store to an existing chain is a privilege, and an increase of the tax on all the stores for the privilege of expanding the chain cannot be condemned as arbitrary; but an increase in the levy not only on a new store but on all the old stores, consequent upon the mere physical fact that the new one lies a few feet over a county line, finds no foundation in reason or in any fact of business experience. There is no more reason for adopting the county line as the measure of the tax than there would be for taking ward lines in cities, or arbitrary lines drawn through the state regardless of county boundaries. It is suggested that the license fee for extending operations into a great and populous city, or for doing business upon crowded business streets, should be greater than for the same privilege in a village or a sparsely settled suburb. But the adoption of a county line can have no reference either to density of population, congregation of the buying public, or any other factor bearing upon the choice of a business site.[74]

To Brandeis the key issue was a much more fundamental one, from a social as well as a constitutional standpoint. His forty-page dissent, something of a tour de force in scholarship and persuasion, sought to show that concern over the impact of the growth of corporate chain stores might serve as a perfectly lawful basis for protecting the community against excessive size. There was no differ-

[73] Liggett v. Lee, 288 U.S. 517, 541 (1933).
[74] *Ibid.*, at 533–34.

ence, he insisted, between curbing the "excrescence" of bigness in business organization and endeavoring to limit size or weight in other business situations. The essence of his constitutional argument may be gleaned from these few sentences:

> Since business must yield to the paramount interests of the community in times of peace as well as in times of war, a State may prohibit a business found to be noxious and, likewise, may prohibit incidents or excrescences of a business otherwise beneficent. . . . Businesses may become as harmful to the community by excessive size, as by monopoly or the commonly recognized restraints of trade. If the State should conclude that bigness in retail merchandising as manifested in corporate chain stores menaces the public welfare, it might prohibit the excessive size or extent of that business as it prohibits excessive size or weight in motor trucks or excessive height in the buildings of a city.[75]

But it is Brandeis' treatment of the broad social issue implicit in Florida's chain store tax which makes his dissenting opinion the impressive excursion into legal economics that it is. Whether one views it as embodying the obsessive apprehensions of the "curse of bigness" or the dispassionate analysis by a deep student of American capitalism, it would be hard to find in judicial literature an utterance to compare with its powerful exposition of the ramifying effects of the corporate system. It is a superb display of the skill which Chief Justice Hughes once said was uniquely Brandeis'—the "skill of the surgeon exploring the operations of the social organism with the purpose of cure." [76] Yet Justice Brandeis never allowed himself to speak directly as the advocate of any particular program. Thus the disquieting picture of economic concentration he painted in Liggett v. Lee was presented by him in the guise of the expert opinion of others. He wrote:

> Able, discerning scholars have pictured for us the economic and social results of thus removing all limitations upon size and activities of business corporations and of vesting in their managers vast powers once exercised by stockholders—results not designed by the States and long

[75] *Ibid.*, at 574.
[76] Frankfurter (ed.), *Mr. Justice Brandeis*, p. 3.

unsuspected. They show that size alone gives to giant corporations a social significance not attached ordinarily to smaller units of private enterprise. Through size, corporations, once merely an efficient tool employed by individuals in the conduct of private business, have become an institution —an institution which has brought such concentration of economic power that so-called private corporations are sometimes able to dominate the State. The typical business corporation of the last century, owned by a small group of individuals, managed by their owners, and limited in size by their personal wealth, is being supplanted by huge concerns in which the lives of tens or hundreds of thousands of employees and the property of tens or hundreds of thousands of investors are subjected, through the corporate mechanism, to the control of a few men. Ownership has been separated from control; and this separation has removed many of the checks which formerly operated to curb the misuse of wealth and power. And as ownership of the shares is becoming continually more dispersed, the power which formerly accompanied ownership is becoming increasingly concentrated in the hands of a few. The changes thereby wrought in the lives of the workers, of the owners and of the general public, are so fundamental and far-reaching as to lead these scholars to compare the evolving "corporate system" with the feudal system; and to lead other men of insight and experience to assert that this "master institution of civilized life" is committing it to the rule of a plutocracy.[77]

Brandeis returned to this theme in the final paragraph of his opinion, this time relating his thesis to the great depression the country was experiencing.

There is a widespread belief that the existing unemployment is the result, in large part, of the gross inequality in the distribution of wealth and income which giant corporations have fostered; that by the control which the few have exerted through giant corporations, individual initiative and effort are being paralyzed, creative power impaired and human happiness lessened; that the true prosperity of our past came not from big business, but through the courage, the energy and the resourcefulness of small men; that only by releasing from corporate control the faculties of the unknown many, only by reopening to them the opportunities for leadership, can confidence in our future be restored and the existing misery be overcome; and that only through participation by the many in the responsibilities and determinations of business, can Americans secure

[77] 288 U.S. 517, 541, at 564–65.

the moral and intellectual development which is essential to the maintenance of liberty.[78]

Holmes was no longer on the Court when Liggett v. Lee was decided. He had resigned on January 12, 1932, informing President Hoover that the time had come for him to "bow to the inevitable." [79] There is good reason to believe, however, that he would have concurred in the views expressed by Brandeis. Of course, those who are familiar with the fact that Holmes once described the Sherman Act as "a humbug based on economic ignorance and incompetence" [80] may be surprised by his record of agreement with Brandeis in the cases in which the latter seemed to favor what might be called the atomization of American society. Not only did Holmes completely

[78] *Ibid.*, at 580.

[79] 284 U.S. VII. The circumstances under which Holmes resigned have been disclosed by Hughes' biographer:

"When the court began its new term the following October [1931], Holmes was slipping fast. 'While he was still able to write clearly, it became evident in the conference of the Justices that he could no longer do his full share in the mastery of the work of the Court.' His drowiness during arguments was so uncontrollable that his head would droop almost to the papers on his desk; then he would start up suddenly, writing with concentrated effort to keep awake. The Chief shielded him whenever possible, giving him only the easier cases. But Holmes' brethren began to fear that he would bring criticism upon the court. In January, 1932, a majority of them asked the Chief Justice to request Holmes' resignation.

". . . He [Hughes] consulted Justice Brandeis, Holmes' closest associate on the court, and Brandeis agreed that the time had come for the Magnificent Yankee to step down. On Sunday, January 11, the Chief summoned all his tact and went to see the grand old man at his home. Gradually coming to the point of his visit, he told Holmes that he was under too heavy a burden; a man who had been forty-nine years on the benches of his state and nation should not strain himself by continuing to carry the load when his strength was no longer equal to it.

"Holmes was the soul of equanimity. Without the slightest indication of resentment, he requested Hughes to get out from the bookshelves the applicable statute and wrote his resignation with his usual felicity of expression." Merlo J. Pusey, *Charles Evans Hughes* (New York: The Macmillan Company, 1951), II, 680–81.

[80] *Holmes-Pollock Letters*, I, 163 (April 23, 1910). Fifteen years later, Holmes wrote to Laski: "We have been having some cases under the Sherman Act, which I loathe and despise. . . . I don't mean to let my disbelief in the act affect my application of it—but I think it has been enlarged by construction in ways that I regret." *Holmes-Laski Letters*, I, 719.

accept Brandeis' position in the *Quaker Cab* case, but at the
same term of Court he filed a dissent in which he expounded a
point of view that might just as well have carried Brandeis' signa-
ture.[81]

In an effort to check the growth of chain drug stores, Pennsylvania
required that no new drug store was to be established or acquired
unless every stockholder or partner was a licensed pharmacist. The
Louis K. Liggett Company was denied permission to open two additional shops in Pennsylvania, an action which the Supreme Court of
the United States, in an opinion by Justice Sutherland, held to have
resulted in an arbitrary invasion of Liggett's property rights. Merely
because drug stores compound prescriptions was no justification for
subjecting a foreign corporation to state laws which conflict with
constitutional guarantees of property. Since it was "a matter of public notoriety" that the stock of chain drug stores was owned largely
by laymen, it was arbitrary for a State under the pretense of protecting public health to do what Pennsylvania did. Holmes, with
whom Brandeis concurred, stated that the police power, which he
regarded as but "one of the incidents of legislative power," clearly
authorized Pennsylvania to adopt the assailed law, "whatever I may
think of its wisdom." This open-mindedness led the Justice to speak
of the legislation in a vein which might have come from one who
personally favored a regime of small business units:

A standing criticism of the use of corporations in business is that it
causes such business to be owned by people who do not know anything
about it. Argument has not been supposed to be necessary in order to
show that the divorce between the power of control and knowledge is an
evil. The selling of drugs and poisons calls for knowledge in a high degree,
and Pennsylvania after enacting a series of other safeguards has provided
that in that matter the divorce shall not be allowed. Of course, notwithstanding the requirement that in corporations hereafter formed all the
stockholders shall be licensed pharmacists, it still would be possible for a
stockholder to content himself with drawing dividends and to take no
hand in the company's affairs. But obviously he would be more likely to

[81] Liggett v. Baldridge, 278 U.S. 105, 114 (1928).

observe the business with an intelligent eye than a casual investor who looked only to the standing of the stock in the market.[82]

VI

Basically, Brandeis' revolt against America's obsession with size reflected a strange contradiction in his thinking. How can one explain that so brilliant an analyst of the forces of his time should have clung so persistently to a point of view which is regarded by many persons as an incongruous and hopeless aim to reverse economic trends? One thing is clear; there was more to his bias than mere antipathy to bigness in business organization. His preference for smallness was an integral part of his social as well as political outlook. Like Jefferson, Brandeis would have liked to see America approximate his image of a decentralized society. Believing strongly that the survival of democracy depended ultimately on a maximum of direct participation by individuals in the decisions that shaped their lives, he was led to stress the virtues of smallness to the point where it looked at times as if, in the words of Judge Jerome N. Frank, he favored the "bermudaization of America." [83] Adolf A. Berle, Jr. summarized the matter well when he said on the occasion of Brandeis' eightieth birthday: "There is his passionate belief in the doctrine that men are entitled to fulfill themselves; hence democracy; hence the desire for preservation of local experimentation; hence the fear of the overmastering big combination; hence also the fear of an overmastering federal government." [84]

Professor Berle—an admirer of the Justice and himself a profound student of American capitalism—went on to speak of the "strange fate in the destiny which sealed Taft, Holmes and Brandeis to life companionship on the Supreme Court bench" and concluded that of the three "Brandeis must loom the largest" because he is "the

[82] *Ibid.*, at 114.
[83] Frank, *Save America First* (New York: Harper and Brothers, 1938), p. 290.
[84] Berle, "The Way of an American," 25 *Survey Graphic* 597 (Nov., 1936).

Modern." [85] Brandeis' modernity consisted, of course, of his remarkable grasp of the actualities of the industrial system and of the ramifying effects of economic power. But even his admirers have wondered whether time will vindicate Brandeis' ideas or whether they have been outstripped by events. Charles A. Beard posed the problem best by placing it in the context of the movement in which Brandeis made his major intellectual contribution: "Is the America of to-morrow to be the society of 'the new freedom', so effectively portrayed by Mr. Brandeis and the President who appointed him? Or will the march of integration in finance and industry override the small enterprises which they sought to preserve against extinction?" [86]

Some liberal-minded students of the American economy—David E. Lilienthal, for one—believe that to dwell on the "curse of bigness" in the contemporary scene is to be guilty of a purely "emotional antagonism." [87] This phrase was used by Mr. Lilienthal to describe a dissent by William O. Douglas, in which the Justice may be said to have spoken as a disciple of the man he succeeded on the Bench. Mr. Lilienthal was taking exception in particular to the following comment by Justice Douglas:

We have the problem of bigness. Its lesson should by now have been burned into our memory by Brandeis. *The Curse of Bigness* shows how size can become a menace—both industrial and social. . ... . In final analysis, size in steel is the measure of the power of a handful of men over our economy. That power can be utilized with lightning speed. It can be benign or it can be dangerous. The philosophy of the Sherman Act is that it should not exist. . . . Industrial power should be decentralized. It should be scattered into many hands so that the fortunes of the people will not be dependent on the whim or caprice, the political prejudices, the emotional stability of a few self-appointed men. The fact that they are not vicious men but respectable and social-minded is irrelevant. That is

[85] *Ibid.*

[86] Beard, "Introduction" to Lief (ed.), *The Social and Economic Views of Mr. Justice Brandeis*, p. xx.

[87] Lilienthal, *Big Business: A New Era* (New York: Harper and Brothers, 1952), p. 4.

the philosophy and the command of the Sherman Act. It is founded on a theory of hostility to the concentration in private hands of power so great that only a government of the people should have it.[88]

Recalling Brandeis' achievement in exposing the "curse of bigness," Mr. Lilienthal inveighed against what he calls "the curse of smallness," arguing that "to assume that small independent business is always a virtue and 'concentration' a synonym for evil can be quite wrong."[89] Holmes, and not Brandeis, Mr. Lilienthal implies, revealed the greater insight as to the future of America's economic welfare:

> The real question for us is whether on the whole Bigness is in the public interest; in other words, are we, the American people, better off for Bigness? If we are—as I believe—and the only possible construction of the Sherman Act makes this illegal, then the comment of a great liberal judge, Mr. Justice Holmes, seems justified that "the Sherman Act is a humbug based on economic ignorance and incompetence."[90]

VII

Yet any suggestion that Brandeis carried his personal predilections to unreasonable lengths would distort the essentially statesmanlike character of his economic philosophy, but especially his conception of the judicial function. The fact is that some of his most powerful dissents were written to protest the action of his colleagues in interposing their veto of efforts to curb competition. That as a judge

[88] Dissenting in United States v. Columbia Steel Co., 334 U.S. 495, 534, at 535–36 (1948). For an excellent discussion of the monopoly problem, analyzing recent judicial as well as economic trends, see Joel B. Dirlam and Alfred E. Kahn, *Fair Competition: The Law and Economics of Antitrust Policy* (Ithaca: Cornell Univ. Press, 1954).

[89] Lilienthal, *op. cit.*, p. 144.

[90] *Ibid.*, p. 168. Mention of Mr. Lilienthal—who was one of the original directors of the Tennessee Valley Authority and its chairman for five years—brings to mind the fact that Brandeis regarded TVA as a great achievement in human inventiveness and regional decentralization. The Justice was particularly interested in the "grass-roots" phase of the enterprise. (Interview with Willard Hurst, New York, Sept. 14, 1951. Professor Hurst was with Justice Brandeis during the 1936–37 term of the Court.)

Brandeis was not going to be an unbending doctrinaire in his approach to the problems of competition was made clear early in his career on the Court.

In the so-called "Hardwood" case, decided in 1921,[91] he dissented vigorously against the Court's ban of the "open competition plan" which a group of hardwood manufacturers had established for the purpose of enabling the members to exchange information concerning production, prices and sales. Dividing six-to-three, the Supreme Court, in an opinion delivered by Justice Clarke, construed this arrangement for pooling trade information to be a combination in restraint of trade in violation of the Sherman Act. Clarke described it as "abnormal conduct on the part of 365 natural competitors" and as simply an expansion of the gentleman's agreement of former days, skillfully devised to evade the law."[92]

Justices Holmes and McKenna joined in Justice Brandeis' dissent. Though agreeing with "the more elaborate discussion of the case by my brother Brandeis," Holmes wrote a separate dissent. His main idea would seem to be contained in his observation that "the Sherman Act did not set itself against knowledge." In obvious sarcasm, he added that he found the Court's decree "surprising in a country of free speech that affects to regard education and knowledge as desirable."[93]

From Brandeis the same case called forth an essay clearly revealing that he was neither the economic dogmatist nor the foe of the profit motive that his detractors so often implied he was. Though he was primarily interested in showing that the Open Competition Plan was not "inherently" a restraint of trade and that there was no evidence that it had that result, his opinion also discloses his broader philosophy of the Sherman Act: "The Sherman Law does not prohibit every lessening of competition; and it certainly does not command that competition shall be pursued blindly, that business rivals

[91] American Column and Lumber Co. v. United States, 257 U.S. 377, 412, 413 (1921).
[92] Ibid., at 410–11.
[93] Ibid., at 413.

shall remain ignorant of trade facts, or be denied aid in weighing their significance. It is lawful to regulate competition in some degree." [94]

Two considerations persuaded Brandeis that the cooperative scheme of the lumbermen was a good thing, and both were in accord with his basic economic outlook. He believed that the Plan, by making possible the interchange of industrial information, made for more rational competition, and rational competition was essential to the maintenance of a truly free economy. "Intelligent conduct of business implies, not only knowledge of trade facts, but an understanding of them." There was always the danger, moreover, that if the hardwood manufacturers were forbidden to cooperate in their trade association they would be tempted to combine. The Justice's statement of these matters will bear quoting:

> The cooperation which is incident to this Plan does not suppress competition. On the contrary it tends to promote all in competition which is desirable. By substituting knowledge for ignorance, rumor, guess and suspicion, it tends also to substitute research and reasoning for gambling and piracy, without closing the door to adventure or lessening the value of prophetic wisdom. In making such knowledge available to the smallest concern it creates among producers equality of opportunity. In making it available also to purchasers and the general public, it does all that can actually be done to protect the community from extortion. . . .
>
> The refusal to permit a multitude of small rivals to cooperate, as they have done here, in order to protect themselves and the public from the chaos and havoc wrought in their trade by ignorance, may result in suppressing competition in the hardwood industry. . . . May not these hardwood lumber concerns, frustrated in their efforts to rationalize competition, be led to enter the inviting field of consolidation? And if they do, may not another huge trust with highly centralized control over vast resources, natural, manufacturing and financial, become so powerful as to dominate competitors, wholesalers, retailers, consumers, employees and, in large measure, the community? [95]

[94] *Ibid.,* at 415.

[95] *Ibid.,* at 418–19. Though unwilling to explicitly overrule its decisions in the *Hardwood* and related cases, the Supreme Court came to adopt, within a short time, Brandeis' view of open price reporting. See Justice Stone's opinions in

The glaring difference between Holmes and Brandeis in the *Hardwood* case has intrigued the interpreters. Walton H. Hamilton thought he was epitomizing it when he stated: "As against Brandeis' detailed presentation of the practical operation of the 'Open Competition Plan,' is to be set Holmes' presumption, 'I should have supposed that the Sherman Act did not set itself against knowledge.' " [96] Probing considerably deeper, Max Lerner has discerned a more far-reaching divergence suggestive of the wide gulf that separated the two Justices in matters of social and economic theory. Coming from an admirer of Holmes, Professor Lerner's estimate stands out as a candid recognition that compared with Brandeis, the master of "economic analysis and economic strategy," Holmes was rather superficial. Mr. Lerner writes:

Holmes's dissent is not one of his best, as that of Brandeis is. The two were based on rather different social values. Brandeis was concerned with the "curse of bigness." He feared that if small independent producers who had banded together into a trade association were not allowed to act together reasonably for common economic ends, they would "be led to enter the inviting field of consolidation," and the result would be a "huge trust" with all of its consequences in concentration of power. Holmes, since he did not share Brandeis' fear of the big trusts, could scarcely restrict himself to this reasoning, although by concurring in Brandeis' "more elaborate discussion" he showed he was not wholly at variance with it. Brandeis' reasoning was tactical: it was part of his strategy for equalizing the position of the small producers as against the big ones, and organizing industrial order. Holmes' reasoning again, as in the Dr. Miles case, assumed a naturally functioning economic norm to which some adjustments had to be made. He saw the action of the Hardwood Association not as "an attempt to override normal market conditions" but as "an attempt to conform to them." [97]

Maple Flooring Manufacturers' Association v. United States, 268 U.S. 563 (1925) and Cement Manufacturers' Protective Assoc. v. United States, 268 U.S. 588 (1925). Holmes may have been thinking of these cases when he informed Laski, on March 5, 1925, that "Brandeis who used to uphold it [the Sherman Act] doesn't think it does any good." *Holmes-Laski Letters*, I, 719. The decisions in these 2 cases were handed down on June 1, 1925.

[96] Hamilton, "The Jurist's Art," in Frankfurter (ed.), *Mr. Justice Brandeis*, p. 219, n. 45.

[97] Lerner, *The Mind and Faith of Justice Holmes*, pp. 247–48.

The fact that Brandeis did not have a completely closed mind on economic matters is confirmed even more strikingly in his dissent in New State Ice Co. v. Liebmann, decided in 1932.[98] An Oklahoma law forbade anyone from entering the business of making and selling ice without first obtaining from the State Corporation Commission a certificate of convenience and necessity. The New State Ice Company sought to restrain Liebmann, a competitor, from entering the business. In his opinion holding the Oklahoma law to be unconstitutional, Justice Sutherland said of the statute that it "does not protect against monopoly, but tends to foster it. The aim is not to encourage competition, but to prevent it; not to regulate the business, but to preclude persons from engaging in it." [99] It was Brandeis, partisan of small business and free competition, who in this case was the spokesman for the theory that in some circumstances limitation of competition and even outright monopoly may be the sound economic policy:

. . . while, ordinarily, free competition in the common callings has been encouraged, the public welfare may at other times demand that monopolies be created. Upon this principle is based our whole modern practice of public utility regulation. It is no objection to the validity of the statute here assailed that it fosters monopoly. That, indeed, is its design. The certificate of public convenience and necessity is a device—a recent social-economic invention—through which the monopoly is kept under effective control by vesting in a commission the power to terminate it whenever that course is required in the public interest.[100]

At first glance, this small debate about the monopoly problem may appear to be a digression on the part of both Justices. Actually, however, it sprang from their disagreement regarding the basic constitutional question as to the extent to which the States were free to use their police power to subject private business to public regulation. A majority of the Court had apparently concluded that there

[98] 285 U.S. 262, 280 (1932). Only Justice Stone joined in the dissent. Justice Cardozo, who had taken his oath as Holmes' successor just a week before, did not participate in the case.
[99] *Ibid.*, at 279.
[100] *Ibid.*, at 304.

was nothing so special about the ice business in Oklahoma as to
justify restriction of competition. As Sutherland remarked, "there is
nothing in the product that we can perceive on which to rest a distinction, in respect of this attempted control, from other products in
common use which enter into free competition." [101] The making of
ice was not a natural monopoly nor did it depend upon public privileges; it was no different from any other occupation the members
of which might wish to prevent others from competing with them.
Hence, there was no basis for experimenting with a measure which
made a monopoly out of the ice business. Sutherland ended his opinion by stressing that there were limits to "experimental legislation"
—"The principle is imbedded in óur constitutional system that there
are certain essentials of liberty with which the state is not entitled
to dispense in the interest of experiments." [102]

These comments on experimentation would seem to have been
intended as a rejoinder to the position taken by Justice Brandeis
that the effective exercise of the "power to regulate" requires freedom to experiment. He rejected any implication that the scope of
governmental regulation depends on the character of the business.
"The notion of a distinct category of business 'affected with a public
interest,' employing property 'devoted to public use,' rests upon
historical error," Brandeis declared.[103] He believed that "The true
principle is that the state's power extends to every regulation of any
business reasonably required and appropriate for the public protection." Only by inquiring into "conditions existing in the community"
could it be determined whether the regulation of a particular business or service was permissible. All that the Constitution required
was that the policy embodied in legislation shall not be "unreasonable" and that the means for effectuating it "shall have a real or
substantial relation to the object sought to be obtained." The Oklahoma law met this test of due process:

. . . where, as here, there is reasonable ground for the legislative conclusion that in order to secure a necessary service at reasonable rates, it may

[101] *Ibid.*, at 279.   [102] *Ibid.*, at 280.
[103] *Ibid.*, at 302.

be necessary to curtail the right to enter the calling, it is, in my opinion, consistent with the due process clause to do so, whatever the nature of the business. The existence of such power in the legislature seems indispensable in our ever-changing society.[104]

Justice Brandeis devoted the last five pages of his long dissent to a discussion of depression problems, a discussion obviously meant to show how vitally necessary was the right to engage in social experiments. Speaking of the catastrophic effects of the great depression—"an emergency more serious than war"—he pointed out that the disaster had led to a search for both causes and remedies. While many economists and businessmen attributed the collapse to "the failure to distribute widely the profits of industry," others blamed overproduction: "But rightly or wrongly, many persons think that one of the major contributing causes has been unbridled competition. Increasingly, doubt is expressed whether it is economically wise, or morally right, that men should be permitted to add to the producing facilities of an industry already suffering from overcapacity." [105] No one can be sure of the outcome of such a policy and it may result in "evils worse than the disease." But government must be free to experiment with various attacks on the grave economic problems facing the country. Progress in the social sciences, even as in the physical sciences, depends on a "process of trial and error"; courts must not interfere with necessary experiments. "I cannot believe," the Justice observed, "that the framers of the Fourteenth Amendment, or the States which ratified it, intended to deprive us of the power to correct the evils of technological unemployment and excess productive capacity which have attended progress in the useful arts." [106] Brandeis concluded his opinion in the *New State Ice Co.* case with as succinct and eloquent a statement of the philosophy of judicial tolerance of social policy as can be found in the literature on the subject:

To stay experimentation in things social and economic is a grave responsibility. Denial of the right to experiment may be fraught with serious

104 *Ibid.*, at 304.   105 *Ibid.*, at 307–08.
106 *Ibid.*, at 311.

consequences to the Nation. It is one of the happy incidents of the federal system that a single courageous State may, if its citizens choose, serve as a laboratory; and try novel social and economic experiments without risk to the rest of the country. This Court has the power to prevent an experiment. We may strike down the statute which embodies it on the ground that, in our opinion, the measure is arbitrary, capricious or unreasonable. We have power to do this, because the due process clause has been held by the Court applicable to matters of substantive law as well as to matters of procedure. But in the exercise of this high power, we must be ever on our guard, lest we erect our prejudices into legal principles. If we would guide by the light of reason, we must let our minds be bold.[107]

[107] *Ibid.*

9

"When a nation is at war"

"Every institution," wrote Emerson, "is the lengthened shadow of one man." The observation is nowhere borne out more strikingly than in judicial doctrines, which often exert an influence truly institutional in scope. . . . A comparable instance in recent times is afforded by Justice Holmes' personal responsibility for the "clear and present danger" formula, a formula which illustrates a facet of its distinguished author's education and habit of mind. . . .

As it finally matured into a doctrine of constitutional law, the "clear and present danger" formula became a measure of legislative power in the choice of values which may be protected against unrestricted speech and publication. . . . the Supreme Court of the United States was, by virtue of the protection which is today thrown about freedom of speech and press by the First and Fourteenth Amendments, the final judge.

Edward S. Corwin [1]

❉   ❉   ❉

The concept of freedom of speech [in Holmes' opinion in the *Schenck* case] received for the first time an authoritative judicial interpretation in accord with the purpose of the framers of the Constitution.

Zechariah Chafee, Jr.[2]

❉   ❉   ❉

[1] Corwin, "Bowing Out 'Clear and Present Danger,'" *XXVII Notre Dame Lawyer 325*, pp. 325, 326 (1952).
[2] Chafee, *Free Speech in the United States* (Cambridge: Harvard Univ. Press, 1941), p. 82.

. . . the court, following the lead of Justice Oliver Wendell Holmes, has persistently ruled that the freedom of speech of the American community may constitutionally be abridged by legislative action. That ruling annuls the most significant purpose of the First Amendment. It destroys the intellectual basis of our plan of self-government.

Alexander Meiklejohn [3]

＊　　＊　　＊

Mr. Justice Holmes' conversion to profound attachment to freedom of expression . . . may be taken to have occurred in 1919, and to have coincided roughly with the advent of Mr. Justice Brandeis' influence.

John Raeburn Green [4]

＊　　＊　　＊

Now that some of the illusions about Holmes are giving way to closer scrutiny of his deeper impulses, the various myths about his liberalism are gradually coming to be recognized for what they are. The liberal image of Holmes has been conveyed through many distortions, but probably the worst of them has been the rather careless effort to depict him as a civil libertarian. His reputation as a champion of human rights would seem to stem from epigrams and cannot be sustained by his record as a judge and citizen.

What the late Oswald Garrison Villard wrote at the time of the Justice's death shows how far from the truth some of his admirers have allowed themselves to wander: "There were no 'buts' in his defense of the fundamentals; none of that hateful, self-contradictory stupidity which says: 'I believe in free speech, but there are limits beyond which it must not go.' " [5] This observation illustrates the hazards of a facile pen, and quite obviously was not the fruit of considered thought. To quote it out of context, however, would be grossly unfair. In a previous paragraph Villard presented a much more sober and balanced view:

[3] Meiklejohn, *Free Speech and Its Relation to Self-Government* (New York: Harper and Brothers, 1948), p. 29.

[4] Green, "The Supreme Court, the Bill of Rights and the States," 97 *Univ. of Penn. L. Rev. 608*, 630 (1949).

[5] Villard, "The Great Judge," *140 The Nation 323* (March 20, 1935).

It is odd, indeed, that this man's [Dr. Oliver Wendell Holmes'] son became known as a great liberal, for that, in most respects, he precisely was not. Like his father, he had no use for reformers and liberals per se. His affection for his classmate, Wendell Phillips Garrison, all his life an editor, or the editor, of The Nation, was never dimmed; but for the crusading spirit and the Godkin-Garrison method of attacking evils, the Justice had no sympathy at all. He could not have endured the militant spirits of radical causes had he come into contact with them; they would have offended him to the core. So he must have pondered with cynical humor upon the fact that he became the idol of the progressives who believed that America must evolve and change. Toward them his attitude was probably like that of a New York editor who once told a group of civic reformers that if he was to continue to support them they must keep away from him.[6]

Holmes' liking for the "non-conformist conscience"[7] was at most a matter of intellectual taste but did not embrace sympathy for the "agitator" and habitual dissident. His assertion "I approve scepticism —though I regret irreverence" is as good a clue to this ambivalence as one can find among his self-revelatory utterances.[8] Morris Raphael Cohen acknowledged an unpleasant fact about Holmes when he wrote, "Indeed, for a thoroughly civilized man, which Holmes was in the best sense of the word, he shows a remarkable absence of sympathy or compassion for the sufferings and faults of mankind."[9] Holmes made no attempt to conceal his disdain for those who did not sufficiently reckon with what he called "the fact of power" and who were moved by the "passion" for equality. "You respect the rights of man—I don't, except those things a given crowd will fight for—which vary from religion to the price of a glass of beer"—he wrote to Laski on June 1, 1927.[10] Nor did he confine his

---

[6] *Ibid.*

[7] The phrase was used by Holmes to describe Charles Evans Hughes at the time of the latter's resignation from the Supreme Court to accept the Republican nomination for President in 1916: "I shall miss him consumedly, for he is not only a good fellow, experienced and wise, but funny, and with doubts that open vistas through the wall of a non-conformist conscience." *Holmes-Pollock Letters*, I, 237.

[8] *Holmes-Laski Letters*, II, 1066.

[9] Cohen, *Faith of a Liberal*, p. 29.   [10] *Holmes-Laski Letters*, II, 948.

high regard for the established order to private correspondence. "What proximate test of excellence can be found," he asked at the turn of the century, "except correspondence to the actual equilibrium of force in the community—that is, conformity to the wishes of the dominant power? Of course, such conformity may lead to destruction, and it is desirable that the dominant power should be wise. But wise or not, the proximate test of a good government is that the dominant power has its way." [11]

It is comments such as the one just quoted which have led many an observer to conclude that Holmes was at heart a totalitarian.[12] The man who claims credit for starting the "battle over Holmes' philosophy and morals" has recently summarized the substance of his original attack by saying that in it he showed that the Justice's "philosophy was akin to Hitler's and that if adopted it would be the death knell of our democracy." [13] Yet it is not necessary to accept all the criticisms of Holmes by the disciples of natural law in order to recognize that he was not given to exalting individual rights above

[11] Holmes, *Collected Legal Papers*, p. 258. These observations are to be found in his introduction to a 1900 reprint of Montesquieu's *L'Esprit des Lois*. In speaking of Montesquieu's essay on fashion in the *Persian Letters*, Holmes says: "We read that the most perfect government is that which attains its ends with the least cost, so that the one which leads men in the way most according to their inclination is best. What have two hundred years added?" (Pp. 257–58.) There then follow the remarks about the "proximate test of excellence."

[12] John C. Ford, S.J., "The Totalitarian Justice Holmes," *159 Catholic World* 114 (May, 1944).

[13] Francis E. Lucey, "Holmes—Liberal—Humanitarian—Believer in Democracy?" *39 Georgetown L. J.* 523, 525 (1951). Father Lucey, who is Regent and Professor of Law at Georgetown University, was here referring to his article of ten years earlier, "Jurisprudence and the Future Social Order," *16 Social Science 211* (1941). The theme has been taken up by both lawyers and laymen. See Ben W. Palmer, "Hobbes, Holmes and Hitler," *31 Amer. Bar Assoc. J. 569* (1945); Harold R. McKinnon, "The Secret of Mr. Justice Holmes," *36 A.B.A.J. 261* (1950); Henry R. Luce, "Reverse Mr. Justice Holmes," *17 Vital Speeches of the Day 596* (July 15, 1951). These attacks naturally have called forth replies. One of the best is Professor Mark DeWolfe Howe's "The Positivism of Mr. Justice Holmes," *64 Harv. L. Rev. 529* (1951). By far the most cogent and balanced analysis of the contradictions in Holmes' treatment of law and ethics is to be found in Professor Henry M. Hart's comment on Professor Howe's article, "Holmes' Positivism—An Addendum," *64 Harv. L. Rev. 929* (1951). Professor Howe's brief rejoinder begins on p. 937.

the assertions of governmental authority. Quite contrary to the view expressed by Mr. Villard, it must be conceded that high in Holmes' hierarchy of social values is the notion that there are limits to freedom. Indeed, it is an integral part of his whole conception of political power.

I

This strain in Holmes' thought was clearly evident while he was still on the Massachusetts Court. His opinion in Commonwealth v. Davis [14] is a leading example. In it he sustained a city ordinance prohibiting anyone from making "any public address" on the Boston Common without first obtaining a permit from the Mayor. "For the Legislature absolutely or conditionally to forbid public speaking in a highway or public park," he held, "is no more an infringement of the rights of a member of the public than for the owner of a private house to forbid it in his house." [15] Failing to perceive any issue of free speech or assembly, he saw the ordinance as being merely "directed toward the modes in which the Boston Common may be used." [16] The decision was affirmed by the United States Supreme Court.[17]

It may be of interest to recall that when the Supreme Court put an end in 1939 to Mayor Hague's attempts to suppress the public activities of the newly formed Committee for Industrial Organization, it ignored the ruling in the *Davis* case.[18] The ordinance which

[14] 162 Mass. 510 (1895).

[15] *Ibid.*, at 511.

[16] Of the same general tenor is his opinion in the *McAuliffe* case containing the now famous dictum: "The petitioner may have a constitutional right to talk politics, but he has no constitutional right to be a policeman." McAuliffe v. New Bedford, 155 Mass. 216, at 220 (1892). A police officer was dismissed because of his political activities. The rest of Holmes' statement read as follows: "There are few employments for hire in which the servant does not agree to suspend his constitutional right of free speech, as well as of idleness, by the implied terms of his contract. The servant cannot complain, as he takes the employment on the terms which are offered him." *Ibid.*

[17] Davis v. Mass., 167 U.S. 43 (1897).

[18] Hague v. Committee for Industrial Organization, 307 U.S. 496 (1939).

served as the pretext for Hague's campaign of repression was not too unlike the one upheld by Holmes. The Jersey City ordinance prohibited meetings "In or upon the public streets, highways, public parks or buildings" without a permit from the Director of Public Safety. It was left for Justice Butler, in his one-sentence dissent, to insist that this ordinance "in principle . . . does not differ from the Boston ordinance, as applied and upheld by this Court, . . . in Davis v. Massachusetts, speaking through Mr. Justice Holmes, in Commonwealth v. Davis." [19]

During Holmes' early years on the United States Supreme Court no change in attitude was discernible. He continued to be unreceptive to the claims of interference with freedom of expression. There comes to mind, for instance, his opinion in Patterson v. Colorado.[20] "In this 1907 opinion," one acute commentator has recently written, "he [Holmes] committed the Court . . . to a proposition . . . which in substance nullified the freedom of the press guaranteed by the First Amendment." [21] Patterson had been convicted of contempt of court for publishing articles in which he questioned the motives and behavior of the Colorado Supreme Court in certain cases that were still pending. Insisting that what he printed was true, he contended that he had a constitutional right to prove the truthfulness of his attacks on the state court. When his case reached the Supreme Court of the United States, it was dismissed for want of jurisdiction. However, in his opinion announcing this result, Holmes interpreted the constitutional guarantee of freedom of the press to be restricted to freedom from previous restraint. The Justice wrote:

. . . the main purpose of such constitutional provisions is "to prevent all such previous restraints upon publications as had been practiced by other governments," and they do not prevent the subsequent punishment of such as may be deemed contrary to the public welfare. . . . The preliminary freedom extends as well to the false as to the true; the subsequent punishment may extend as well to the true as to the false.[22]

[19] *Ibid.*, at 533.   [20] 205 U.S. 454, (1907).
[21] Green, *op. cit.*, p. 629.
[22] 205 U.S. 454, at 462.

Holmes was echoing here Blackstone's view of the matter. According to Blackstone, "the liberty of the press . . . consists in laying no previous restraints upon publications and not in freedom from censure for criminal matter when published." [23] Though Holmes "never expressly recanted" [24] his position in the *Patterson* case, he deviated from it on many subsequent occasions. One such "recantation" is to be found in the decision in the *Schenck* case: "It well may be that the prohibition of laws abridging the freedom of speech is not confined to previous restraints, although to prevent them may have been the main purpose, as intimated in Patterson v. Colorado." [25]

The Supreme Court has quite completely abandoned the view that the guarantee of freedom of the press protects only against previous restraint. Thus Chief Justice Hughes wrote in his notable opinion in Near v. Minnesota: "The criticism upon Blackstone's statement has not been because immunity from previous restraint upon publication has not been regarded as deserving of special emphasis, but chiefly because that immunity cannot be deemed to exhaust the conception of the liberty guaranteed by State and federal constitutions." [26] Even more emphatic is Justice Black's comment in the *Bridges* case: "To assume that English common law in this field became ours is to deny the generally accepted historical belief that 'one object of the Revolution was to get rid of the English common law on liberty of speech and of the press.' More specifically, it is to forget the environment in which the First Amendment was ratified." [27]

[23] Quoted in Chafee, *op. cit.*, p. 9. Professor Chafee has explained Blackstone's statement in these words: "The line where legitimate suppression begins is fixed chronologically at the time of publication. The government cannot interfere by a censorship or injunction before the words are spoken or printed, but can punish them as much as it pleases *after* publication, no matter how harmless or essential to the public welfare the discussion may be." *Ibid.*

[24] For an interesting account of this "process of recantation," see John Raeburn Green, *op. cit.*, p. 630.

[25] Schenck v. United States, 249 U.S. 47, at 51–52 (1919).

[26] 283 U.S. 697, at 714 (1931).

[27] Bridges v. California, 314 U.S. 252, at 264 (1941).

Two years after the decision in Patterson v. Colorado, we find Holmes again vindicating governmental power against the assertion of individual rights. The occasion was a rather dramatic one, Moyer v. Peabody,[28] a case illustrating the extent to which Holmes believed that in the last analysis government means force. Moyer, who headed the Western Federation of Miners, was held in military custody for ten weeks following the outbreak of labor trouble. Holmes summarized the situation as follows: "the Governor had declared a county to be in a state of insurrection, had called out troops to put down the trouble, and had ordered that the plaintiff [Moyer] should be arrested as a leader of the outbreak, and should be detained until he could be discharged with safety, and that then he should be delivered to the civil authorities to be dealt with according to law." In his suit against the former Governor and officials of the National Guard, Moyer maintained that as there had been no particular complaint against him and as the civil courts were open during the whole time, he had been deprived of liberty without due process of law. It is obvious that these allegations interested Holmes very little; he saw the case entirely from the standpoint of the need for upholding executive authority in times of emergency. As he said, "When it comes to a decision by the head of the State upon a matter involving its life, the ordinary rights of individuals must yield to what he deems the necessities of the moment. Public danger warrants the substitution of executive process for judicial process."[29]

Under the constitution and laws of the State, the Governor was authorized to order the National Guard to "repel or suppress" any invasion or insurrection "made or threatened." It is Holmes' construction of this provision which indicates how far he was prepared to allow the Executive to go. It meant, the Justice said, that the Governor "may kill persons who resist and, of course, . . . he may use the milder measure of seizing the bodies of those whom he considers to stand in the way of restoring peace. Such arrests are not necessarily for punishment, but are by way of precaution to prevent

[28] 212 U.S. 78 (1909).
[29] Ibid., at 85.

the exercise of hostile power. So long as such arrests are made in good faith and in the honest belief that they are needed in order to head the insurrection off, the Governor is the final judge and cannot be subjected to an action after he is out of office." [30]

In Fox v. Washington, decided in 1915,[31] Holmes spoke for a unanimous Court when it sustained the constitutionality of a state law which made it unlawful to advocate the commission of crime. More specifically, the Washington statute made it unlawful to publish or circulate any matter "advocating, encouraging or inciting, or having a tendency to encourage or incite the commission of any crime." Fox had been convicted for publishing articles which denounced those who would suppress nudism and threatened that a boycott would be organized against those who interfered with the freedom of the nudist colony. Brushing aside the argument that punishment of those responsible for the article was a denial of freedom of the press, Justice Holmes accepted the State Court's interpretation of the statute as directed against "an actual breach of the law" and the jury's finding that the article "by indirection but unmistakably . . . encourages and incites a persistence in what we must assume would be a breach of the state laws against indecent exposure." [32]

Professor Corwin has called attention to the fact that in Holmes' opinion in Fox v. Washington—written just four years before the decision in the *Schenck* case—"nothing was said about the degree of danger that breach of the law would result from the publication." He states further that "The plain implication is that incitement to crime or encouragement thereof is sufficient, without reference to its actual consequences." [33]

II

The pertinence of Holmes' views in the *Fox* case is, of course, that the *Schenck* case [34] also grew out of a prosecution in which the

[30] *Ibid.*, at 84–85.
[32] *Ibid.*, at 277.
[34] 249 U.S. 47 (1919).

[31] 236 U.S. 273 (1915).
[33] Corwin, *op. cit.*, p. 327.

defendant found himself in trouble as the result of circulating a document which was said to urge illegal conduct. The indictment charged that in order to obstruct the recruitment and enlistment service of the United States, Schenck had "willfully conspired to have printed and circulated to men who had been called and accepted for military service . . . a document, . . . calculated to cause such insubordination and obstruction." [35] Schenck, who was General Secretary of the Socialist Party and in command of the party's headquarters at Chicago, was indicted for mailing to men already accepted for military service circulars counseling them to assert their constitutional rights—rights which the draft was said to violate.

In view of the seminal importance which Holmes' opinion in the *Schenck* case has attained, it may not be amiss to quote in full his version of the circulars which formed the basis for the indictment. The Justice described them as follows:

The document in question upon its first printed side recited the first section of the Thirteenth Amendment, said that the idea embodied in it was violated by the Conscription Act and that a conscript is little better than a convict. In impassioned language it intimated that conscription was despotism in its worst form and a monstrous wrong against humanity in the interest of Wall Street's chosen few. It said "Do not submit to intimidation," but in form at least confined itself to peaceful measures such as a petition for the repeal of the act. The other and later printed side of the sheet was headed "Assert Your Rights." It stated reasons for alleging that any one violated the Constitution when he refused to

[35] Section 3 of Title I of the Espionage Act of June 15, 1917 created three new offenses: "(1) Whoever, when the United States is at war, shall willfully make or convey false reports or false statements with intent to interfere with the operation or success of the military or naval forces of the United States or to promote the success of its enemies (2) and whoever, when the United States is at war, shall willfully cause or attempt to cause insubordination, disloyalty, mutiny, or refusal of duty, in the military or naval forces of the United States, (3) or shall willfully obstruct the recruiting or enlistment service of the United States, to the injury of the service or of the United States, shall be punished by a fine of not more than $10,000 or imprisonment for not more than twenty years, or both." Quoted in Chafee, *op. cit.,* p. 39.

recognize "your right to assert your opposition to the draft," and went on "If you do not assert and support your rights, you are helping to deny or disparage rights which it is the solemn duty of all citizens and residents of the United States to retain." It described the arguments on the other side as coming from cunning politicians and a mercenary capitalist press, and even silent consent to the conscription law as helping to support an infamous conspiracy. It denied the power to send our citizens away to foreign shores to shoot up the people of other lands, and added that words could not express the condemnation such cold-blooded ruthlessness deserves, &c., &c., winding up "You must do your share to maintain, support and uphold the rights of the people of this country." [36]

There then follows a statement which easily could have disposed of the case even if nothing had been said about "clear and present danger." Holmes added: "Of course the document would not have been sent unless it had been intended to have some effect, and we do not see what effect it could be expected to have upon persons subject to the draft except to influence them to obstruct the carrying of it out." [37] This observation by Holmes, argues Professor Corwin, shows that the Justice was not at all troubled by the "circumstance" that no evidence was presented as to the "possible or probable effect" of the circulars, "apart from their contents and the fact of their publication." [38] As further proof, he cites this additional comment from the opinion: "If the act, (speaking, or circulating a paper,) its tendency and the intent with which it is done are the same, we perceive no ground for saying that success alone warrants making the act a crime." [39]

Since it was claimed that the circulars were protected by the First Amendment's guarantee of freedom of expression, the crucial problem was the test to be applied in assessing the "effect" of their distribution in the circumstances disclosed by the case. Holmes' contribution in the *Schenck* case is generally said to have consisted precisely in formulating a new criterion—"Whether the words used

---

[36] 249 U.S. 47, at 50–51.   [37] *Ibid.*, at 51.
[38] Corwin, *op. cit.*, p. 329.
[39] 249 U.S. 47, at 52.

are used in such circumstances and are of such a nature as to create a clear and present danger that they will bring about the substantive evils that Congress has a right to prevent." Yet fundamentally, it was merely a way of stating the practical need for striking a balance between the effective prosecution of war and the constitutional protection of freedom of expression. Holmes' basic assumption is that freedom of expression is not an absolute right, any more than are other rights upon which governmental action inevitably impinges.[40]

A close look at the paragraph in which Holmes introduces the idea of "clear and present danger" shows that he was not primarily concerned with propounding a new test of constitutionality. The emphasis was definitely on the exigencies of government, the profoundly important practical considerations which, he seemed to be saying, made no other approach possible. Holmes wrote:

We admit that in many places and in ordinary times the defendants in saying all that was said in the circular would have been within their constitutional rights. But the character of every act depends upon the circumstances in which it is done. . . . The most stringent protection of free speech would not protect a man in falsely shouting fire in a theatre and causing a panic. It does not even protect a man from an injunction against uttering words that may have all the effect of force. . . . The question in every case is whether the words used are used in such circumstances and are of such a nature as to create a clear and present danger that they will bring about the substantive evils that Congress has a right to prevent. It is a question of proximity and degree. When a nation is at war many things that might be said in time of peace are such a hindrance to its effort that their utterance will not be endured so long as men fight and that no Court could regard them as protected by any Constitutional right.[41]

[40] It is this view of the Amendment—Holmes' refusal, that is to say, to read the language of the First Amendment as an absolute command—which has led Alexander Meiklejohn to accuse him of distorting its historic import. See *Free Speech and Its Relation to Self-Government,* especially ch. II. For an eminently fair criticism of Mr. Meiklejohn's thesis, coupled with a defense of the value of the "clear and present danger" doctrine, see Zechariah Chafee, Jr., Book Review: *62 Harv. L. Rev. 891* (1949).

[41] 249 U.S. 47, at 52.

After almost four decades of discussion, there is still wide disagreement as to just what meaning and purpose Holmes had in mind when he formulated this measure of the limits of free speech. As Justice Jackson has said, "All agree that it means something very important, but no two seem to agree on what it is." [42] Only recently Edward S. Corwin has insisted that "in the final analysis" the doctrine announced in the *Schenck* case is "indistinguishable" from that followed in Fox v. Washington. Presumably, Professor Corwin means to say that the test of criminality in both cases was the same, since it was published words which were alleged to be fraught with the danger of inducing illegal acts.[43] Writing at exactly the same time, another careful student of the problem professed to see a much more creative purpose: "The great contribution of Mr. Justice Holmes was that he looked through the deceptively simple language of the First Amendment to its plain purpose—the safeguarding of society's thinking processes." [44] But the fact is that until his dissent in the *Abrams* case,[45] Holmes always discussed free speech from the standpoint of the interest of society in curbing it. If it is true, as Holmes is clearly saying in the *Schenck* case, that the allowable area of free discussion is circumscribed by the general conditions in which the community finds itself, then it is obvious that words in and of themselves may be restrained. "The real issue in every free speech controversy," our leading authority on the subject has written, "is this: whether the state can punish all words which have some tendency, however remote, to bring about acts in violation of law, or only words which directly incite to acts in violation of law." [46]

There can be little doubt that Justice Holmes found Judge Learned Hand's famous dictum of World War I entirely satisfac-

[42] Concurring in Dennis v. United States, 341 U.S. 494, 561, at 567, n. 9 (1951).

[43] Corwin, *op. cit.*, p. 329.

[44] Wallace Mendelson, "Clear and Present Danger—From Schenck to Dennis," 52 *Col. L. Rev.* 313, 317 (1952).

[45] Abrams v. United States, 250 U.S. 616, 624 (1919).

[46] Chafee, *Free Speech in the United States*, p. 23.

tory. The judge who, in Professor Chafee's estimate, "gave the fullest attention to the meaning of free speech," [47] had this to say regarding the relation of words to action: "One may not counsel or advise others to violate the law as it stands. Words are not only the keys of persuasion, but the triggers of action, and those which have no purport but to counsel the violation of law cannot by any latitude of interpretation be a part of that public opinion which is the final source of government in a democratic state." [48] Holmes' opinions for a unanimous Court in the *Frohwerk* and *Debs* cases, [49] coming just a week after the *Schenck* case, clearly demonstrate his belief that the Constitution did not bar punishment for words which were potentially "triggers" of unlawful action. As Professor Corwin has observed, apropos of the *Schenck* decision, "advocates of 'clear and present danger' always quote the part about shouting 'fire in a theatre,' but usually omit the reference to the *Gompers* case where speech was held restrainable in enforcement of an anti-labor injunction." [50]

Like Schenck, Frohwerk was indicted for conspiring to violate the Espionage Act of 1917. He was charged with preparing and circulating twelve newspaper articles with the intent of obstructing the draft. The articles were bitterly critical of America's entry into the war, praised Germany and denounced the conscription of men for service in foreign lands. [51]

[47] *Ibid.*, p. 42.
[48] Masses Publishing Co. v. Patten, 244 F. 535, at 540 (1917).
[49] Frohwerk v. United States, 249 U.S. 204 (1919); Debs v. United States, 249 U.S. 211 (1919).
[50] Corwin, *op. cit.*, p. 328. Professor Corwin was referring to this passage in the *Schenck* opinion: "The most stringent protection of free speech would not protect a man in falsely shouting fire in a theatre and causing a panic. It does not even protect a man from an injunction against uttering words that may have all the effect of force. Gompers v. Buck's Stove and Range Co., 221 U.S. 418, 439." 249 U.S. 47, at 52.
[51] Holmes' summary of two of the articles conveys a pretty clear picture of "the kind of matter" which the Court had before it. He wrote:
"The first begins by declaring it a monumental and inexcusable mistake to send our soldiers to France, says that it comes no doubt from the great trusts, and later that it appears to be outright murder without serving anything prac-

The mere circulation of the articles was held to be violative of the Espionage Act. It well may be, as Professor Chafee suggests, that the Supreme Court's decision in the *Frohwerk* case was largely due to poor work on the part of the lawyers for the defense.[52] ". . . on the inadequately prepared record as it stood, the evidence might conceivably have been sufficient to sustain a conviction, since the circumstances and the intention, though not the words *per se*, might satisfy the danger test."[53] It is hard to reconcile this hypothesis with Holmes' assertion in his *Frohwerk* opinion—"a person may be

---

tical; speaks of the unconquerable spirit and undiminished strength of the German nation, and characterizes its own discourse as words of warning to the American people. . . . Later, . . . came discussion of the causes of war, laying it to the administration and saying 'that a few men and corporations might amass unprecedented fortunes we sold our honor, our very soul,' with the usual repetition that we went to war to protect the loans of Wall Street. Later, after more similar discourse, comes 'We say therefore, cease firing.'

". . . the paper goes on to give a picture . . . of the sufferings of a drafted man, of his then recognizing that his country is not in danger and that he is being sent to a foreign land to fight in a cause that neither he nor any one else knows anything of, and reaching the conviction that this is but a war to protect some rich men's money. Who then, it is asked, will pronounce a verdict of guilty upon him if he stops reasoning and follows the first impulse of nature: self-preservation; and further, whether, while technically he is wrong in his resistance, he is not more sinned against than sinning; and yet again whether the guilt of those who voted the unnatural sacrifice is not greater than the wrong of those who now seek to escape by ill-advised resistance." 249 U.S. 204, at 207–08.

[52] "The next decision, the Frohwerk case, illustrates one of the commonest reasons why appeals from sedition convictions prove unsuccessful—the lack of good old-fashioned lawyerlike work by the defense counsel. An unpopular pacifist or radical often finds it hard to get a competent lawyer. Eloquent praise of the blessings of free speech amounts to little, unless counsel also possesses a firm grasp of the technical issues clearly involved and tries the case so as to bring out those issues clearly and get them on the printed record which goes to the appellate court. The main issue in such a prosecution is usually not the unconstitutionality of the statute as a whole, but whether what the defendant said or did, when connected with the surrounding circumstances, falls within the terms of the statute as properly construed in the light of the free speech clause. Therefore, it is essential for counsel for the accused to establish at the trial with accuracy and completeness just what the accused said or did, among what persons and when and where and how. The prisoner's lawyer keeps his eyes on the jury, but he must always keep his mind on the appellate court." Chafee, *Free Speech in the United States*, pp. 82–83.

[53] *Ibid.*, p. 83.

convicted of a conspiracy to obstruct recruiting by words of persuasion"[54]—an assertion which he backed with a citation of the *Schenck* case, though he did not mention "clear and present danger." The least that can be said, however, is that Holmes relied on an incomplete record to draw inferences as to both intention and circumstances. The Justice said:

It may be that all this might be said or written even in time of war in circumstances that would not make it a crime. We do not lose our right to condemn either measures or men because the Country is at war. . . . But we must take the case on the record as it is, and on that record it is impossible to say that it might not have been found that the circulation of the paper was in quarters where a little breath would be enough to kindle a flame and that the fact was known and relied upon by those who sent that paper out.[55]

On the more fundamental issue of the constitutional protection of free speech, Holmes' remarks are even more unequivocal:

. . . the First Amendment while prohibiting legislation against free speech as such cannot have been and obviously was not, intended to give immunity for every possible use of language. . . . We venture to believe that neither Hamilton nor Madison, nor any other competent person then or later, ever supposed that to make criminal the counseling of a murder within the jurisdiction of Congress would be an unconstitutional interference with free speech.[56]

The most spectacular of the prosecutions under the Espionage Act of 1917 was without doubt that of Eugene V. Debs, militant head of the American Socialist Party. "I hated to have to write the *Debs* case and still more those of the other poor devils before us the same day and the week before," Holmes wrote to Herbert Croly, on May 12, 1919, adding:

. . . I could not see the wisdom of pressing the cases, especially when the fighting was over and I think it quite possible that if I had been on the jury I should have been for acquittal but I cannot doubt that there

[54] 249 U.S. 204, at 206.   [55] *Ibid.*, at 208–09.
[56] *Ibid.*, at 206.

was evidence warranting a conviction on the disputed issues of fact. More-over I think that *clauses under consideration* not only were constitutional but were proper enough while the war was on. When people are putting out all their energies in battle I don't think it unreasonable to say we won't have obstacles intentionally put in the way of raising troops—by persuasion any more than by force. But in the main I am for aeration of all effervescing convictions—there is no way so quick for letting them get flat.[57]

To Pollock he had written a month earlier:

. . . I am beginning to get stupid letters of protest against a decision that Debs, a noted agitator, was rightly convicted of obstructing the recruiting service so far as the law was concerned. I wondered that the Government should press the case to a hearing before us, as the inevitable result was that fools, knaves, and ignorant persons were bound to say he was convicted because he was a dangerous agitator and that obstructing the draft was a pretence. How it was with the Jury of course I don't know, but of course the talk is silly as to us. There was a lot of jaw about free speech, which I dealt with somewhat summarily in an earlier case— *Schenck v. U.S.* . . . also *Frohwerk v. U.S.* . . . As it happens I should go farther probably than the majority in favor of it, and I daresay it was partly on that account that the C. J. assigned the case to me.[58]

While there is more than one bit of evidence that Holmes was somewhat disturbed by the professional criticism of his role in the *Debs* case, the opinion itself is entirely free of doubt. It contains no confession of "anxiety" over the inadequacy of the record, as there was in the *Frohwerk* case. More strange still is the fact that as in the *Frohwerk* case, the author of the clear and present danger doctrine completely ignored his own brain-child.

Following his delivery of a speech in Canton, Ohio, on June 16, 1918, Debs was indicted for attempting to cause insubordination in the armed forces and for attempting to obstruct the recruiting service. There is good reason for accepting Professor Chafee's

[57] *Holmes-Laski Letters*, I, 203–04. These comments were prompted by Ernst Freund's article in the *New Republic* critical of the *Debs* decision, "The Debs case and Freedom of Speech," *19 New Republic 13* (May 3, 1919).

[58] *Holmes-Pollock Letters*, II, 7 (April 5, 1919).

inference that Debs was convicted by the jury largely because of his "exposition of socialism." [59] But in his opinion sustaining the conviction, Holmes disclaims any such motivation on the part of the Court: "The main theme of this speech was socialism, its growth, and a prophecy of its ultimate success. With that we have nothing to do, but if a part or the manifest intent of the more general utterances was to encourage those present to obstruct the recruiting service and if in passages such encouragement was directly given, the immunity of the general theme may not be enough to protect the speech." [60] What, then, was there in Debs' speech which could be said to produce the consequences outlawed by the Espionage Act? In the main, the passages to which the Justice was taking exception were the ones in which the speaker lauded, by name, some Socialists who were serving prison terms allegedly for interfering with the carrying out of the draft law. Some of the more objectionable comments were summarized by Holmes as follows:

The speaker began by saying that he had just returned from a visit to the workhouse in the neighborhood where three of their most loyal comrades were paying the penalty for their devotion to the working class . . . who had been convicted of aiding and abetting another in failing to register for the draft. . . .

. . . he took up the case of Kate Richards O'Hare, convicted of obstructing the enlistment service, praised her for her loyalty to socialism and otherwise. . . . The defendant spoke of other cases, and then, after dealing with Russia, said that the master class has always declared the war and the subject class has always fought the battles—that the subject class has had nothing to gain and all to lose, including their lives; that the working class, who furnish the corpses, have never yet had a voice in declaring war and have never yet had a voice in declaring peace. "You have your lives to lose; you certainly ought to have the right to declare war if you consider a war necessary." . . .

There followed personal experiences and illustrations of the growth of socialism, a glorification of minorities, and a prophecy of the success of the international socialist crusade, with the interjection that "You need

[59] Chafee, *op. cit.*, p. 84.
[60] 249 U.S. 211, at 212.

to know that you are fit for something better than slavery and cannon fodder." [61]

Holmes also quoted part of Debs' address to the jury which convicted him: "I have been accused of obstructing the war. I admit it. Gentlemen, I abhor war. I would oppose war if I stood alone."

Holmes' opinion in the *Debs* case held that it was entirely proper to admit in evidence the record of the conviction of the persons Debs had praised in his speech, since only thereby would it be possible "to show what he was talking about, to explain the true import of his expression of sympathy and to throw light on the intent of the address." It was also permissible to introduce at the trial the Anti-War Proclamation and Program that had been adopted at St. Louis in April of 1917, a declaration which gave capitalism as the cause of the war and blamed "predatory capitalists" for forcing the United States to enter the struggle. Debs had endorsed the document both in his Canton speech and before the jury. Holmes found the Proclamation's call for "continuous, active and public opposition to the war, through demonstrations, mass petitions and all other means within our power" especially significant. As he said, "Evidence that the defendant accepted this view and this declaration of his duties at the time that he made this speech is evidence that if in that speech he used words tending to obstruct the recruiting service he meant that they should have that effect." [62]

Even more difficult to explain than this statement about "words tending to obstruct" is the reason the Justice gave for being sure that the jury knew what it was doing. The jury was "most carefully instructed," he added reassuringly, "that they could not find the defendant guilty for advocacy of any of his opinions unless the words used had as their natural tendency and reasonably probable effect to obstruct the recruiting service, &c., and unless the defendant had the specific intent to do so in his mind." [63] At no point

[61] *Ibid.*, at 213–14.
[62] *Ibid.*, at 216.
[63] *Ibid.*

in the decision, however, is there any attempt to demonstrate that in the circumstances in which Debs made his speech there was any imminence of danger that the "effect" he was alleged to have intended would be produced. "Debs was convicted of an attempt to cause insubordination in the army and obstruct recruiting," notes Professor Chafee, "yet no provocation to any such definite and particular acts was proved. . . . Not one word was designed for soldiers, not one word urged his hearers to resist the draft, objectionable as he considered it." [64] In fact, right after quoting Debs' remarks to the jury, Holmes states quite categorically that even without this personal expression of opposition to war, the jury would have been justified in finding the defendant guilty of seeking to obstruct the war effort. The crux of his opinion in the *Debs* case is to be found in his emphatic declaration that the jury was altogether warranted "in finding that one purpose of the speech, whether incidental or not does not matter, was to oppose not only war in general but this war, and that the opposition was so expressed that its natural and intended effect would be to obstruct recruiting. If that was intended and if, in all the circumstances, that would be its probable effect, it would not be protected by reason of its being part of a general program and expressions of a general and conscientious belief." [65]

After reading Holmes' opinions in the *Frohwerk* and *Debs* cases, one can understand why Professor Corwin has said that they "went far to dispel whatever impression may have been created by the earlier opinion [in the *Schenck* case] that there is a constitutional requirement that 'clear and present danger' of some 'substantive evil' be proved where intent to incite a crime is found to exist." Equally justifiable is his summary of all three cases: "In short, we find three cases, decided within a period of two weeks, in which convictions for violation of the Espionage Act were unanimously sustained for utterances of such general nature that they might all

[64] Chafee, *op. cit.*, p. 85.
[65] 249 U.S. 211, at 214–15.

have borne innocent interpretations if made in other circumstances, but which were deemed to be unlawful because the circumstances warranted the finding that their probable and intended effect would be to obstruct the war effort." [66]

If one accepts Professor Chafee's view that as tests of criminality "bad tendency" and "presumed intent" are "wholly inconsistent with freedom of speech and any genuine discussion of public affairs," [67] it also must be acknowledged that for all practical purposes these were the very criteria on which Holmes relied in the *Frohwerk* and *Debs* cases. Judging from the Justice's attitude in these decisions, moreover, it would almost seem that the reference to "clear and present danger" in the *Schenck* case was a casual remark, a bit of neat verbalization on the part of a man given to terse expression; a mere "rationalization," as Robert E. Cushman has called it. Professor Cushman's explanation of the "official" status of the clear and present danger concept would appear to be both plausible and accurate:

The Court went along with Holmes in the three wartime free speech cases in which he wrote the opinions (Schenck, Frohwerk, and Debs). This is not significant. The three defendants were all held to be validly convicted, and the rest of the Court, agreeing with this result, were content to let Holmes' remarks about clear and present danger stand as a bit of rationalization. It is unlikely that in these first cases they fully grasped the significance of Holmes' doctrine.[68]

The more perplexing question, however, is whether Holmes himself "fully grasped the significance"—or shall we say, potentialities—of his now famous formula. On the basis of the three opinions just discussed, the answer would have to be in the negative. Indeed, were it not for the important occasions on which Holmes came to

[66] Corwin, *op. cit.*, p. 331.
[67] Chafee, *op. cit.*, p. 85.
[68] Cushman, " 'Clear and Present Danger' in Free Speech Cases: A Study in Judicial Semantics," in *Essays in Political Theory*, edited by Milton R. Konvitz and Arthur E. Murphy (Ithaca: Cornell Univ. Press, 1948), p. 311, at pp. 316–17.

invoke the clear and present danger doctrine in dissent, one would be forced to agree with Justice Frankfurter that it was merely a "felicitous" [69] or "literary" [70] phrase. Starting with his dissenting opinion in the *Abrams* case and with the powerful support of Justice Brandeis, Holmes was succeeding in projecting "clear and present danger" into the discussion of free speech problems. Apart from his moving eloquence and the drama of the legal controversies themselves, he achieved this effect by accusing court majorities of having gone astray through disregard of the test. Yet within the Supreme Court itself his success was very limited. As Professor Corwin has reminded us, in the twelve years that elapsed between the *Abrams* case and Holmes' retirement from the Court, he "succeeded in enrolling under his banner" only Justice Brandeis.[71] However, Brandeis' own notable dissents in free speech cases show that he took the theory much more seriously than did Holmes, so that there is reason to wonder whether the influence may not have worked the other way around.

III

By a vote of seven to two, the Supreme Court upheld the conviction of Abrams and his fellow defendants, who had been convicted for conspiring to violate the Espionage Act of 1917, as amended by the so-called Sedition Act of 1918.[72] They were

[69] "To talk about 'clear and present danger' as the touch-stone of allowable educational policy by the states whenever school curricula may impinge upon the boundaries of individual conscience, is to take a felicitous phrase out of the context of the particular situation where it arose and for which it was adapted." Frankfurter, J., Dissenting in West Virginia State Board of Education v. Barnette, 319 U.S. 624, 646, at 663 (1943).

[70] "It [clear and present danger] was a literary phrase not to be distorted by being taken from its context." Frankfurter, J., Concurring in Pennekamp v. Florida, 328 U.S. 331, 350, at 353 (1946).

[71] Corwin, *op. cit.*, p. 334.

[72] The Amendments have been summarized by Professor Chafee as follows: "This amendment of May 16, 1918 (repealed in 1921), which is sometimes called the Sedition Act, inserted 'attempts to obstruct' in the third of the original offenses, and added nine more offenses, as follows: (4) saying or doing

charged principally with two offenses: (1) printing circulars intended to encourage resistance to the United States in its war with Germany, and (2) inciting and advocating in these circulars resort to a general strike by munition workers for the purpose of curtailing production of ammunition essential to the prosecution of the war with Germany, "with intent by such curtailment to cripple or hinder the United States in the prosecution of the war." Since the undisguised aim of the pamphleteers was to prevent interference with the cause of the Russian Revolution, the knotty problem for the Supreme Court majority was to establish their specific "intent" to hinder the war with Germany. Justice Clarke met the challenge with the aid of the following piece of roundabout reasoning:

> It will not do to say . . . that the only intent of these defendants was to prevent injury to the Russian cause. Men must be held to have intended, and to be accountable for, the effects which their acts were likely to produce. Even if their primary purpose and intent was to aid the cause of the Russian Revolution, the plan of action which they adopted necessarily involved, before it could be realized, defeat of the war program of the United States, for the obvious effect of this appeal, if it should become effective, as they hoped it might, would be to persuade persons . . . not to aid government loans and not to work in ammunition factories.[73]

---

anything with intent to obstruct the sale of United States bonds, except by way of bona fide and not disloyal advice; (5) uttering, printing, writing, or publishing any disloyal, profane, scurrilous, or abusive language, or language intended to cause contempt, scorn, contumely or disrepute as regards the form of government of the United States; (6) or the Constitution; (7) or the flag; (8) or the uniform of the Army or Navy; (9) or any language intended to incite resistance to the United States or promote the cause of its enemies; (10) urging any curtailment of production of any things necessary to the prosecution of the war with intent to hinder its prosecution; (11) advocating, teaching, defending, or suggesting the doing of any of these acts; and (12) words or acts supporting or favoring the cause of any country at war with us, or opposing the cause of the United States therein. Whoever committed any one of these offenses during the war was liable to the maximum penalty of the original Act, $10,000 fine or twenty years' imprisonment, or both." Chafee, *Free Speech in the United States,* pp. 40–41.

[73] 250 U.S. 616, at 621.

Holmes' now classic dissent in the *Abrams* case, in which he was also speaking for Brandeis, is much more than an attempt to refute Clarke's logic on the crucial issue of intent. It is a passionate defense of the high value of freedom of expression, all the more remarkable because coming from a source which fairly could not be considered as either "soft" or "sentimental" on the subject. Holmes advanced two reasons for questioning the soundness of the Court's decision. In the first place, he was not convinced that the Government had proved that the defendants actually intended to "hinder" the war effort against Germany. "I am aware of course," he writes, "that the word intent as vaguely used in ordinary legal discussion means no more than knowledge at the time of the act that the consequences said to be intended will ensue." He conceded that even less was demanded by common law principles: "A man may have to pay damages, may be sent to prison, at common law might be hanged, if at the time of his act he knew facts from which common experience showed that the consequences would follow, whether he individually could foresee them or not." [74] But the master of the common law called for a new view of the meaning of intent, arguing that an accused person ought not to be charged with having done something with the intent of bringing about the illegal result "unless the aim to produce it is the proximate motive of the specific act, although there may be some deeper motive behind."

Holmes could not find in the words of the defendants any evidence of an "actual intent" to commit the offenses with which they were charged. There was no "hint of resistance" to the United States in its war, since the "resistance" within the meaning of the Espionage Act must be "some forcible act of opposition to some proceeding of the United States in pursuance of the war." As to the intent to curtail munitions, Holmes admitted that it seemed "too plain to be denied" that the second leaflet urged "curtailment of production of things necessary to the prosecution of the war,"

[74] *Ibid.*, at 626–27.

but insisted that to make the conduct criminal it should be, in the language of the Espionage Act, "with intent by such curtailment to cripple or hinder the United States in the prosecution of the war." He found no proof of any such intent: "An intent to prevent interference with the Revolution in Russia might have been satisfied without any hindrance to carrying on the war in which we were engaged." [75]

This approach to the problem of intent, presumably in the interest of greater freedom of utterance, evoked a sharp rebuke from even so calm and fair-minded an observer as Professor Corwin. In a contemporaneous review of the Supreme Court's work, he said quite bluntly that Holmes' conception of intent "standing by itself . . . will hardly hold water." [76] He reminded the Justice that "common sense no less than common law exact that a man be held to intend the necessary means to his objectives." After pointing out that the published debates on the Espionage Act demonstrate that Congress had used the word "intent" in its usual legal sense, Professor Corwin suggested that Holmes' "unconventional view" of intent was really not meant to stand alone but was offered as a necessary instrument for enforcing the doctrine of clear and present danger. He took Holmes to task for adducing no proof for the assumption that Congress can punish only "utterances that constitute criminal attempts" and charged that "the pretended limitation is apparently made up out of whole cloth." [77]

Before discussing the freedom of speech issue—the "more important aspect of the case"—Holmes summarized the state of the law on the subject. In doing so, he was interpreting for us, of course, the decisions of which he himself was the author. For this reason, his résumé is indeed worth recalling:

[75] *Ibid.*, at 628.
[76] Corwin, "Constitutional Law in 1919–1920," *14 Amer. Pol. Sci. Rev. 635, 656* (Nov., 1920). Professor Corwin repeated his criticism in his more widely quoted article "Freedom of Speech and Press under the First Amendment," *30 Yale L. J. 40* (1920); reprinted in 2 *Selected Essays 1060*.
[77] *14 Amer. Pol. Sci. Rev. 635, 657.*

I never have seen any reason to doubt that the questions of law that alone were before this Court in the cases of *Schenck, Frohwerk and Debs,* . . . were rightly decided. I do not doubt for a moment that by the same reasoning that would justify punishing persuasion to murder, the United States constitutionally may punish speech that produces or is intended to produce a clear and imminent danger that it will bring about forthwith certain substantive evils that the United States constitutionally may seek to prevent. The power undoubtedly is greater in time of war than in time of peace because war opens dangers that do not exist at other times.

But as against dangers peculiar to war, as against others, the principle of the right to free speech is always the same. It is only the present danger of immediate evil or an intent to bring it about that warrants Congress in setting a limit to the expression of opinion where private rights are not concerned. Congress certainly cannot forbid all efforts to change the mind of the country.[78]

Holmes' second reason for dissenting—probably his fundamental objection—was that the facts of the case did not establish that the words used in the leaflets gave rise to any clear and present danger that the unlawful objectives would be realized. "Nobody can suppose that the surreptitious publishing of a silly leaflet by an unknown man, without more, would present an immediate danger that its opinions would hinder the success of the Government arms or have any appreciable tendency to do so." The imposition of a twenty year sentence, moreover, apparently only served to convince him that the defendants were prosecuted not because of the alleged danger flowing from their conduct but for the ideas they advocated:

Even if I am technically wrong and enough can be squeezed from these poor and puny anonymities to turn the color of legal litmus paper; I will add, even if what I think the necessary intent were shown; the most nominal punishment seems to me all that possibly could be inflicted, unless the defendants are to be made to suffer not for what the indictment alleges but for the creed that they avow—a creed that I believe to be the creed of ignorance and immaturity when honestly held, as I see no reason to doubt that it was held here, but which, although made the subject of examination at the trial, no one has a right even to consider in dealing with the charges before the Court.[79]

[78] 250 U.S. 616, at 627–28.   [79] *Ibid.,* at 629–30.

In closing, Holmes penned a paragraph on the worth of freedom of thought which inevitably has led observers to compare his *Abrams* dissent with the great tracts on toleration. It is likely to endure as long as human freedom itself remains a faith which men live by. It has been justly characterized by Max Lerner as "the greatest utterance on intellectual freedom by an American ranking in the English tongue with Milton and Mill." [80] Holmes wrote:

Persecution for the expression of opinions seems to me perfectly logical. If you have no doubt of your premises or your power and want a certain result with all your heart you naturally express your wishes in law and sweep away all opposition. To allow opposition by speech seems to indicate that you think the speech impotent, as when a man says that he has squared the circle, or that you do not care whole-heartedly for the result, or that you doubt either your power or your premises. But when men have realized that time has upset many fighting faiths, they may come to believe even more than they believe the very foundations of their own conduct that the ultimate good desired is better reached by free trade in ideas—that the best test of truth is the power of the thought to get itself accepted in the competition of the market, and that truth is the only ground upon which their wishes safely can be carried out. That at any rate is the theory of our Constitution. It is an experiment, as all life is an experiment. Every year if not every day we have to wager our salvation upon some prophecy based upon imperfect knowledge. While that experiment is part of our system I think that we should be eternally vigilant against attempts to check the expression of opinions that we loathe and believe to be fraught with death, unless they so imminently threaten immediate interference with the lawful and pressing purposes of the law that an immediate check is required to save the country. . . . Only the emergency that makes it immediately dangerous to leave the correction of evil counsels to time warrants making any exception to the sweeping command, "Congress shall make no law . . . abridging the freedom of speech." [81]

Referring to this passage in the *Abrams* dissent, on which so much homage has since been heaped, one eminent commentator said at the time: "This disquisition on Truth seems sadly out of

---

[80] Lerner, *The Mind and Faith of Justice Holmes*, p. 306.
[81] 250 U.S. 616, at 630–31.

place. To weigh in juxtaposition the dastardly sentiments of these
circulars and the great theme of world-wide justice for which our
armies were sacrificing themselves, and then to assume the sacred
cause of Truth as equally involved in both, is to misuse high
ideals." [82] The critic was John H. Wigmore, the noted authority
on evidence, then Dean of the School of Law at Northwestern
University, who had served on the staff of the Provost Marshal
General during the war. He began his sensational attack on what
he persisted in calling the "Minority Opinion" by declaring that it
"represents poor law and poor policy" and by announcing that he
wished to point out its dangerous implications. The reason he gave
for thinking it "worth analysis" set the tone of the whole article:
"It is shocking in its obtuse indifference to the vital issues at stake
in August, 1918, and it is ominous in its portent of like indifference
to pending and coming issues."

Wigmore then proceeded to castigate Holmes and Brandeis—
without ever mentioning them by name—for saying that the circulation of the leaflets constituted no "present danger," a conclusion
he attributed to the fact that the two Justices were oblivious to
the desperate plight of the United States and her Allies in the
summer of 1918. After relating the events leading up to the stalemate
on the Western Front and the "supreme effort" to prepare for the
final offensive against the Germans, Dean Wigmore pointed out
that the manufacture of military supplies was not only slow in
starting but that "for the enlarged American army that was to be
ready to continue the initial successes of the Allied offensive of
July–October, 1918, the supply never equalled the need, until the
end of September." The minority simply was overlooking the fact
that it was during this same "crucial August, 1918" that "Abrams
and this band of alien parasites, and a hundred other such bands,
were doing all in their power to curtail this production and cripple

[82] John H. Wigmore, "Abrams v. United States: Freedom of Speech and
Freedom of Thuggery in War-Time and Peace-Time," XIV Ill. L. Rev. 539, 551
(1920).

our fighting men." In short, Wigmore maintained that Holmes and Brandeis were indifferent to the military situation of the country in August, 1918, and that for this reason they were in no position to assess the danger stemming from the activity of Abrams and his associates in urging curtailment of war production. He wrote:

> The point is that this situation did not impress the Minority Opinion as one of "present danger" in August, 1918. The national agonies of those six months from April to October were apparently unsensed by the Minority Opinion. It was blind to the crisis—blind to the last supreme needs of the fighters in the field, blind to the straining toil of the workers at home, obtuse to the fearful situation which then obsessed the whole mind and heart of our country.[83]

Perhaps even more so than the contradictory conclusions drawn by the majority and minority Justices in the *Abrams* case, Wigmore's diatribe—a remarkable mixture of fact and emotion, philosophy and poetry, law and polemic—illuminates in rather dramatic fashion the underlying cause of dissension in free-speech cases. For it showed that the outcome depended upon how the general situation to which the offending utterances were addressed was appraised. As Wigmore himself admitted, "the opposite interpretations of the majority and the minority were due, . . . to differences of temperament and attitude towards the issues involved."

Neither the majority nor the minority questioned the constitutionality of the legislation under which the indictment was brought; the disagreement between them turned on the evaluation of the circumstances from which danger could be inferred. Thomas Reed Powell was not merely indulging his justly famed wit as a constitutional commentator when he suggested that Holmes rejected the decision in the *Abrams* case "because of the silliness of the leaflet and the unimportance of its authors."[84] Although he found Holmes' dissent "difficult to deal with" because it did not make clear how much of it is "based on the Constitution," Professor

[83] *Ibid.*, p. 549.
[84] Powell, "Constitutional Law in 1919–1920," *19 Mich. L. Rev. 283, 292* (1921).

Powell finally concluded that to the minority "the circumstances do not as a matter of inference show that degree of danger which is necessary before freedom of speech can be curtailed consistently with the First Amendment."

Another significant difference between the majority and the minority in the war-time cases was discerned by Professor Corwin when he paused in 1920 to summarize the results of these cases. He found that a minority of the Court was asking for more extensive supervision of the verdicts of juries in this class of cases, whereas the majority was refusing to scrutinize them more strictly than jury findings in ordinary criminal cases. Professor Corwin expressed the judgment that "the cause of freedom of speech and press is largely in the custody of legislative majorities and of juries." [85]

IV

This prophetic analysis was confirmed rather strikingly in a case [86] in which is to be found the first contribution to the discussion of "clear and present danger" by the "co-architect of the great constitutional structure of civil liberties," [87] as Justice Brandeis has been called. Schaefer and several other persons connected with the publication of the Philadelphia *Tageblatt* were convicted for publishing in this German-language newspaper false reports with the intent of furthering the success of Germany in the war. They were charged with deliberately altering news accounts from other papers in order to depress patriotic fervor and support for the nation's war effort. Speaking through Justice McKenna, the Supreme Court reversed the conviction of Schaefer and one of his associates but allowed the conviction of the others to stand. The case presented a "curious spectacle," the Justice declared, of people invoking the protection of the Constitution "to justify the activities of anarchy or of the

[85] Corwin, *op. cit.*, in 2 *Selected Essays 1060, 1068.*
[86] Schaefer v. United States, 251 U.S. 466, 482 (1920).
[87] Mr. Justice Frankfurter, concurring in Pennekamp v. Florida, 328 U.S. 331, 350, at 352 (1946).

enemies of the United States." [88] Inspired by such a feeling, it is not surprising that he should have concluded that the inevitable "tendency" of the incriminating publications was to interfere with the prosecution of the war.

In McKenna's treatment of one of the articles—a dispatch entitled "Yankee Bluff" which questioned the sincerity of the American promise to send troops to Europe—is to be found the Court's basic position: "To them [the readers] its derisive contempt may have been truly descriptive of American feebleness and inability to combat Germany's prowess, and thereby chill and check the ardency of patriotism and make it despair of success and in hopelessness relax energy both in preparation and action." [89] The Espionage Act had been passed as a precaution, and it was therefore not necessary to wait for the full effect to be felt of the regular and systematic publication of derisive and false news reports of the capacity or intention of the United States to aid her allies. As McKenna put it, "The incidence of its violation might not be immediately seen, evil appearing only in disaster, the result of the disloyalty engendered and the spirit of mutiny." [90]

What stands out in this statement is the Court's complete refusal to concern itself with the degree of the danger allegedly created by the publication of the articles. Perhaps it was McKenna's cavalier disregard of the need to weigh the "effect" of the words which explains Brandeis' forceful invocation of the clear and present danger test. "The extent to which Congress may, under the Constitution, interfere with free speech," he began, "was in Schenck v. United States . . . declared by a unanimous Court to be this: . . ." He then quoted Holmes' sentence about clear and present danger. Calling it a "rule of reason," he argued that even though it gave a wide latitude to the jury in applying it to a particular situation, both trial and appellate judges—but ultimately the appellate courts

[88] 251 U.S. 466, at 477.
[89] *Ibid.*, at 478.
[90] *Ibid.*, at 479.

—had the responsibility of seeing to it that it was not misused. He felt that "no jury acting in calmness" could have found the defendants guilty of printing things which produced an immediate threat to the nation's war effort.

Brandeis' vigorous elaboration of the clear and present danger concept as a rule of reason is one more illustration of the way casual dicta may come to be raised to the level of purposeful legal doctrines. The Justice wrote:

This is a rule of reason. Correctly applied, it will preserve the right of free speech both from suppression by tyrannous, well-meaning majorities and from abuse by irresponsible, fanatical minorities. Like many other rules for human conduct, it can be applied correctly only by the exercise of good judgment; and to the exercise of good judgment, calmness is, in times of deep feeling and on subjects which excite passion, as essential as fearlessness and honesty. The question whether in a particular instance the words spoken or written fall within the permissible curtailment of free speech is, under the rule enunciated by this court, one of degree. And because it is a question of degree the field in which the jury may exercise its judgment is, necessarily, a wide one. But its field is not unlimited. The trial provided for is one by judge *and* jury; and the judge may not abdicate his function. If the words were of such a nature and were used under such circumstances that men, judging in calmness, could not reasonably say that they created a clear and present danger that they would bring about the evil which Congress sought and had a right to prevent, then it is the duty of the trial judge to withdraw the case from the consideration of the jury; and if he fails to do so, it is the duty of the appellate court to correct the error.[91]

Taking up the Court's view of the recurring items in the *Tageblatt* which cast doubt upon the ability of the government to fulfill all of its promises to the Allies, Brandeis pointed out that some of these statements contained the very type of propaganda which many American patriotic societies circulated in order to stimulate support of the war. In his opinion not even "Yankee Bluff" could "rationally" be held to obstruct recruiting. Interestingly enough, the Justice quoted Professor Chafee by way of underscoring the

[91] *Ibid.*, at 482–83.

weight of authority against the test of "remote tendency" in free
speech cases: "as this Court has declared and as Professor Chafee
has shown . . . the test to be applied—as in the case of criminal
attempts and incitements—is not the remote or possible effect. There
must be clear and present danger." [92]

A week later—in Pierce v. United States [93]—Brandeis again voiced
his objection to the wide discretion allowed juries in free speech
cases. Pierce and three others were convicted for distributing
copies of "The Price We Pay," a four-page leaflet issued by the
national headquarters of the Socialist Party and written by Irwin
St. John Tucker, a well-known Episcopal clergyman. They were
found guilty of conspiring to cause disloyalty in the military forces
of the United States and to disseminate false statements with intent
to interfere with the success of those forces. Through Justice Pitney,
a majority of the Supreme Court held that the pamphlet could be
construed as a "protest" against the further prosecution of the war
and that it was up to the jury to determine whether the statements
contained in the leaflet were likely to have that effect. In rejecting
the testimony of the defendants that their sole aim was to win
converts for socialism, Pitney stressed that the "jury very reasonably
might find—as evidently they did—that the protestations of inno-
cence were insincere and that the real purpose of defendants—
indeed, the real object of the pamphlet—was to hamper the Government in the prosecution of the war." [94]

As he had in the *Schaefer* case, so in the *Pierce* case Brandeis
devoted most of his opinion to a close examination of the incriminating documents. He quoted one statement in the leaflet to this
effect: "Our entry into it [the war] was determined by the certainty
that if the Allies did not win, J. P. Morgan's loans to the Allies will
be repudiated, and those American investors who bit on his promises
would be hooked." Observing that the forces behind modern wars

[92] *Ibid.*, at 486. The reference was to Professor Chafee's article, "Freedom
of Speech in War Time," 32 *Harv. L. Rev. 932, 963* (1919).
[93] 252 U.S. 239, 253 (1920).
[94] *Ibid.*, at 250.

are so complex that not even historians always agree on the causes of any particular war, Brandeis argued at some length that the statement in the Tucker leaflet concerning the effect of the loans to the Allies was a mere expression of opinion and that the same suspicion had been voiced in Congress. Since such declarations are not capable of being proved false in fact, but were mere "matters of opinion and judgment," they should not have been submitted to the jury. It would be a serious threat to freedom of political discussion, the Justice contended, if juries were left free to draw their own inferences from the expression of opinions on controversial political questions. As he said, "To hold that a jury may make punishable statements of conclusions or opinion, . . . by declaring them to be statements of facts and to be false would practically deny members of small political parties freedom of criticism and of discussion in times when feelings run high and the questions involved are deemed fundamental." [95]

Turning to the constitutional issue, Brandeis insisted that merely because the leaflet contained "lurid and exaggerated pictures of the horrors of war" that in itself did not prove that it would produce the harmful results condemned by the Espionage Act. Noting that the offending leaflet acknowledged the "hopelessness of protest" and the military might of the Government, he went on to say that it was not conceivable that "any man of ordinary intelligence and normal judgment" could be induced thereby to commit the grave offenses banned by the Espionage Act. Justice Brandeis concluded his dissenting opinion in the *Pierce* case with this plea for tolerance:

The fundamental right of free men to strive for better conditions through new legislation and new institutions will not be preserved, if efforts to secure it by argument to fellow citizens may be construed as criminal incitement to disobey the existing law—merely, because the argument presented seems to those exercising judicial power to be unfair in its portrayal of existing evils, mistaken in its assumptions, unsound in reasoning or intemperate in language.[96]

[95] *Ibid.*, at 269.
[96] *Ibid.*, at 273.

The next time Justice Brandeis dissented on a free-speech issue he was not joined by his usual companion in dissent, Holmes concurring in the result reached by the majority. In Gilbert v. Minnesota,[97] the Supreme Court found valid the law which the legislature of Minnesota passed in 1917 prohibiting public speaking against enlistment and the teaching of opposition to war. The official report of this decision carries this brief announcement: "The Chief Justice, being of the opinion that the subject-matter is within the exclusive legislative power of Congress, when exerted, and that the action of Congress has occupied the whole field, therefore dissents."[98] For some undisclosed reason—perhaps because of Brandeis' version of the constitutional guarantee of free speech—Chief Justice White did not concur in his dissent. On the merits of the controversy over the infringement of freedom of speech, therefore, Brandeis stood quite alone in Gilbert v. Minnesota. In connection with the votes of Holmes and White, it may be of interest to recall a suggestive comment by Professor Chafee: "Here Chief Justice White, who was a Confederate drummer boy, supported national supremacy, while Justice Holmes, who fought in the Union Army, upheld states' rights."[99] There is some indication that Brandeis was rather puzzled by Holmes' failure to support him in this case; for he referred to a case decided just a month before in which Holmes had acted as the Court's spokesman in an opinion taking the national side of an issue of conflict between state and federal powers. Justice Brandeis thought it sufficiently germane to quote from it in his *Gilbert* dissent, though he refrained from mentioning Holmes as the author of the decision.[100]

[97] 254 U.S. 325, 334 (1920).   [98] *Ibid.*, at 334.
[99] Chafee, *Free Speech in the United States*, p. 290.
[100] "In Johnson v. Maryland, . . . [254 U.S. 51] this court held that the power of Congress to establish post roads precluded the State from requiring of a post-office employee using the state highway in the transportation of mail the customary evidence of competency to drive a motor truck, although the danger to public safety was obvious and it did not appear that the Federal Government had undertaken to deal with the matter by statute or regulation. The prohibition of state action rests, as the court pointed out there, 'not upon

Gilbert, an official of the Nonpartisan League, was convicted for violating the Minnesota Statute as the result of saying the following at a meeting of the organization:

We are going over to Europe to make the world safe for democracy, but I tell you we had better make America safe for democracy first. You say, What is the matter with our democracy? I tell you what is the matter with it: Have you had anything to say as to who should be President? Have you had anything to say as to who should be Governor of this State? Have you had anything to say as to whether we would go into this war? You know you have not. If this is such a great democracy, for Heaven's sake why should we not vote on conscription of men? We were stampeded into this war by newspaper rot to pull England's chestnuts out of the fire for her. I tell you if they conscripted wealth like they have conscripted men, this war would not last over forty-eight hours.[101]

In answer to Gilbert's objection that Minnesota had invaded a field within the exclusive domain of Congress, Justice McKenna replied for the majority that each member of the Union had the power of cooperation against the enemies of all. As for the contention that the statute interfered with freedom to discuss governmental functions, the *Schenck* and other cases were cited to show that that right could be limited. McKenna no doubt thought that he was disposing of the whole "curious spectacle" presented by the case when he declared: "The Nation was at war with Germany, armies were recruiting, and the speech was the discouragement of that." [102]

Although it is obvious that Justice Brandeis was deeply disturbed over the interference with freedom of expression, he devoted most of his dissenting opinion to showing that the Minnesota law encroached on the Federal Government's powers and functions. Yet

---

any consideration of degree but upon the entire absence of power on the part of the States to touch . . . the instrumentalities of the United States.' As exclusive power over enlistments in the Army and the Navy of the United States and the responsibility for the conduct of war is vested by the Federal Constitution in Congress, legislation by a State on this subject is necessarily void unless authorized by Congress." 254 U.S. 325, 334, at 341–42.

[101] Quoted in Chafee, *op. cit.*, pp. 289–90.
[102] 254 U.S. 325, at 333.

in stressing at the outset that it was more repressive than the Espionage Act, he only underscored that this was the more serious constitutional objection: "Unlike the Federal Espionage Act . . . it applies equally whether the United States is at peace or at war. It abridges freedom of speech and of the press, not in a particular emergency, in order to avert a clear and present danger, but under all circumstances. The restriction imposed relates to the teaching of the doctrine of pacifism and the legislature in effect prescribes it for all time." [103] Brandeis complained that the prohibition of public speaking against enlistment was so sweeping or absolute that it made no difference what the motive or purpose of the speaker was. As he said, "It applies alike to the preacher in the pulpit, the professor at the university, the speaker at a political meeting, the lecturer at a society or club gathering." He regarded the provision forbidding the teaching of opposition to war to be even more obnoxious: "Thus the statute invades the privacy and freedom of the home. Father and mother may not follow the promptings of religious belief, of conscience or of conviction, and teach son or daughter the doctrine of pacifism." [104] But his fundamental criticism of the Minnesota law was that by curtailing freedom of speech and assembly, it interfered with rights essential to effective citizen participation in public affairs. The passage in which Justice Brandeis says this is one of the most graceful and eloquent to come from his pen:

Full and free exercise of this right [the right of the people to assemble for the purpose of petitioning the Government for redress of grievances] by the citizen is ordinarily also his duty; for its exercise is more important to the Nation than it is to himself. Like the course of the heavenly bodies, harmony in national life is a resultant of the struggle between contending forces. In frank expression of conflicting opinion lies the greatest promise of wisdom in governmental action; and in suppression lies ordinarily the greatest peril. There are times when those charged with the responsibility of Government, faced with clear and present danger, may conclude that suppression of divergent opinion is imperative; because

[103] *Ibid.*, at 334.   [104] *Ibid.*, at 335–36.

the emergency does not permit reliance upon slower conquest of error by truth. And in such emergencies the power to suppress exists.[105]

Whether intentionally or not, in the statement just quoted Brandeis was making a significant extension of the test of clear and present danger. In the war-time free speech cases, the formula was a limitation on the enforcement of legislation—a restriction upon the executive and administrative officers. Brandeis' dissent in the *Gilbert* case, on the other hand, leaves little room for doubting that he for one was prepared to employ "clear and present danger" as a test of the constitutional limits of legislative policy itself. His opinion is important for another reason. He used the occasion to urge that it was time that freedom of speech were made part of the "liberty" guaranteed by the Fourteenth Amendment against abridgment by the States:

As the Minnesota statute is in my opinion invalid because it interferes with federal functions and with the right of a citizen of the United States to discuss them, I see no occasion to consider whether it violates also the Fourteenth Amendment. But I have difficulty in believing that the liberty guaranteed by the Constitution, which has been held to protect against state denial the right of an employer to discriminate against a workman because he is a member of a trade union, . . . the right of a business man to conduct a private employment agency, . . . or to contract outside the State for insurance of his property, . . . although the Legislature deems it inimical to the public welfare, does not include liberty to teach, either in the privacy of the home or publicly, the doctrine of pacifism; so long, at least, as Congress has not declared that the public safety demands its suppression. I cannot believe that the liberty guaranteed by the Fourteenth Amendment includes only liberty to acquire and to enjoy property.[106]

V

From this survey of the war-time free speech cases, it should be apparent that Holmes' celebrated concept of clear and present

[105] *Ibid.*, at 338.
[106] *Ibid.*, at 343. When Chief Justice Warren recently led the Court in holding Pennsylvania's Sedition Act to have been "superseded" by the Smith Act, he sought to distinguish the *Gilbert* decision. See Pennsylvania v. Nelson, 350 U.S. 497 (1956).

danger did not emerge as possessing any clear-cut meaning or content. Under the influence of the dissenters and the lawyers engaged in the battle to win greater protection for freedom of utterance, the test came in time to dominate the thinking about the problem. "When the small group of courageous men who fought these prosecutions [war-time Espionage Act cases] gave up the extreme position that speech was never punishable unless it was shown to have actually resulted in inciting criminal acts," Herbert Wechsler has informed us, "they seized upon Justice Holmes' formula for their next stand; and in the cases that have arisen since, the most persistent contention made in attacking limitations on freedom of speech and assembly has been couched in terms of the clear and present danger test." [107] It was to be expected that the responses of the Justices to this pressure would produce a plethora of "judicial semantics," as the verbal gyrations in the interpretation of Holmes' formula have been justly labelled.[108]

In one respect, however, the responsibility thrust upon the courts by the test of clear and present danger is characteristic of the judicial process generally. Regardless of the subject matter of the litigation or the criteria employed, the construction of constitutional provisions requires the Supreme Court to weigh and, if possible, to resolve conflicting interests. Faced by clashes between demands for public safety and the social interest in the search for truth, argues Professor Chafee, the Court has been greatly aided by the standard of clear and present danger as it seeks to fix "the precise point where restrictions on speech become permissible." He suggests that the test reduces itself to a quest for proof of two vital elements: "The essential features of his [Holmes'] test are (1) a substantial evil (2) closely connected with the utterance in question. As Holmes stated the test, it demands a close chronological connection—'present'." [109]

[107] Wechsler, "Symposium on Civil Liberties," 9 *Amer. Law School Rev.* 881, 882 (1941).

[108] Cushman, *op. cit.*, p. 311.

[109] Chafee, *Government and Mass Communications* (Chicago: Univ. of Chicago Press, 1947), I, 59.

Granted that it is the temporal element in the clear and present danger test which makes it a significant weapon for the protection of untrammeled speech, the recognition of this fact is only the beginning of the search for its effective use. Actually, its application involves not one but two questions. There is a difference, after all, between saying that the words used, if tolerated, may in time bring about the apprehended evil, and saying that the threat is immediate in the sense of inducing the "substantive evil" the government has a right to guard against, for example, obstruction of a national war effort. The Espionage Act cases themselves illustrate that the semantic problem was a very real one. When Holmes and Brandeis said in those cases that the acid test was whether the language used by the defendants was uttered under "circumstances" which would "create" a "clear and present danger" that the evil which it was lawful for Congress to forestall would arise, what did they mean by "circumstances"? Were they referring to the general condition of the country —an actual state of war—or the particular situation in which the forbidden words were used? To answer this question, it may be helpful to put two facets of the problem in juxtaposition. If alongside Dean Wigmore's stress upon the desperate need for men and munitions is placed Justice McKenna's insistence that the Espionage Act was passed to prevent as well as to punish the offenses it established, it becomes a little more difficult to know what constituted a "clear and present danger" during the years of the First World War. In the perspective of two decades of so-called peace and in the shadow of a new world convulsion, Professor Wechsler was able in 1940 to see a phase of the problem which has escaped many of the critics:

It is worth a moment to pause on these war time cases which reached the Supreme Court after the peace. In all of them, the challenged speech was addressed to an unquestionably immediate issue, the continuance and conduct of the war. If action was proposed in resistance to the policy of the government, it was immediate action; if there was danger that the publication would lead to unlawful resistance, it was a danger at that time; if such resistance was intended, it was intended then. Thus the clear and present danger test could have only a minimal operation to place beyond the pale of liability those statements which were patently impotent and were motivated by some other purpose than to promote obstruction of the conduct of the war.[110]

By not distinguishing clearly between these two different meanings of "circumstances," Holmes and Brandeis themselves contributed to the semantic confusion. Holmes' responsibility was the greater, since it was he who led the Court in contradictory directions. The source of the ambiguity is the *Schenck* decision itself; it is not at all clear that the "circumstance" that Schenck's circular had reached draftees was the decisive factor in the case. Holmes may have revealed, perhaps unwittingly, the really controlling consideration when he declared—"When a nation is at war many things that might be said in time of peace are such a hindrance to its effort that their utterance will not be endured so long as men fight and that no Court could regard them as protected by any constitutional right." [111]

[110] Wechsler, *op. cit.*, pp. 82–83.
[111] 249 U.S. 47, at 52.

10

"If authority is to be reconciled
with freedom"

"Paradoxical as it may seem, we are in an age of rebellion against liberty."—Robert H. Jackson [1]

* * *

I

It is in the *Gitlow* case,[2] decided in 1925, that the issue over the imminence of the "danger" stemming from the challenged words became much more clearly delineated than in any of the war-time cases. Since the disputed language called for action to implement a political creed, it is understandable why Holmes' dissent upholding the right to speak such language should have come to play so important a part in the discussion of efforts to curb extremist political views and organizations. As Justice Frankfurter has remarked, "It would be disingenuous to deny that the dissent in *Gitlow* has been treated with the respect usually accorded to a decision." [3]

[1] Jackson, *The Supreme Court in the American System of Government* (Cambridge: Harv. Univ. Press, 1955), p. 7.
[2] Gitlow v. New York, 268 U.S. 652, 672 (1925).
[3] Concurring in Dennis v. United States, 341 U.S. 494, 517, at 541.

Gitlow, a member of the Left Wing of the Socialist Party and later a leader of the Communist Party, was convicted in the New York courts for violating the State's Criminal Anarchy Act of 1902, which the New York Legislature had adopted following the assassination of President McKinley. It defined criminal anarchy as the "doctrine that organized government should be overthrown by force or violence . . . or by any unlawful means" and made the advocacy of such a doctrine either in print or by word of mouth punishable as a felony. Gitlow and three other defendants were charged with having written a pamphlet called "the Left Wing Manifesto" and with having printed and distributed it in the paper *The Revolutionary Age.* The Manifesto first spoke of some recent revolutionary struggles: "Strikes are developing which verge on revolutionary action, and in which the suggestion of proletarian dictatorship is apparent, the strike-workers trying to usurp functions of municipal government as in Seattle and in Winnipeg. The mass struggle of the proletariat is coming into being." It then called for destruction of the bourgeois parliamentary state by "mass strikes," "mass action" and "expropriation of the bourgeoisie" and establishment of "the dictatorship of the proletariat."

Justice Sanford wrote the Supreme Court's opinion which affirmed Gitlow's conviction, and only Justices Holmes and Brandeis dissented. The chief issue on which the Court divided is suggested by Sanford's summary of the principal argument against application of the Criminal Anarchy Act to what Gitlow said and did. "The sole contention," Sanford stated, "is essentially, that as there was no evidence of any concrete result flowing from publication of the Manifesto or of circumstances showing the likelihood of such result, the statute as construed and applied by the trial court penalizes the mere utterance, as such, of 'doctrine' having no quality of incitement, without regard either to the circumstances of its utterance or to the likelihood of unlawful sequences." Over and over again, Sanford tried to show that Gitlow was not convicted for the ideas or "doctrine" he advocated:

The statute does not penalize the utterance or publication of abstract "doctrine" or academic discussion having no quality of incitement to any concrete action. It is not aimed against mere historical or philosophical essays. It does not restrain the advocacy of changes in the form of government by constitutional and lawful means. What it prohibits is language advocating, advising or teaching the overthrow of organized government by unlawful means. . . . It is not the abstract "doctrine" of over-throwing organized government by unlawful means which is denounced by the statute, but the advocacy of action for the accomplishment of that purpose.[4]

Evidently by way of proving that the conviction was due to the action called for by the Manifesto and not to the principles it urged, Sanford quoted the two sentences with which the Manifesto concluded: "The proletarian revolution and the Communist reconstruction of society—the struggle for these—is now indispensable. . . . The Communist International calls the proletariat of the world to the final struggle." Was this exhortation a "call to action," as Sanford characterized it, or a restatement of traditional Marxist-Leninist ideology? To a majority of the Court, it was a dangerous invitation to immediate action. After quoting the final sentences from the Left Wing Manifesto, Sanford declared: "This is not the expression of philosophical abstraction, the mere prediction of future events; it is the language of direct incitement."[5] And later he added:

That utterances inciting to the overthrow of organized government by unlawful means, present a sufficient danger of substantive evil to bring their punishment within the range of legislative discretion, is clear. Such utterances, by their very nature, involve danger to the public peace and to the security of the State. They threaten breaches of the peace and ultimate revolution. And the immediate danger is none the less real and substantial, because the effect of a given utterance cannot be accurately foreseen. The State cannot reasonably be required to measure the danger from every such utterance in the nice balance of a jeweler's scale. A single revolutionary spark may kindle a fire that, smouldering for a time, may burst into a sweeping and destructive conflagration. It cannot be said that

[4] 268 U.S. 652, at 664–65.
[5] *Ibid.,* at 665.

the State is acting arbitrarily or unreasonably when in the exercise of its judgment as to the measures necessary to protect the public peace and safety, it seeks to extinguish the spark without waiting until it has en-kindled the flame or blazed into the conflagration. It cannot reasonably be required to defer the adoption of measures for its own peace and safety until the revolutionary utterances lead to actual disturbances of the public peace or imminent and immediate danger of its own destruc-tion; but it may, in the exercise of its judgment, suppress the threatened danger in its incipiency.[6]

Paraphrasing Cardozo's well known stricture on the exaggeration of similes—"Historians may find hyperbole in the sanguinary simile"[7]—it may be said that in the *Gitlow* case the Supreme Court disposed of an important constitutional issue on the basis of an incendiary simile. Holmes' retort to the talk of "incitement" was simply that "every idea is an incitement." But his fundamental quarrel with the majority can be deduced from his assertion that Gitlow's Left Wing Manifesto "had no chance of starting a present conflagration." In his view, the Court's decision failed to meet the test of clear and present danger. After quoting his own words from the *Schenck* case, he admits that the criterion he there formu-lated was departed from in the *Abrams* case, but adds, "the con-victions I express in that case are too deep for it to be possible for me as yet to believe that it and *Schaefer v. United States . . .* have settled the law."[8] If his test were applied correctly, he maintained, it would be obvious that Gitlow's pamphlet said things which looked to "some indefinite time in the future" and did not urge immediate destruction of the government. He saw "no present danger of an at-tempt to overthrow the government by force on the part of the admittedly small minority who shared the defendant's views."

[6] *Ibid.*, at 669.

[7] Dissenting in Jones v. Securities & Exchange Commission, 298 U.S. 1, 29, at 33 (1936). This comment was in the nature of a rejoinder to the remarks by Sutherland, in his opinion for the Court, in which he had likened the conduct of the Commission to "those intolerable abuses of the Star Chamber, which brought that institution to an end at the hands of the Long Parliament in 1640." *Ibid.*, at 28.

[8] 268 U.S. 652, 672, at 673.

Holmes rejected Sanford's easy assimilation of revolutionary speech into revolutionary action and expressed the belief that "the only meaning of free speech" is that even the advocacy of "proletarian dictatorship" must be tolerated. He wrote:

It is said that this manifesto was more than a theory, that it was an incitement. Every idea is an incitement. It offers itself for belief and if believed it is acted on unless some other belief outweighs it or some failure of energy stifles the movement at its birth. The only difference between the expression of an opinion and an incitement in the narrower sense is the speaker's enthusiasm for the result. Eloquence may set fire to reason. But whatever may be thought of the redundant discourse before us it had no chance of starting a present conflagration. If in the long run the beliefs expressed in proletarian dictatorship are destined to be accepted by the dominant forces of the community, the only meaning of free speech is that they should be given their chance and have their way.[9]

Perhaps without realizing it, Holmes added a new element to the measure of clear and present danger—an "attempt" to bring about the evil apprehended. For he ended his opinion by saying:

If the publication of this document had been laid as an attempt to induce an uprising against government at once and not at some indefinite time in the future it would have presented a different question. The object would have been one with which the law might deal, subject to the doubt whether there was any danger that the publication could produce any result, or in other words, whether it was not futile and too remote from possible consequences. But the indictment alleges the publication and nothing more.[10]

This more sharply focused concern over the imminence of the threat is no doubt explained in part by the fact that unlike the utterances involved in the war-time cases, the post-war attempts at suppression were by and large unrelated to any general situation of immediate danger in which the country could be said to find itself. As it became clearer that what was really at stake was the airing of political and economic theories, the picture of conflicting values became less blurred. The dissenters were able to speak of

[9] Ibid.
[10] Ibid.

"clear and present danger" with somewhat greater precision. Thus the opinion of Justice Brandeis in the *Whitney* case,[11] in 1927, was almost entirely given over to a definition of "imminence" under the test. Yet the fact that he did not actually dissent would indicate that not even in the *Whitney* case is his criticism of the Court's use of the test altogether free of ambiguity. It was apparently too late to challenge on appeal the testimony which tended to show that the actions of the Communist Labor Party would further the plan of the Industrial Workers of the World to commit "present" serious crimes. "Because we may not inquire into the errors now alleged, I concur in affirming the judgment of the state court." [12]

Nevertheless, Brandeis wrote a long opinion, in which Justice Holmes joined, undertaking to demonstrate that if the criterion of clear and present danger were correctly applied, Anita Whitney's conduct would have to be viewed as entirely lawful. The late Anita Whitney—described by Professor Chafee as "a woman nearing sixty, a Wellesley graduate long distinguished in philanthropic work" [13]— was convicted under California's Criminal Syndicalism Act of 1919 for helping to organize the Communist Labor Party in the State. Obviously aimed at the activities of the I.W.W., this law made it a felony to organize or knowingly become a member of an organization formed to advocate the commission of crime, sabotage, or acts of violence as a means of bringing about industrial or political change. Again Justice Sanford spoke for the court, summing up the decision in these words: "We cannot hold that, as here applied, the Act is an unreasonable or arbitrary exercise of the police power of the State, unwarrantably infringing any right of free speech, assembly or association, or that those persons are protected from punishment by the due process clause who abuse such rights by joining and furthering an organization thus menacing the peace and welfare of the State." [14]

[11] Whitney v. California, 274 U.S. 357, 372 (1927).
[12] *Ibid.*, at 380.
[13] Chafee, *Free Speech in the United States*, p. 343.
[14] 274 U.S. 357, at 372.

Justice Brandeis came to grips immediately with a basic issue raised by Sanford in the *Gitlow* case but there ignored by Holmes. On the question of the constitutionality of the New York Criminal Anarchy Act, Sanford's opinion in the *Gitlow* case held that it was the legislature which had "determined" that the mere advocacy of the overthrow of government constituted a danger, and that this "determination" was a reasonable exercise of the State's police power. "By enacting the present statute," Sanford had written, "the State has determined, through its legislative body, that utterances advocating the overthrow of organized government by force, violence and unlawful means, are so inimical to the general welfare and involve such danger of substantive evil that they may be penalized in the exercise of its police power. That determination must be given great weight. Every presumption is to be indulged in favor of the validity of the statute." [15] As has been seen, this was also the majority position in the *Whitney* case.

Brandeis' view, on the other hand, was that the constitutional safeguards of freedom of speech limit the legislature's power to determine when free speech may be curtailed. His *Whitney* opinion is quite unequivocal on this point:

It is said to be the function of the legislature to determine whether at a particular time and under the particular circumstances the formation of, or assembly with, a society organized to advocate criminal syndicalism constitutes a clear and present danger of substantive evil; and that by enacting the law here in question the legislature of California determined that question in the affirmative. . . . The legislature must obviously decide, in the first instance, whether a danger exists which calls for a particular protective measure. But where a statute is valid only in case certain conditions exist, the enactment of the statute cannot alone establish the facts which are essential to its validity. Prohibitory legislation has repeatedly been held invalid, because unnecessary, where the denial of liberty involved was that of engaging in a particular business. The power of the courts to strike down an offending law is no less when the interests involved are not property rights, but the fundamental personal rights of free speech and assembly.[16]

[15] 268 U.S. 652, at 668.   [16] 274 U.S. 357, 372, at 374.

From the very start of his unusually eloquent opinion, Justice Brandeis made it emphatically clear that to him the vital issue in the case concerned the imminence of the danger to interests the State of California had a constitutional right to protect. He began by contrasting the Criminal Syndicalism Act with other criminal conspiracy laws and suggested that there must be more than mere "advocacy" before suppression can be justified:

Thus the accused is to be punished, not for contempt, incitement or conspiracy, but for a step in preparation, which, if it threatens the public order at all, does so only remotely. The novelty in the prohibition introduced is that the statute aims, not at the practice of criminal syndicalism, nor even directly at the preaching of it, but at association with those who propose to preach it.[17]

He agreed that while the rights of free speech and assembly were "fundamental" they were not "absolute." But he argued that if what he called the test of "clear and imminent danger" were properly applied, these rights would not be curtailed unless the restriction were required to protect the state from "destruction or from serious injury, political, economic, or moral."

There is strong indication that Brandeis was led to file his concurring yet dissenting opinion because of the Court's failure to clarify the meaning of the test. "This Court has not yet fixed the standard by which to determine when a danger shall be deemed clear; how remote the danger may be and yet be deemed present; and what degree of evil shall be deemed sufficiently substantial to justify resort to abridgment of free speech. and assembly as the means of protection." Brandeis' attempt to define the standard for assessing the degree and imminence of the threat to established institutions shows that the evidence of peril he demanded would have to be very persuasive indeed:

To justify suppression of free speech there must be reasonable ground to fear that serious evil will result if free speech is practiced. There must be reasonable ground to believe that the danger apprehended is imminent.

[17] *Ibid.*, at 373.

There must be reasonable ground to believe that the evil to be prevented is a serious one. . . . But even advocacy of violation, however reprehensible morally, is not a justification for denying free speech where the advocacy falls short of incitement and there is nothing to indicate that the advocacy would be immediately acted on. The wide difference between advocacy and incitement, between preparation and attempt, between assembling and conspiracy, must be borne in mind. In order to support a finding of clear and present danger it must be shown either that immediate serious violence was to be expected or was advocated, or that the past conduct furnished reason to believe that such advocacy was then contemplated.[18]

Nor would Brandeis confine the defendant to a mere refutation of the incriminating evidence. A defendant was entitled to introduce facts to attack the whole definition of "danger" embodied in the statute itself. "Whenever the fundamental rights of free speech and assembly are alleged to have been invaded," the Justice wrote, "it must remain open to a defendant to present the issue whether there actually did exist at the time a clear danger, whether the danger, if any, was imminent; and whether the evil apprehended was one so substantial as to justify the stringent restriction interposed by the legislature." [19]

But even if Brandeis had not essayed so searching an examination of the meaning of "clear and present danger," his opinion would have been notable for another reason. In it is to be found one of the most moving expositions of America's heritage of freedom. The passages in which he states his libertarian creed do indeed reveal him to be, in Professor Chafee's phrase, one of the "strongest conservators of Americanism." [20] Particularly striking is the paragraph in which he links his own conception of the standard of clear and present danger with the faith and fortitude of the generation that fought the American Revolution:

Those who won our independence by revolution were not cowards. They did not fear political change. They did not exalt order at the cost

[18] *Ibid.*, at 376. [19] *Ibid.*, at 378–79.
[20] Chafee, *op. cit.*, p. 348.

of liberty. To courageous, self-reliant men, with confidence in the power of free and fearless reasoning applied through the processes of popular government, no danger flowing from speech can be deemed clear and present, unless the incidence of the evil apprehended is so imminent that it may befall before there is opportunity for full discussion. If there be time to expose through discussion the falsehood and fallacies, to avert the evil by the processes of education, the remedy to be applied is more speech, not enforced silence. Only an emergency can justify repression. Such must be the rule if authority is to be reconciled with freedom. Such, in my opinion, is the command of the Constitution. It is therefore always open to Americans to challenge a law abridging free speech and assembly by showing that there was no emergency justifying it.[21]

II

It is this clear-cut recognition of the right to challenge the legislature's appraisal of public danger which, in the view of Mark DeWolfe Howe, demonstrates the extent to which Brandeis elaborated Holmes' formula. In a critical review of Professor Chafee's 1941 revision of his now classic work on freedom of speech,[22] Professor Howe has written:

When Professor Chafee wrote in 1920 there was no necessity for him to consider the meaning of that portion of the Holmes formula which referred to "the substantive evils that Congress had a right to prevent." The evils then feared were of the traditional sort which I have mentioned—violence, sedition, and obstruction of the draft. Both Holmes and Professor Chafee were quite appropriately concerned to show the frequent absurdity of the pretension that the imminence of those evils was substantially increased by the words of the wartime defendants. In 1927 Justice Brandeis looked beyond the question of fact as to the propinquity of danger to the question of law as to the quality of the preventible evil.[23]

Professor Howe chided Professor Chafee for failing to deal adequately with the implications of Justice Brandeis' approach, espe-

---

[21] 274 U.S. 357, 372, at 377.
[22] Chafee, *Freedom of Speech* (New York: Harcourt, Brace & Company, 1920).
[23] Howe, Book Review: 55 *Harv. L. Rev.* 695, 698 (1942).

cially as revealed by the Roosevelt Court's attitude in the decisions protecting picketing and the distribution of leaflets under the free speech guarantees. He added:

> In those decisions Brandeis's suggestion has suddenly borne fruit. It has become evident that the present majority is not satisfied to have a defendant's rights depend entirely on a jury's quite probably biased finding of fact that the evil feared by the legislature had sufficient clarity and sufficient proximity to justify the imposition of the threatened penalty. A question of law must also be considered: was the immediate evil thus found by the jury to exist of a serious or a trivial sort? The littering of streets is an evil, and interference with free access to an employer's place of business is an evil, but neither is sufficient, though it be clear and present, to warrant the suppression of handbills or the banning of pickets.[24]

These criticisms help to point up an issue in both the *Gitlow* and *Whitney* cases which has continued to perplex and divide the Court and the disciples of the Holmes-Brandeis brand of judicial liberalism. Strictly speaking, the decisions in these two cases held that the state laws forbidding the "advocacy" of the overthrow of government had been enacted in the reasonable exercise of the police power, and that the legislature's judgment was entitled to respect unless shown to be capricious. For the liberals, the invocation of constitutional presumption raised a most difficult and embarrassing dilemma. Holmes, the Court's chief exponent of deference to the legislative choice in matters of economic regulation, did not bother to answer Sanford on the matter in the *Gitlow* case. The source and nature of the dilemma has been sketched by Professor Cushman in a few simple sentences:

> . . . by the nineteen-twenties the American judicial mind, and especially that of the Supreme Court, had been fully won over to the doctrine that legislative exercises of the police power must be presumed by the courts to be valid, and should be upheld as long as the question of their validity is reasonably debatable. Mr. Justice Holmes had devoted a lifetime of effort to the accomplishment of this bit of judicial education, and it was

[24] *Ibid.*

no small achievement. In the numerous cases in which the police power had been used to promote social and economic progress the doctrine had the wholesome effect of restraining judges from substituting their own social and economic opinions for those of the legislature. The doctrine came to be associated with Holmes' name, and was widely heralded as an important asset of liberalism.[25]

But of course, the canon of constitutional presumption did not always have the "wholesome effect" of which Professor Cushman speaks. The fact is that the doctrine was something of a double-edged sword, a convenient and flexible bit of verbalization, used by both liberals and conservatives as the strategy of the occasion dictated. The late Harry Shulman once demonstrated—after examining the opinions in two significant cases decided at the same term of Court, a free speech case and one concerned with economic regulation—that "Every member of the Court changed his attitude, shifting from one rule of presumption in the one case to an opposite rule of presumption in the other." [26] Both liberals and conservatives have

[25] Cushman, " 'Clear and Present Danger' in Free Speech Cases: A Study in Judicial Semantics," in Konvitz & Murphy (eds.), *Essays in Political Theory,* p. 321.

[26] Shulman, "The Supreme Court's attitude toward Liberty of Contract and Freedom of Speech," *41 Yale L. J. 262* (1931); reprinted in 2 *Selected Essays 1098, 1101.* With the concurrence of Hughes, Holmes, Stone and Roberts, Justice Brandeis spoke for the Court (in a very short opinion) in upholding a New Jersey statute prohibiting insurance companies from paying to local agents commissions in excess of those paid to other local agents. Starting with the assumption that the power to annul legislation was to be exercised only in the "clearest" cases, Brandeis concluded that since it did not "appear upon the face of the statute, or from any facts of which the Court must take judicial notice" that evils "did not exist" for which the statute was "an appropriate remedy," the "presumption of constitutionality" governed the case. O'Gorman v. Hartford Ins. Co., 282 U.S. 251, 258, at 257–58 (1931). Van Devanter, McReynolds, Sutherland and Butler dissented in a joint opinion. Invoking the principle of the *Adkins* case that "freedom of contract is the general rule, restraint the exception," they argued that the statute was unconstitutional because no grounds had been presented to justify the exception it embodied.

Five months later came Near v. Minnesota, 283 U.S. 697, 723 (1931). In this case, the same majority of five struck down a Minnesota law authorizing injunctions restraining the continued publication of newspapers which had printed "malicious, scandalous and defamatory matters." For himself and his fellow dissenters in the *O'Gorman* case, Justice Butler contended that the

taken refuge in this essentially "opportunistic" formula which, in
the blunt words of Judge Learned Hand, has served them as a
"facile opportunity to enforce their will." [27]

On the so-called pre-Roosevelt Court, it was the conservatives
who ignored the claims of presumption in opposing legislative
policies limiting the freedom of action of the property owner. These
decisions frequently evoked stern dissents evincing high regard for
the prerogatives of the people's representatives. In many a case
concerned with governmental restrictions upon personal rights
other than property, however, the liberals remained silent on the
deference owed to the legislative process and the conservatives
posed as champions of constitutional presumption. After 1937, some
of the Justices began to take note of this "latent equivocation," as
the contradiction has been termed by Judge Learned Hand.[28]

Justice Stone, whose now classic rebuke to his more conservative
colleagues—"the only check upon our exercise of power is our
own sense of self-restraint" [29]—came to be hailed as a veritable
epitome of judicial humility, soon enunciated a dictum furnish-

---

Minnesota law had been enacted "in the exertion of the State's power of police"
and that the Supreme Court "by well established rule" must assume "until the
contrary is clearly made to appear, that there exists in Minnesota a state of
affairs that justifies the preservation of the peace and good order of the State."
(At 731). The dissenters cited the *O'Gorman* decision as precedent for their
view of the presumption of the validity of the Minnesota statute. The contrary
position of the majority, as presented by Chief Justice Hughes, was that in
view of the fundamental importance of the immunity of the press from previous
restraint "when dealing with official misconduct," the particular abuse of this
freedom was not great enough to justify interference by the legislature. Near's
defamatory accusations against public officials "unquestionably create a public
scandal, but the theory of the constitutional guaranty is that even a more
serious public evil would be caused by authority to prevent publication."
(At 722.)

[27] Hand, "Chief Justice Stone's Conception of the Judicial Function," *46 Col.
L. Rev. 696, 697* (1946).

[28] *Ibid.*

[29] "While unconstitutional exercise of power by the executive and legislative
branches of the government is subject to judicial restraint, the only check upon
our exercise of power is our own sense of self-restraint." Stone, J., dissenting in
United States v. Butler, 297 U.S. 1, 78, at 79 (1936).

ing a most appealing reason for the expansion of the power of judges. Two years later he ventured to suggest, even if ever so cautiously, that there might be "narrower scope for operation of the presumption of constitutionality" in cases involving laws restrictive of the personal freedoms guaranteed by the first ten amendments.[30] Legislation regulating "ordinary commercial transactions" was to be assumed to be constitutional unless it could not be shown that it rested "upon some rational basis within the knowledge and experience of the legislators." Stone contemplated the possibility that laws hampering "those political processes which can ordinarily be expected to bring about repeal of undesirable legislation" and statutes directed against religious, national or racial minorities "may call for a . . . more searching judicial inquiry." He made the distinction more explicit when, in his lone dissent in the first flag-salute case, he urged his colleagues to protect a politically helpless religious sect against the demands of the "popular will." [31]

Justice Frankfurter has been the Court's leading critic of the tendency to make judicial respect for legislative authority depend upon the character of the constitutional right alleged to be infringed. His dissent against the Court's action overruling the flag-salute decision, only three years later, was an eloquent and forceful plea for "judicial self-restraint" and for consistency in the application of the constitutional standard of reasonableness.[32] "The Constitution does not give us greater veto power when dealing with one phase of 'liberty' than with another," he declared.[33] Regardless of the regulation under attack, the only inquiry proper for judges is "whether legislators could in reason have enacted such a law." [34]

But ever since the rift among the Roosevelt-appointed Justices became visible, it has been apparent that some of them favored spe-

[30] United States v. Carolene Products Co., 304 U.S. 144, 152–53, n. 4 (1938).
[31] Minersville School District v. Gobitis, 310 U.S. 586, 601, at 606 (1940).
[32] West Virginia State Board of Education v. Barnette, 319 U.S. 624, 646, at 648 (1943).
[33] *Ibid.*
[34] *Ibid.*, at 647.

cial guardianship for the freedoms of the First Amendment. The "crusading conception of the judicial function" in behalf of civil liberty manifested by Justices Black, Douglas, Murphy and Rutledge—the four "libertarian activists," as Professor Pritchett calls them [35]—made it entirely logical, if not inevitable, for them to seize upon the implications of Stone's famous footnote in the *Carolene Products Company* case. In 1944, the vote of Justice Jackson gave them a majority for an opinion which rationalized the emerging doctrine of the presumed invalidity of legislation interfering with civil liberties. It announced the principle that the four freedoms of the First Amendment occupied a "preferred place" under the American constitutional system. Dissenting were Justices Roberts, Reed and Frankfurter and, surprisingly enough, also Chief Justice Stone. The case was Thomas v. Collins,[36] and the issue was one peculiarly capable of being resolved by the use of presumption. It was concerned with a Texas statute requiring the registration of union organizers, the Supreme Court of Texas having sustained it as an exercise of the State's police power for the protection of workers against impostors. R. J. Thomas, then President of the United Automobile Workers, had come to Texas to challenge the law and was cited for contempt for violating a court order not to address a meeting at which he solicited members without first registering with the appropriate authorities.

Justice Rutledge was the Court's spokesman when it reversed the conviction. His opinion stated the abortive doctrine as to the preferential treatment for civil rights in unequivocal terms:

The case confronts us again with the duty our system places on this Court to say where the individual's freedom ends and the State's power begins. Choice on that border, now as always delicate, is perhaps more so where the usual presumption supporting legislation is balanced by the

[35] C. Herman Pritchett, "Libertarian Motivations on the Vinson Court," *47 Amer. Pol. Sci. Rev. 321,* 325 (June, 1953). For Professor Pritchett's more elaborate discussion of recent trends, see his *Civil Liberties and The Vinson Court* (Chicago: Univ. of Chicago Press, 1954), especially chs. X–XII.

[36] 323 U.S. 516, 548 (1944).

preferred place given in our scheme to the great, the indispensable democratic freedoms secured by the First Amendment. . . . That priority
gives these liberties a sanctity and a sanction not permitting dubious
intrusions. And it is the character of the right, not of the limitation, which
determines what standard governs the choice. . . .

For these reasons any attempt to restrict those liberties must be justified
by clear public interest, threatened not doubtfully or remotely, but by
clear and present danger. The rational connection between the remedy
provided and the evil to be curbed, which in other contexts might support
legislation against attack on due process grounds, will not suffice. These
rights rest on firmer foundation. Accordingly, whatever occasion would
restrain orderly discussion and persuasion, at appropriate time and place,
must have clear support in public danger, actual or impending. Only
the gravest abuses, endangering paramount interests, give occasion for
permissible limitation. It is therefore in our tradition to allow the widest
room for discussion, the narrowest range for its restriction, particularly
when this right is exercised in conjunction with peaceable assembly. It
was not by accident or coincidence that the rights to freedom in speech
and press were coupled in a single guaranty with the rights of the people
peaceably to assemble and to petition for redress of grievances. All these,
though not identical, are inseparable. They are cognate rights, . . .[37]

What were the implications of the special status which Justice
Rutledge would have assigned to the first Amendment in the
hierarchy of constitutional values? Obviously, the Supreme Court's
responsibility in passing upon the validity of laws restraining freedom of expression is much greater than its ordinary duty in reviewing legislation. Laws invading the liberties secured by the First
Amendment, Rutledge emphasized, "must be justified by clear public interest, threatened not doubtfully or remotely, but by clear and
present danger." More explicit still as to the import for the judicial
function is the insistence of Justice Douglas, in dissent, that "even
a reasonable regulation of the right to free speech is not compatible
with the First Amendment." [38] In effect, "liberty of the mind" [39]—to

[37] *Ibid.,* at 529–30.
[38] Poulos v. New Hampshire, 345 U.S. 395, 422, at 425 (1953).
[39] Palko v. Connecticut, 302 U.S. 319, at 327 (1937). In essence, the preferred-position thesis is but an extension of the "rationalizing principle" which
Justice Cardozo saw as the basis of the Supreme Court's "absorption" into the

use Justice Cardozo's catch-all phrase for the four freedoms of the First Amendment—is the "rule" of a free society, and the burden of proving the need for curtailment of that liberty was cast upon those defending exceptions to the rule. Thus the attitude once exhibited by the conservatives toward the "sanctity" of freedom of contract was now to be applied to freedom of expression. As a practical matter, the high regard for free speech would give courts a legal as well as a moral justification for substituting their judgment for that of the other branches of the government in determining when conditions warrant limitations on the rights protected by the First Amendment. The late Justice Frank Murphy probably penned his own epitaph as a fervent defender of human rights when he observed midway in his tenure on the Court: "The law knows no finer hour than when it cuts through formal concepts and transitory emotions to protect unpopular citizens against discrimination and persecution." [40]

At no time, however, has the philosophy of preference for certain constitutional rights commanded the support of the full Court. Indeed, the record confirms Justice Frankfurter's claim that the "preferred-position" theory "never commended itself to a majority of this Court." [41] The Justice regards the phrase as a "mischievous"

"liberty" of the Fourteenth Amendment (and therefore restraining the States) of some of the rights guaranteed by the Bill of Rights against abridgment by Congress. As he put it: "We reach a different plane of social and moral values when we pass to the privileges and immunities that have been taken over from the earlier articles of the federal bill of rights and brought within the Fourteenth Amendment by a process of absorption. These in their origin were effective against the Federal Government alone. If the Fourteenth Amendment has absorbed them, the process of absorption has had its source in the belief that neither liberty nor justice would exist if they were sacrificed. . . . This is true, for illustration, of freedom of thought, and speech. Of that freedom one may say that it is the matrix, the indispensable condition, of nearly every other form of freedom. . . . So it has come about that the domain of liberty, withdrawn by the Fourteenth Amendment from encroachment by the States, has been enlarged by latter-day judgments to include liberty of the mind as well as liberty of action." 302 U.S. 319, at 326–27.

[40] Dissenting in Falbo v. United States, 320 U.S., 549, 555, at 561 (1944).

[41] Kovacs v. Cooper, 336 U.S. 77, 89, at 95 (1949). Justice Frankfurter's concurring opinion in this case contains a full chronological account of the history of the preferred position doctrine. (At pp. 90–94.)

one and primarily because "it carries the thought, which it may subtly imply, that any law touching communication is injected with presumptive invalidity." [42]

Justice Jackson's vote for reversal in *Thomas v. Collins* apparently did not signify acceptance of the doctrine, as he himself later revealed. "We cannot give some constitutional rights a preferred position," he said in 1949, "without relegating others to a deferred position; we can establish no firsts without thereby establishing seconds." [43] For Jackson, this logic represented repudiation of views he had expressed earlier, both before and after coming to the Court. In the book which he wrote just before being named to the Supreme Court in 1941, the future Justice gave his blessing to a tendency he had observed on the recently reconstituted Court:

There is nothing covert or conflicting in the recent judgments of the Court on social legislation and on legislative repressions of civil rights. The presumption of validity which attaches in general to legislative acts is frankly reversed in the case of interferences with free speech and free assembly, and for a perfectly cogent reason. Ordinarily, legislation whose basis in economic wisdom is uncertain can be redressed by the processes of the ballot box or the pressures of opinion. But when the channels of opinion and of peaceful persuasion are corrupted or clogged, these political correctives can no longer be relied on, and the democratic system is threatened at its most vital point. In that event the Court, by intervening, restores the processes of democratic government; it does not disrupt them.[44]

Two years later, in his opinion for the Court in the second flag salute case, Justice Jackson was even more specific, this time stating his position in constitutional rather than philosophic terms. He wrote:

The right of a State to regulate, for example, a public utility may well include, so far as the due process test is concerned, power to impose all of the restrictions which a legislature may have a "rational basis" for adopting. But the freedoms of speech and press, of assembly, and of

[42] *Ibid.*, at 90.
[43] Dissenting in Brinegar v. United States, 338 U.S. 160, 180 (1949).
[44] Jackson, *The Struggle for Judicial Supremacy*, pp. 284–85.

worship may not be infringed on such slender grounds. They are susceptible of restriction only to prevent grave and immediate danger to interests which the State may lawfully protect.[45]

III

The continuing controversy over the respect to be accorded to the legislative will as embodied in laws impinging upon freedom of discussion erupted into something of a "full-dress" debate when the Supreme Court affirmed the convictions of the leaders of the Communist Party in 1951.[46] It is in the long and scholarly opinion of Justice Frankfurter that the issue is faced most explicitly. As he put it, "Who is to make the adjustment?—who is to balance the relevant factors and ascertain which interest [free speech or national security] is in the circumstances to prevail?" [47] But Chief Justice Vinson's opinion announcing the judgment of the Court, the concurring opinion of Justice Jackson and the dissents by Justices Black and Douglas —all show that the relative competence of courts and legislatures in assessing threats to national security was a major problem dividing the jurists.

This dispute is particularly significant for the future of the Holmes-Brandeis concept of clear and present danger as a test of the constitutional limits of checks on political freedom. According to one chronicler of the Supreme Court's labors, the outcome in the *Dennis* case seems to mark the famous formula for the discard. "Whether the clear and present danger doctrine will survive much longer under the crushing weight of the Chief Justice's loving devotion," writes David Fellman, "remains to be seen, but the question

[45] West Virginia State Board of Education v. Barnette, 319 U.S. 624, at 639 (1943).

[46] Dennis v. United States, 341 U.S. 494, 517, 561, 579, 581 (1951). Justices Rutledge and Murphy were no longer on the Court, the vacancies caused by their deaths having been filled by President Truman with the appointment of Sherman Minton and Tom C. Clark. However, Justice Clark, who was attorney general when the defendants were indicted, did not participate in the *Dennis* case.

[47] *Ibid.*, 517, at 525 (concurring opinion).

is fairly debatable." [48] Another political scientist has concluded that the net effect of Chief Justice Vinson's approval of Judge Learned Hand's substitution of "probable" for "present" is to "reject time as a determinate factor in the equation" and therefore to "undermine the central premise of the clear and present danger principle." [49] Summarizing the consensus of the views of the legal commentators, John P. Frank has noted that few of them "are persuaded that there is really much resemblance between the Holmes-Brandeis position . . . and the Vinson doctrine." [50]

Vinson did not shrink from the necessity of discussing the meaning of "clear and present danger." On the contrary, he handled the issue with considerable relish, as indeed he had the previous year in his opinion upholding the non-Communist provisions of the Taft-Hartley Act.[51] "In this case," his *Dennis* opinion declares, "we are squarely presented with the application of the 'clear and present danger' test, and must decide what that phrase imports." The Chief Justice also acknowledged that "Although no case subsequent to *Whitney* and *Gitlow* has expressly overruled the majority opinions in those cases, there is little doubt that subsequent opinions have inclined toward the Holmes-Brandeis rationale." [52] Vinson spoke as a believer in the Holmes-Brandeis tradition; yet the irony of his position in the *Dennis* case is that by the time he was through with his labor of exegesis, it was clear that the doctrine had been deprived of much of its original vitality and significance, especially as contemplated by Justice Brandeis. But then the disciple also exclaimed: "To those who would paralyze our Government in the face of impending threat by encasing it in a semantic straitjacket we must reply that all concepts are relative." [53]

[48] Fellman, "Constitutional Law in 1950–51," *XLVI Amer. Pol. Sci. Rev. 158, 162* (March, 1952).
[49] Robert G. McCloskey, "Free Speech, Sedition and the Constitution," *XLV Amer. Pol. Sci. Rev. 662, 668* (Sept., 1951).
[50] Frank, "Fred Vinson and the Chief Justiceship," *21 Univ. of Chicago L. Rev. 212, 216* (1954).
[51] American Communications Association v. Douds, 339 U.S. 382 (1950).
[52] 341 U.S. 494, at 507.   [53] *Ibid.,* at 508.

Justice Jackson dismissed the whole concept of clear and present danger as "a judge-made verbal trap" and Justice Frankfurter described it as a "euphemistic disguise for an unresolved conflict." [54] Not the least interesting fact about Justice Frankfurter's opinion is that he finally faced the ultimate implication of his persistent attack upon the indiscriminate use of the test. "It were far better that the phrase be abandoned," he was frank to say, "than that it be sounded once more to hide from the believers in an absolute right of free speech the plain fact that the interest in speech, profoundly important as it is, is no more conclusive in judicial review than other attributes of democracy or than a determination of the people's representatives that a measure is necessary to assure the safety of government itself." [55] Quoting from his own opinion in *Bridges v. California*,[56] Justice Black reiterated his belief that, "At least as to speech in the realm of public matters, . . . the 'clear and present danger' test does not mark the further-most constitutional boundaries of protected expression, but does 'no more than recognize a minimum compulsion of the Bill of Rights.'" [57] To Justice Douglas, Brandeis' "classic statement" of the rule in the *Whitney* case was still sound doctrine.[58]

The basic problem in the *Dennis* case was whether, notwithstanding the safeguards of the First Amendment, the Communist leaders

[54] "Few questions of comparable import have come before this Court in recent years. The appellants maintain that they have a right to advocate a political theory, so long, at least, as their advocacy does not create an immediate danger of obvious magnitude to the very existence of our present scheme of society. On the other hand, the Government asserts the right to safeguard the security of the Nation by such a measure as the Smith Act. Our judgment is thus solicited on a conflict of interests of the utmost concern to the well-being of the country. This conflict of interests cannot be resolved by a dogmatic preference for one or the other, nor by a sonorous formula which is in fact only a euphemistic disguise for an unresolved conflict. If adjudication is to be a rational process, we cannot escape a candid examination of the conflicting claims with full recognition that both are supported by weighty title-deeds." Frankfurter, J., concurring, 341 U.S. 494, 517, at 518–19.

[55] *Ibid.*, at 544.

[56] 314 U. S. 252, at 263 (1941).

[57] 341 U.S. 494, 579, at 580.

[58] *Ibid.*, at 585.

could be punished for their part in reconstituting the American Communist Party in the period between 1945 to 1948. At stake was the constitutionality of the Smith Act of 1940. As pointed out by Justice Frankfurter, the Smith Act is "nearly identical" with the New York Criminal Anarchy Act involved in the *Gitlow* case. Section 2 of the Smith Act makes it a crime to teach or advocate the overthrow of the government by force or violence and to organize any group for the purpose of teaching or advocating the destruction of government. Section 3 makes it unlawful "to attempt to commit, or to conspire to commit" the acts prohibited by Section 2.[59] The leaders of the Communist Party had been indicted for conspiring "to organize or help to organize any society, group, or assembly of persons who teach, advocate, or encourage the overthrow or destruction of any government in the United States by force or violence." On appeal, their lawyers argued that the defendants had a constitutional right to advocate their political theories, so long as such advocacy did not seriously threaten existing institutions with immediate destruction.

From the very outset of the Chief Justice's opinion, it was obvious that the effort to use the Holmes-Brandeis version of clear and present danger as a basis for winning a reversal of the convictions had failed to convince a majority of the Justices. Donning the mantle of the legal historian, Vinson undertook a chronological survey of the clear and present danger test. The entire trend of that

[59] Section 2 of the Smith Act makes it unlawful for any person "(1) to knowingly or willfully advocate, abet, advise, or teach the duty, necessity, desirability, or propriety of overthrowing or destroying any government in the United States by force or violence, or by the assassination of any officer of any such government; (2) with intent to cause the overthrow or destruction of any government in the United States, to print, publish, edit, issue, circulate, sell, distribute, or publicly display any written or printed matter advocating, advising, or teaching the duty, necessity, desirability, or propriety of overthrowing or destroying any government in the United States by force or violence; (3) to organize or help to organize any society, group, or assembly of persons who teach, advocate, or encourage the overthrow or destruction of any government in the United States by force or violence; or to be or become a member of, or affiliate with, any such society, group, or assembly of persons, knowing the purposes thereof." Quoted in 341 U.S. 494, at 496.

résumé pointed toward a new meaning of an old doctrine. Noting that it was not until Justice Holmes' "classic dictum" in the *Schenck* case that "speech *per se*" received special emphasis in a majority opinion, he called attention to the fact that the phrase "bore no connotation that the danger was to be any threat to the safety of the Republic." The "insubstantial gesture toward insubordination"— Schenck's circulation of "some" leaflets—"was held to be a clear and present danger of bringing about the evil of military insubordination." We were reminded that Holmes was the author of the unanimous opinions in the *Schenck, Frohwerk* and *Debs* cases and that Holmes and Brandeis dissented in the *Abrams, Schaefer* and *Pierce* cases over a question of evidence: "The basis of their dissents was that, because of the protection which the First Amendment gives to speech, the evidence in each case was insufficient to show that the defendants had created the requisite danger under *Schenck*. But these dissents did not mark a change of principle. The dissenters doubted only the probable effectiveness of the puny efforts toward subversion." [60] From these war-time cases, the Chief Justice deduced this rule: "Where an offense is specified by a statute in nonspeech or nonpress terms, a conviction relying upon speech or press as evidence of violation may be sustained only when the speech or publication created a 'clear and present danger' of attempting or accomplishing the prohibited crime, e.g., interference with enlistment." [61]

Turning next to the *Gitlow* decision, Vinson maintained that the majority in that case refused to apply "clear and present danger" as a test of the constitutionality of the Criminal Anarchy Act and that it treated the question raised by Gitlow's conviction as fundamentally different from the issue in the wartime cases. In the Espionage Act cases of World War I, the problem before the Court was to determine whether the evidence was sufficient to sustain the charge that the defendants had by their conduct violated a

[60] *Ibid.*, at 505.
[61] *Ibid.*

statute deemed constitutional. In the *Gitlow* case, on the other hand, the prohibited language—advocacy of the overthrow of the government—was forbidden by the statute itself, so that all the Court had to do was to decide whether the legislation was a "reasonable" exercise of the State's police power. And how did Vinson explain the fact that Holmes and Brandeis dissented in the *Gitlow* case? He wrote:

. . . there [in the *Gitlow* case] a legislature had found that a certain kind of speech was, itself, harmful and unlawful. The constitutionality of such a state statute had to be adjudged by this Court just as it determined the constitutionality of any state statute, namely, whether the statute was "reasonable." Since it was entirely reasonable for a state to attempt to protect itself from violent overthrow, the statute was perforce reasonable. . . . Justices Holmes and Brandeis refused to accept this approach, but insisted that wherever speech was the evidence of the violation, it was necessary to show that the speech created the "clear and present danger" of the substantive evil which the legislature had the right to prevent. Justices Holmes and Brandeis, then, made no distinction between a federal statute which made certain acts unlawful, the evidence to support the conviction being speech, and a statute which made speech itself the crime. . . . In their concurrence [in the *Whitney* case] they repeated that even though the legislature had designated certain speech as criminal, this could not prevent the defendant from showing that there was no danger that the substantive evil would be brought about.[62]

There is a conspicuous hiatus in the Chief Justice's analysis. Though he conceded that the Holmes-Brandeis view of clear and present danger had come to be treated by the Court as the correct view, he proceeded to accept the approach of the majority in the *Gitlow* and *Whitney* cases, but without saying so. The fact is, however, that he was not unaware of the contradiction. He went on to rationalize it by arguing that such cases as those concerned with the distribution of leaflets, peaceful picketing and the flag-salute were all instances in which the public interest to which free speech was being subordinated was "too insubstantial to warrant

[62] *Ibid.*, at 506-7.

restriction of speech." In contrast stands the vital interest in the prevention of the forcible overthrow of the government: "Overthrow of the Government by force and violence is certainly a substantial enough interest for the Government to limit speech. Indeed, this is the ultimate value of any society, for if a society cannot protect its very structure from armed internal attack, it must follow that no subordinate value can be protected." [63]

This observation brought Vinson to the question as to whether the activities of the Communist leaders which formed the basis of their indictment under the Smith Act could be said to give rise to a clear and present danger to "the substantial interest" in protecting the government from being destroyed. He answered it by adopting Judge Harold R. Medina's chief instruction to the jury and Judge Learned Hand's gloss on the meaning of clear and present danger. In his charge to the jury, Judge Medina had said: "It is not the abstract doctrine of overthrowing or destroying organized government by unlawful means which is denounced by this law, but the teaching and advocacy of action for the accomplishment of that purpose, by language reasonably and ordinarily calculated to incite persons to such action, . . . as speedily as circumstances would permit." [64] Vinson's infusion of this interpretation into the discussion of "attempt" and of the time factor is probably the most serious distortion of the Holmes test of clear and present danger, especially as it had come to be sharpened by Brandeis. The Chief Justice explained:

Obviously, the words cannot mean that before the Government may act, it must wait until the *putsch* is about to be executed, the plans have been laid and the signal is awaited. If Government is aware that a group aiming at its overthrow is attempting to indoctrinate its members and to commit them to a course whereby they will strike when the leaders feel the circumstances permit, action by the Government is required. . . . Certainly an attempt to overthrow the Government by force, even though doomed from the outset because of inadequate numbers or power

[63] *Ibid.*, at 509.
[64] United States v. Foster, 9 F.R.D. 367, at 391 (1949).

of the revolutionists, is a sufficient evil for Congress to prevent. The damage which such attempts create both physically and politically to a nation makes it impossible to measure the validity in terms of the probability of success, or the immediacy of a successful attempt.[65]

Accordingly, Judge Medina was correct in instructing the jury that they could not convict the Communist leaders unless they were satisfied that they intended to overthrow the Government "as speedily as circumstances would permit."

But perhaps the most crucial aspect of the Chief Justice's reliance on Holmes and Brandeis is his insistence that the situation with which they were concerned in the *Gitlow* case was fundamentally different from the problem in the *Dennis* case. His statement of the distinction between the two situations may be regarded as the ultimate justification for the new look given clear and present danger. "The situation with which Justices Holmes and Brandeis were concerned in *Gitlow* was a comparatively isolated event, bearing little relation in their minds to any substantial threat to the safety of the community. . . . They were not confronted with any situation comparable to the instant one—the development of an apparatus designed and dedicated to the overthrow of the Government, in the context of world crisis after crisis." [66]

Both Justices Frankfurter and Jackson shared the view that the considerations which impelled Holmes and Brandeis to dissent in the *Gitlow* case did not apply to the problem in the *Dennis* case. Justice Frankfurter put it this way:

The result of the *Gitlow* decision was to send a left-wing Socialist to jail for publishing a Manifesto expressing Marxist exhortations. It requires excessive tolerance of the legislative judgment to suppose that the *Gitlow* publication in the circumstances could justify serious concern.

In contrast, there is ample justification for a legislative judgment that the conspiracy now before us is a substantial threat to national order and security. . . .[67]

[65] 341 U.S. 494, at 509.
[66] *Ibid.*, at 510.
[67] *Ibid.*, at 541–42.

With his characteristic bluntness, Justice Jackson argued that we would be outwitted by the "Communist stratagem" if we were to try to assess the perils arising from the techniques of totalitarian parties by means of the test developed by Holmes and Brandeis for dealing with the relatively "trivial" situations with which they were concerned. "Either by accident or design," he commented, "the Communist stratagem outwits the anti-anarchist pattern of statutes aimed against 'overthrow by force and violence' if qualified by the doctrine that only 'clear and present danger' of accomplishing that result will sustain the prosecution." [68] The Justice pointed out that the "coup d'état" in Czechoslovakia proved that unlike the old-style revolutionary parties, the modern Communist parties do not rely on force and violence in coming to power. Infiltration and subversion are used to prepare the way. Justice Jackson summarized his thesis in these words: "Force would be utilized by the Communist Party not to destroy government but for its capture. The Communist recognizes that an established government in control of modern technology cannot be overthrown by force until it is about ready to fall of its own weight. Concerted uprising, therefore, is to await that contingency and revolution is seen, not as a sudden episode, but as the consummation of a long process." [69]

[68] *Ibid.*, at 567.

[69] *Ibid.*, at 565. Justice Jackson's suggested revision of the clear and present danger test is worth recalling: "I would save it, unmodified, for application as a 'rule of reason' in the kind of case for which it was devised. When the issue is criminality of a hot-headed speech on a street corner, or circulation of a few incendiary pamphlets, or parading by some zealots behind a red flag, or refusal of a handful of school children to salute our flag, it is not beyond the capacity of the judicial process to gather, comprehend, and weigh the necessary materials for decision whether it is a clear and present danger of substantive evil or a harmless letting off of steam. It is not a prophecy, for the danger in such cases has matured by the time of trial or it was never present. The test applies and has meaning where a conviction is sought to be based on a speech or writing which does not directly or explicitly advocate a crime but to which such tendency is sought to be attributed by construction or by implication from external circumstances. The formula in such cases favors freedoms that are vital to our society, and, even if sometimes applied too generously, the consequences cannot be grave. But its recent expansion has extended, in particular to Communists, unprecedented immunities. Unless we are to hold our Gov-

Chief Justice Vinson found Judge Learned Hand's interpretation of clear and present danger an entirely satisfactory criterion for appraising the conditions which justified the Government in prosecuting the leaders of the Communist Party. In his opinion for the United States Court of Appeals, affirming the convictions, Judge Hand had formulated this rule for the guidance of courts: "In each case [courts] must ask whether the gravity of the 'evil,' discounted by its improbability, justifies such invasion of free speech as is necessary to avoid the danger." [70] In answer to the question as to when the "conspiracy" with which the Communist leaders were charged became a "present danger," Judge Hand said: "The jury has found that the conspirators will strike as soon as success seems possible, and obviously, no one in his senses would strike sooner." After discussing the character of the Communist Party and the world tensions prevailing at the time the defendants were indicted, he added: "Nothing short of a revived doctrine of *laissez faire*, which would have amazed even the Manchester School at its apogee, can fail to realize that such a conspiracy creates a danger of the utmost gravity and of enough probability to justify its suppression. We hold that it is a danger 'clear and present.'" [71] The jury having found that the defendants had violated the Smith Act, the issue as to "whether the mischief of the repression is greater than the gravity of the evil, discounted by its improbability" was a question of law for the courts to decide.

Vinson construed Judge Learned Hand's view of clear and present danger—described by one critic as "a perhaps and probable test" [72]—to mean that overthrow of the government is a sufficiently grave "evil" to permit Congress to seek to avert it even if the

---

ernment captive in a judge-made verbal trap, we must approach the problem of a well-organized, nation-wide conspiracy . . . as realistically as our predecessors faced the trivialities that were being prosecuted until they were checked with a rule of reason." *Ibid.*, at 568–69.

[70] United States v. Dennis, 183 F. 2nd 201, at 212 (1950).

[71] *Ibid.*, at 213.

[72] Chester J. Antieau, "Dennis v. United States—Precedent, Principle or Perversion?" 5 *Vanderbilt L. Rev. 141, 142–43* (1952).

likelihood was that the evil itself would never come to pass. It is the nature of the Communist Party, in the context of world conditions, which justified Judge Medina in finding, "as a matter of law," that the "requisite danger" was present when the Communist leaders were indicted. The Chief Justice wrote:

The mere fact that from the period 1945 to 1948 petitioners' activities did not result in an attempt to overthrow the Government by force and violence is of course no answer to the fact that there was a group ready to make the attempt. The formation by petitioners of such a highly organized conspiracy, with rigidly disciplined members subject to call when the leaders, these petitioners, felt that the time had come for action, coupled with the inflammable nature of world conditions, similar uprisings in other countries, and the touch-and-go nature of our relations with countries with whom petitioners were in the very least ideologically attuned, convince us that their convictions were justified on this score. And this analysis disposes of the contention that a conspiracy to advocate, as distinguished from the advocacy itself, cannot be constitutionally restrained, because it comprises only the preparation. It is the existence of the conspiracy which creates the danger. . . . If the ingredients of the reaction are present, we cannot bind the Government to wait until the catalyst is added.[73]

No one can mistake the meaning of the Justices who voted to affirm the convictions. In the light of the "cold war" prevailing at the time the Justice Department moved against the leaders of the Communist Party, they were saying, the mere existence of the party—in view of its conspiratorial structure and its ties with the Soviet Union—constituted a sufficiently serious threat to the security of the United States to warrant the Government in invoking the Smith Act. However, since the Communist leaders had been indicted for conspiring to advocate the overthrow of the Government, and not for attempting to destroy it, Vinson's treatment of the constitutional issue was not exactly "responsive" to the main problem in the case, as Justice Douglas has phrased it. That problem was, after all, whether under the Holmes–Brandeis test of clear and

[73] 341 U.S. 494, at 510–11.

present danger, the mere advocacy of revolutionary action may be punished. As Mark DeWolfe Howe has suggested, the really fundamental question is, "Have the policies which lie behind the clear and present danger test become a constitutional standard by which the Court will measure the scope not only of the right of speech but of the right of political association?" [74]

IV

Regardless of one's estimate of the true character of the Communist Party or of its potential capacity for mischief, the logical inadequacy of the majority's position in the *Dennis* case is rather obvious. Probably the clearest statement of what the case actually holds was made by Justice Douglas in one of his extra-judicial utterances. "The theory underlying the cases," he has written, "is that if an act can be punished, its advocacy can be, *provided* the utterance is a call to action immediately or as speedily as circumstances permit, and not merely a reflection of a philosophical attitude." [75] In the *Dennis* case itself, both Justices Douglas and Black maintained that the application of such a rule spells the end of the clear and present danger test. Justice Black would hold the conspiracy section of the Smith Act both "on its face and as applied" to be a "virulent form of prior censorship." [76] The communist leaders had been indicted for merely setting up an organization which was planning to use speech and press to disseminate Communist doctrines:

These petitioners were not charged with an attempt to overthrow the Government. They were not charged with overt acts of any kind designed to overthrow the Government. They were not even charged with saying anything or writing anything designed to overthrow the Government. The charge was that they agreed to assemble and to talk and publish certain

[74] *63 Yale L. J. 132*, 134–35.
[75] William O. Douglas, *An Almanac of Liberty* (Garden City: Doubleday and Company, 1954), p. 124.
[76] 341 U.S. 494, at 579.

ideas at a later date: The indictment is that they conspired to organize the Communist Party and to use speech or newspapers and other publications in the future to teach and advocate the forcible overthrow of the Government.[77]

He attributed the resulting "jettisoning" of the clear and present danger rule to "the expressed fear that the advocacy of Communist doctrine endangers the safety of the Republic" but did not discuss the basis for the fear.[78]

Justice Douglas, in his much more elaborate dissent, did deal with the threat of communism and criticized the Court for refusing to weigh the evidence supporting the finding of danger. In his view, there was no basis in fact for the assumption that the Communist Party menaced the security of the country:

> The nature of Communism as a force on the world scene would, of course, be relevant to the issue of clear and present danger of petitioners' advocacy within the United States. But the primary consideration is the strength and tactical position of petitioners and their converts in this country. On that there is no evidence in the record. If we are to take judicial notice of the threat of Communists within the nation, it should not be difficult to conclude that *as a political party* they are of little consequence.[79]

Quoting Brandeis' summary in the *Whitney* case of the conditions which must exist to justify restraint of speech, Justice Douglas emphasized over and over again that the record in the case was barren of any "evidence" that the activities of the Communist leaders in organizing their party resulted in any "immediate injury" to American society. This was no doubt his way of underscoring the Court's failure to reconcile its decision with the central hypothesis of Brandeis' opinion in the *Whitney* case: "The wide difference between advocacy and incitement, between preparation and attempt, between assembling and conspiracy, must be borne in mind." [80]

[77] *Ibid.*
[78] *Ibid.*, at 580.
[79] *Ibid.*, at 588.
[80] Whitney v. California, 274 U.S. 357, 372, at 376.

Consistently with their belief in the "exalted position" of free speech—the phrase is Justice Douglas'—the dissenters in the *Dennis* case were candid in claiming for the judiciary the last word as to when the First Amendment is violated. "So long as this Court exercises the power of judicial review of legislation," Justice Black stated, "I cannot agree that the First Amendment permits us to sustain laws suppressing freedom of speech and press on the basis of Congress' or our own notions of mere 'reasonableness.' Such a doctrine waters down the First Amendment so that it amounts to little more than an admonition to Congress."[81] To Justice Douglas "the command of the First Amendment is so clear that we should not allow Congress to call a halt to free speech except in the extreme case of peril from the speech itself."[82]

Justice Frankfurter, in keeping with his well articulated philosophy of judicial self-limitation, used the occasion to stress the inadequacy of the judicial process for dealing with the danger of communism and the importance of allowing the "people's representatives" to cope with so complex an issue. This is the recurring theme of his *Dennis* opinion, and it is difficult to choose among his many utterances on the matter. Most pertinent, perhaps, is his comment on the need for judicial restraint even where freedom of speech is at stake:

> Free speech cases are not an exception to the principle that we are not legislators, that direct policy-making is not our province. How best to reconcile competing interests is the business of legislatures, and the balance they strike is a judgment not to be displaced by ours, but to be respected unless outside the pale of fair judgment.[83]

Returning to the same subject toward the close of his opinion, the Justice referred to the impossibility of having the judiciary resolve the issue on a more informed basis than that open to Congress:

> To make validity of legislation depend on judicial reading of events still in the womb of time—a forecast, that is, of the outcome of forces at

[81] 341 U.S. 494, 579, at 580.
[82] *Ibid.*, at 590.
[83] *Ibid.*, at 539–40.

best appreciated only with knowledge of the topmost secrets of nations—
is to charge the judiciary with duties beyond its equipment. We do not
expect courts to pronounce historic verdicts on bygone events. Even historians have conflicting views to this day on the origins and conduct of
the French Revolution, or, for that matter, varying interpretations of "the
glorious Revolution" of 1688. It is as absurd to be confident that we can
measure the present clash of forces and their outcome as to ask us to read
history still enveloped in clouds of controversy.[84]

Thus what Eugene V. Rostow has said about the *Dennis* case generally is especially true concerning the attitude of Justice Frankfurter: "In the end, the *Dennis* case is strongly colored—perhaps
determined—by the view that cloistered and appointed Justices
should not pit their judgment of the Constitution against that of
the elected representatives of the people." [85]

What, then, it may be asked, will be the effect of the *Dennis*
decision upon the future of the Holmes–Brandeis concept of clear
and present danger? One thing seems assured. It is likely to continue
to be used in cases arising from attempts to restrain the isolated
dissident. As Justice Frankfurter observed, "Our decision today
certainly does not mean that the Smith Act can constitutionally be
applied to facts like those in *Gitlow v. New York.*" [86] But the *Dennis*
case does little to help resolve the underlying dilemma of freedom
in our age of revolution. That dilemma has been expressed by

[84] *Ibid.,* at 551–52.
[85] Rostow, "The Democratic Character of Judicial Review," *66 Harv. L. Rev.*
193, 223 (1952). Justice Frankfurter's trenchant opinion in the *Dennis* case
seems to have evoked more interest and attention than has any of the others.
Calling it a "remarkable" opinion, Sidney Hook has praised it highly and commended it especially for its philosophy of judicial restraint. See Hook, *Heresy,
Yes—Conspiracy, No* (New York: The John Day Company, 1953), p. 105. Alexander Meiklejohn has devoted a whole twenty-page article to an attack on its
"underlying political and social theory" and particularly the Justice's refusal
to construe the First Amendment as imposing an absolute prohibition upon
Congress to limit political freedom. Meiklejohn, "What Does the First Amendment Mean?" *20 Univ. of Chicago L. Rev. 461* (1953). For a fuller discussion of
the relative competence of courts and legislatures to deal with the problem
of setting limits to free speech, see Elliot L. Richardson, "Freedom of Expression and the Function of Courts," *65 Harv. L. Rev. 1* (1951).
[86] 341 U.S. 494, 517, at 542.

Mark DeWolfe Howe in these simple words: "The issue of paramount importance, perhaps, has been that concerning the extent
to which the leaders and members of the Communist Party are
entitled to demand that the formulas of liberty be applied to them
as they had been applied to other radical dissenters." [87]

The position of the majority in the *Dennis* case was, of course,
that the Communist leaders were not convicted for disseminating
their belief in the right of Americans to stage another revolution,
but for erecting a most effective instrument for inculcating the
dogma among its converts and for teaching them how to act on
the road to power. Justice Jackson's reliance on the law of conspiracy—"The Constitution does not make conspiracy a civil right" [88]
—was perhaps the inevitable climax to the Court's logic. Yet this
seemingly realistic approach—Sidney Hook's distinction between
"heresy" and "conspiracy" [89]—is itself question-begging, at least as
applied to the problem before the Court in the *Dennis* case. If the
challenged statute were one which outlawed the Communist Party,
it would have been more pertinent to dwell on the techniques of the
party and on the ways in which Communists have subverted other
free governments.

So long as we have a First Amendment, any effort to stifle the
Party's proselytizing activities is bound to make many of those who
cherish the constitutional right of political dissent wonder whether
it was a mere manifestation of the irrational impulse toward political conformity. The presence in the same case of learned and
persuasive opinions depicting the Communist Party in the United
States as a fearsome engine of subversion and eloquent pleas for
tolerance of the group's "politically impotent" leaders—who are
described as "miserable merchants of unwanted ideas" [90]—can only

[87] Howe, Book Review: *63 Yale L. J. 132.*
[88] 341 U.S. 494, 561, at 572.
[89] Hook, *op. cit.*, particularly pp. 17–36 and 94–119. For a short but trenchant
criticism of Professor Hook's distinction between heresy and conspiracy as well
as of Justice Jackson's use of the law of conspiracy, see Mark DeWolfe Howe,
Book Review: *63 Yale L. J. 132* (1953).
[90] 341 U.S. 494, 581, at 589 (Justice Douglas dissenting).

nurture doubts and confusion. Said Justice Douglas: "Communism in the world scene is no bogeyman: but Communism as a political faction or party in this country plainly is." [91] But perhaps the fundamental key to the outcome and alignments in the *Dennis* case is contained in a posthumously published comment by Justice Jackson: "I find little indication that they [the framers of the Bill of Rights] foresaw a technique by which those liberties might be used to destroy themselves by immunizing a movement of a minority to impose upon the country an incompatible scheme of values which did not include political and civil liberties. The resort to that technique in this country, however fruitless, contemporaneously with the collapse or capture of free governments abroad, has stirred American anxieties deeply." [92]

[91] *Ibid.*, at 588.
[92] Jackson, *The Supreme Court in the American System of Government*, p. 4.

11

"No preestablished harmony"

"Brandeis and I are so apt to agree," Holmes wrote to Laski, on February 18, 1928, "that I was glad to have him dissent in my case, as it shows that there is no preestablished harmony." [1] But in June the Justice affirmed what he denied in February: "Brandeis and I are together as we are so apt to be, by a sort of preestablished harmony." [2] Some years earlier, Holmes asked Brandeis' law clerk to deliver a message to his Justice: "I am sure I admire him, but I do not emulate him." [3] While this was said with reference to Brandeis' penchant for footnotes, it is fair to assume that the sentiment carried deeper implications.

Both comments to Laski, though they would appear to be mutually contradictory, are yet basically not irreconcilable. For Holmes was obviously voicing a genuine ambivalence with respect to his relationship to Brandeis. His conception of his own function as a judge ordinarily led him to agree with Brandeis, so consistently, indeed, that the impression was bound to be created that the two men were of one mind on all significant issues. But of course, Holmes was aware that there were fundamental differences between them,

[1] *Holmes-Laski Letters*, II, 1027.
[2] *Ibid.*, p. 1060.
[3] Interview with Warren S. Ege, who was with Brandeis in 1924–25. (Washington, D.C., May 17, 1951.)

and it is this knowledge which may be the real reason why the talk of a "preestablished harmony" made him uncomfortable.

Differences between them there were, but in the judicial sphere they were reflective in the main of the fact that the two jurists looked at and handled public questions differently. Nevertheless, the idea persists that they were often deeply divided on the Court. This is simply not true. What does stand out is the fact that the occasions on which they diverged from each other were conspicuously few and that the divergences themselves were not fundamental. Holmes would probably have said that their disagreements were over "differences of degree."

I

In the well known case of Meyer v. Nebraska [4] Holmes and Brandeis found themselves on opposite sides of the Court on an issue of minority rights. It is debatable, however, whether Holmes' dissent, in which he was joined by Justice Sutherland, was necessarily the product of a reactionary point of view. Fred Rodell calls it Holmes' "most illiberal view and vote." [5] But the honors for Holmes' most illiberal constitutional opinion would probably have to go to his dissent from the opinion of Justice Hughes holding Alabama's "peonage" statute to be unconstitutional.[6] As Max Lerner has observed, "For those who still cling to a lingering belief that Holmes was a humanitarian liberal in his impulses, the 'Alabama peonage' case should be required reading." [7]

No doubt as an aftermath of anti-German feeling of the First World War, some of the Middle Western States adopted laws prohibiting the teaching of German in the schools. Nebraska forbade the use of any modern language other than English in the first

[4] 262 U.S. 390 (1923). Holmes' dissenting opinion is to be found in Bartels v. Iowa, 262 U.S. 404, 412 (1923).
[5] Rodell, Nine Men (New York: Random House, 1955), p. 205.
[6] Bailey v. Alabama, 219 U.S. 219, 245 (1911).
[7] Lerner, The Mind and Faith of Justice Holmes, pp. 336–37.

eight grades. Meyer, a teacher in a parochial school, was convicted under the statute for teaching a child of ten how to read in German. Justice McReynolds spoke for the majority, which included Brandeis, in holding that the Nebraska law deprived Meyer of his "liberty" guaranteed to him by the Fourteenth Amendment. He relied almost entirely on the cases in which regulatory measures had been stricken down as unduly interfering with freedom of contract, among them, Lochner v. New York, Adams v. Tanner, and Truax v. Corrigan.

So broad is the conception of liberty which McReynolds espoused that it is not altogether clear which phase of it Nebraska was unreasonably curtailing. Some things are definitely included in the meaning of liberty:

Without doubt, it [liberty] denotes not merely freedom from bodily restraint but also the right of the individual to contract, to engage in any of the common occupations of life, to acquire useful knowledge, to marry, establish a home and bring up children, to worship God according to the dictates of his own conscience, and generally, to enjoy those privileges long recognized at common law as essential to the orderly pursuit of happiness by free men.[8]

McReynolds seemed to be thinking not only of the right to pursue the occupation of a teacher, possibly as a phase of property, but also of the need for guarding against excessive state regimentation of education. Thus in speaking of the role of school teachers, he said that "The calling always has been regarded as useful and honorable" and later he added: "His [the language teacher's] right thus to teach and the right of parents to engage him so to instruct their children, we think, are within the liberty of the Amendment."[9] After referring to Plato's idea "That the wives of our guardians are to be common, and their children are to be common, and no parent is to know his own child, nor any child his parent" and the practice in Sparta of assembling all male children at the age of seven in barracks and entrusting their education to official guardians, Mc-

---

[8] 262 U.S. 390, at 399.   [9] *Ibid.*, at 400.

Reynolds commented: "Although such measures have been deliberately approved by men of great genius, their ideas touching the relation between individual and State were wholly different from those upon which our institutions rest; and it hardly will be affirmed that any legislature could impose such restrictions upon the people of a State without doing violence to both letter and spirit of the Constitution." [10]

The majority in the Meyer case recognized that it was within the power of the legislature to seek to foster a "homogeneous people with American ideals." Indeed, McReynolds acknowledged that the legislature may have been trying to deal with special conditions existing in Nebraska: "It is also affirmed that the foreign born population is very large, that certain communities commonly use foreign words, follow foreign leaders, move in a foreign atmosphere, and that the children are thereby hindered from becoming citizens of the most useful type and the public safety is imperiled." [11] But by declaring the statute to be invalid, the Court was denying to the legislature the right to use a particular educational device for achieving the legitimate purpose it had in mind: "Perhaps it would be highly advantageous if all had ready understanding of our ordinary speech, but this cannot be coerced by methods which conflict with the Constitution—a desirable end cannot be promoted by prohibited means." [12]

For Holmes the attack on the Nebraska law was just one more instance of the resort to judicial review to check legitimate legislative discretion. Though he appreciated the objection to it, he felt that it dealt with a matter concerning which "men reasonably might differ" and therefore did not think that the Constitution barred the State from trying the experiment. "We all agree, I take it," Holmes began, "that it is desirable that all the citizens of the United States should speak a common tongue, and therefore that the end aimed

[10] *Ibid.*, at 401–2.
[11] *Ibid.*, at 401.
[12] *Ibid.*

at by the statute is a lawful and proper one." [13] The only debatable point was the lawfulness of the means adopted toward that end, and as to that the Justice felt that the Court should defer to those better acquainted with local conditions:

I cannot bring my mind to believe that in some circumstances, and circumstances existing it is said in Nebraska, the statute might not be regarded as a reasonable or even necessary method of reaching the desired result. The part of the act with which we are concerned deals with the teaching of young children. Youth is the time when familiarity with a language is established and if there are sections of the State where a child would hear only Polish or French or German spoken at home I am not prepared to say that it is unreasonable to provide that in his early years he shall hear and speak only English at school.[14]

Does the fact that Brandeis voted with the majority in the Meyer case necessarily prove that it was harder to convince him than Holmes of the need for limiting individual freedom? On the total record, the question would have to be answered in the negative. Most of the time they were together on such an issue. All that can be said with certainty is that Holmes was somewhat more self-consistent. Max Lerner's view of the case would seem to be the correct one:

There have been some who have expressed surprise at Holmes's opinion . . . on the ground that his civil liberties views should have put him on the side of freedom of teaching, and therefore against the validity of the statutes, as his liberal colleague Justice Brandeis was. Yet I feel that Holmes had a consistent position. He believed in judicial tolerance of state legislative action, even when he disapproved of the state policies. The question here again, as in so many of the economic cases, was whether the end the state sought to achieve was legitimate, and whether the means were not unreasonably related to the end.[15]

The simple statistical fact is that in all of the really crucial civil liberties cases, Holmes and Brandeis stood together on the side of the claimed right. Holmes was the author of the opinion com-

[13] 262 U.S. 404, 412. [14] *Ibid.*
[15] Lerner, *op. cit.*, p. 318.

mitting the Court to the guardianship of civilized standards in the administration of justice in state criminal trials,[16] thus transforming one of his famous dissents of an earlier day into prevailing doctrine.[17] There is much to be said for the view of Judge Charles E. Wyzanski that Holmes' contribution in this field may have been more significant than his role in free speech cases. Judge Wyzanski has written:

To my mind the most important change [in the Court's attitude toward civil liberty] was not in the field of free speech as is sometimes asserted. It was the recognition that fair procedure in criminal trials conducted in state as well as federal courts is a civil liberty so fundamental to our democracy that it is covered by the constitutional assurance of "due process." When this point was first pressed it was denied by the Supreme Court of the United States. Indeed, as recently as 1915, in Frank v. Mangum, where the defendant had been convicted by a Georgia state jury which was terrorized by a mob surrounding the courtroom, only Justices Holmes and Hughes thought that the Federal Supreme Court was warranted in invoking the due process clause or any other constitutional provision to set aside the sentence. . . . Today the dissent of Holmes is regarded as almost self-evident. And from Holmes' doctrine have stemmed the myriad of cases which lay down as fundamentals of our democratic system protected by the Supreme Court the right of a defendant in any criminal court in the land to a trial which is open to the public and free of outside pressure, which admits no evidence secured by torture or by third degree methods or by perjury known to the prosecution and which assures a defendant the right to the assistance of counsel in meeting a charge of undeniable gravity.[18]

Both Holmes and Brandeis dissented in the cases in which the Court sustained the right of the Federal Government to use evidence obtained through the tapping of telephone wires [19] and to deny

[16] Moore v. Dempsey, 261 U.S. 86 (1923).

[17] Frank v. Mangum, 237 U.S. 309, 345 (1915). For an interesting account of the collaboration between Justices Holmes and Hughes in the writing of this dissent, see Pusey, *Charles Evans Hughes*, I, 289–90.

[18] Wyzanski, "The Democracy of Justice Oliver Wendell Holmes," reprinted in *The Holmes Reader*, edited by Julius J. Marke (New York: Oceana Publications, 1955), p. 263.

[19] Olmstead v. United States, 277 U.S. 438, 469, 471 (1928).

citizenship to persons with conscientious scruples against war.[20] To Holmes wiretapping was "dirty business" because of the shabby role played by the Federal government; it was against the law in the State of Washington, where the bootleggers had their headquarters, to intercept telephone conversations. Those who see the Justice as a man devoid of sentiment might well reflect on his assertion, "I think it less evil that some criminal should escape than that the government should play an ignoble part."[21] Brandeis, co-author of a pioneer disquisition on the legal protection of the right to privacy,[22] was disturbed by the effect of the *Olmstead* decision upon "the right to be let alone—the most comprehensive of rights and the right most valued by civilized men." The passage in which this observation occurs is reflective of the Justice's deepest convictions concerning the proper relation between government and the individual, and for this reason ought to be recalled:

The makers of our Constitution undertook to secure conditions favorable to the pursuit of happiness. They recognized the significance of man's spiritual nature, of his feelings and of his intellect. They knew that only a part of the pain, pleasure and satisfactions of life are to be found in material things. They sought to protect Americans in their beliefs, their thoughts, their emotions and their sensations. They conferred, as against

[20] United States v. Schwimmer, 279 U.S. 644, 653 (1929).

[21] 277 U.S. 438, 469, at 470. Ironically, the case which Holmes thought proved that there was no "preestablished harmony" between him and Brandeis was one in which Holmes wrote the Court's opinion sustaining the Government and Brandeis dissented because he believed that "the prosecution must fail because officers of the Government instigated the commission of the alleged crime." Casey v. United States, 276 U.S. 413, 421 (1928). Casey, a Seattle lawyer, suspected of supplying narcotics to his clients among the inmates of a prison, was trapped by Federal agents and convicted of buying morphine in violation of the Harrison Anti-Narcotic Act. "We are not persuaded," Holmes wrote, "that the conduct of the officials was different from or worse than ordering a drink of a suspected bootlegger." (At 419.) Justice Brandeis concluded his dissent in this case—which was decided just two months prior to Olmstead v. United States—in these words: "This prosecution should be stopped, not because some right of Casey's has been denied, but in order to protect the Government. To protect it from illegal conduct of its officers. To preserve the purity of its courts." (At 425.)

[22] Samuel D. Warren and Louis D. Brandeis, "The Right to Privacy," *4 Harv. L. Rev.* 193 (1890); reprinted in *The Curse of Bigness*, p. 289.

the Government, the right to be let alone—the most comprehensive of rights and the right most valued by civilized men. To protect that right, every unjustifiable intrusion by the Government upon the privacy of the individual, whatever the means employed, must be deemed a violation of the Fourth Amendment. And the use, as evidence in a criminal proceeding, of facts ascertained by such intrusion must be deemed a violation of the Fifth.[23]

The man who was thrice wounded in the Civil War and who believed that war was both "inevitable and rational"[24] gave dramatic proof of his objectivity as a judge when he dissented in the *Schwimmer* case. "I would suggest," Holmes there said, "that the Quakers have done their share to make the country what it is, . . . and that I had not supposed hitherto that we regretted our inability to expel them because they believe more than some of us do in the teachings of the Sermon on the Mount."[25] His *Schwimmer* opinion was his last dissent in a free speech case, and appropriately enough he put into it a sentence containing what is perhaps the very core of the philosophy of toleration: "If there is any principle of the Constitution that more imperatively calls for attachment than any other it is the principle of free thought—not free thought for those who agree with us but freedom for the thought that we hate."[26]

Neither Holmes nor Brandeis made a fetish of his customary deference to the will of the community's policy-makers. Their constitutional oaths as well as their own social values made that impossible. Occasions were bound to arise when their "attachment" to principles they deemed fundamental would lead them to use their power as judges to restrain attacks upon basic liberties. Holmes may have been contemptuous of the "drool" preached by the "malcontents" whose right to speak their minds he was upholding, but there was also the pull of the ideals of freedom enshrined

[23] 277 U.S. 438, 471, at 478–79.
[24] *Holmes-Pollock Letters*, II, 230.
[25] 279 U.S. 644, 653, at 655.
[26] *Ibid.*, at 654–55.

in the Constitution. "I suspect," he wrote to Laski in 1923, "you don't like the bill of rights of former days—whereas I have been rather led to the belief that we have grown so accustomed to the enjoyment of those rights that we forget that they had to be fought for and may have to be fought for again." [27]

What Justice Frankfurter has said about Holmes is probably even more true of Brandeis—"Mr. Justice Holmes was far more ready to find legislative invasion where free inquiry was involved than in the debatable area of economics." [28] Indeed, a judge for whom the social consequences of adjudication were as compelling as they were for Brandeis may be assumed not to have worried about logical consistency. His conception of flexibility in the interpretation of the Constitution would suggest that he was not troubled by the contradiction between his sympathy for legislative experimentation with economic rights and his readiness to restrain government from interfering with other fundamental freedoms. The rationale he once advanced for overturning undesirable decisions is probably the key to his attitude toward consistency in constitutional matters generally: "In cases involving constitutional issues . . . this Court must, in order to reach sound conclusions, feel free to bring its opinions into agreement with experience and with facts newly ascertained." [29]

---

[27] *Holmes-Laski Letters,* I, 529–30.

[28] Concurring in Kovacs v. Cooper, 336 U.S. 77, 89, at 95 (1949).

[29] Dissenting in Burnet v. Coronado Oil & Gas Co., 285 U.S. 393, 405, at 412 (1932). In discussing *stare decisis* in constitutional law, Brandeis likened the Court's interpretations of such provisions of the Constitution as the due process, equal protection and commerce clauses to the actions of juries in applying general rules to the facts or circumstances of a particular case. Hence, he saw no reason why the Court should hesitate to reconsider or even overrule earlier cases when "the lessons of experience" indicated that they had been decided erroneously: "The decision of the Court, if, in essence, merely the determination of a fact, is not entitled, in later controversies between other parties, to that sanction which, under the policy of *stare decisis,* is accorded to the decision of a proposition purely of law. For not only may the decision of the fact have been rendered upon an inadequate presentation of then existing conditions, but the conditions may have changed meanwhile. . . . Moreover, the judgment of the Court in the earlier decision may have been influenced by prevailing views as to economic or social policy which have since been abandoned." *Ibid.*

II

It is in the economic field that some observers have professed to see even more far-reaching differences between the two Justices. A study of their private predilections does reveal, to be sure, a striking contrast between an old-fashioned Republican's faith in the ultimate social utility of laissez-faire and the twentieth-century progressive's zest for the use of governmental power for purposes of reform. But it is one thing to take note of the wide gulf between Holmes and Brandeis as reflected in their economic and social theories; it is misleading to magnify the significance of these differences as they bear upon the judicial process.

On one of the first occasions on which Holmes and Brandeis found themselves on opposite sides of an important issue, Holmes was for judicial protection of the claimed property right and Brandeis spoke for the superior competence of the legislature to deal with the matter.[30] The case arose as a suit to restrain the International News Service from copying news items appearing on bulletin boards and in early editions of newspapers which were members of the Associated Press. In allowing the restraining order to stand, Justice Pitney, for a majority of the Supreme Court, stressed that news "must be regarded as *quasi* property" entitled to be protected from piracy as long as it remained fresh. Holmes saw the failure to credit the source of the news as a subtle form of deception which the law ought to be able to reach even as more obvious methods of unfair competition are restrainable: "The falsehood is a little more subtle, the injury a little more indirect, than in ordinary cases of unfair trade, but I think that the principle that condemns the one condemns the other." [31] He thought that the International News Service should either acknowledge the source or wait some hours after the news items were published by the Associated Press papers.

[30] International News Service v. Associated Press, 248 U.S. 215, 246, 248 (1918).
[31] *Ibid.*, at 247.

In his long dissenting opinion, Brandeis argued that it was dangerous to create a new property right by judicial fiat and that courts were in no position to safeguard the public interest in the dissemination of news. "The rule for which the plaintiff [the Associated Press] contends," he declared, "would effect an important extension of property rights and a corresponding curtailment of the free use of knowledge and of ideas; and the facts of this case admonish us of the danger involved in recognizing such a property right in news, without imposing upon news-gatherers corresponding obligations." [32] He suggested some of the considerations which legislators might take into account in striking a balance between private and public interests in news gathering and concluded his opinion by emphasizing that courts lacked machinery for working out a practical accommodation:

Courts are ill-equipped to make the investigations which should precede a determination of the limitations which should be set upon any property right in news or of the circumstances under which news gathered by a private agency should be deemed affected with a public interest. Courts would be powerless to prescribe the detailed regulations essential to full enjoyment of the rights conferred or to introduce the machinery required for enforcement of such regulations. Considerations such as these should lead us to decline to establish a new rule of law in the effort to redress a newly-disclosed wrong, although the propriety of some remedy appears to be clear.[33]

Another significant case in which Holmes and Brandeis differed even more sharply is Pennsylvania Coal Co. v. Mahon.[34] Holmes wrote the decision setting aside a law restricting property rights and Brandeis dissented. Their disagreement in this case is sometimes discussed as if it were the inevitable product of their clashing philosophies. Actually, however, their conflicting views merely illustrate that the two jurists drew different inferences from the same set of facts. As Holmes himself said of the issue on which he and Brandeis came to opposite conclusions, "this is a question of de-

[32] *Ibid.*, at 263.
[33] *Ibid.*, at 267.
[34] 260 U.S. 393, 416 (1922).

gree—and therefore cannot be disposed of by general propositions." [35] He apparently resented the opinion in liberal circles that
Brandeis' dissent was the more "statesmanlike" position.[36] An un-
signed editorial in the *New Republic* on the *Mahon* case had expressed the belief that "Justice Brandeis's view seems the superior
statesmanship." [37]

The *Mahon* case was concerned with the constitutionality of a
1921 Pennsylvania statute which prohibited the mining of anthracite coal in such a way as to cause subsidence of any dwelling
in which people lived or worked. Holmes took the view that by
limiting the right to mine, the Kohler Act practically destroyed
the value of the property. He pointed out that the Pennsylvania
Coal Co. had reserved to itself "in express terms" the right to
remove the coal when it sold the surface rights to the land. The
nub of his argument was that Mahon assumed the risk of subsidence
when he acquired the land on which his house stood and that the
State's police power could not be "stretched" so far as to shift the
burden to the mine owner. Such a "diminution" in the value of
property for the benefit of other private persons is a "taking" for
which the Constitution requires compensation. Thus did the great
apostle of the police power call a halt to its exercise by Pennsylvania:

It is our opinion that the act cannot be sustained as an exercise of the
police power, so far as it affects the mining of coal under streets or cities
in places where the right to mine such coal has been reserved. . . .
What makes the right to mine coal valuable is that it can be exercised
with profit. To make it commercially impracticable to mine certain coal
has very nearly the same effect for constitutional purposes as appropriating
or destroying it.[38]

Brandeis' cogent dissent might just as well have been written by

[35] *Ibid.,* at 416.
[36] *Holmes-Laski Letters,* I, 474.
[37] Holmes told Laski that the editorial had been written by Dean Acheson,
who had served as Brandeis' law secretary for two years, 1919–21. *Ibid.*
[38] 260 U.S. 393, at 414.

Holmes, so much does it invoke respect for the lawmakers' familiarity with local needs. Though he agreed that there were limits to the exercise of the police power, he felt that in its attempt to safeguard the public interest Pennsylvania had not exceeded those limits. All rights, including property, are relative and depend on changing social conditions. Property values may increase as well as decrease because of changes in the community, and the Fourteenth Amendment does not demand that the community pay for diminutions in property values resulting from measures taken to protect the public against dangers to their safety. Brandeis rejected Holmes' argument that if the object were merely to protect personal safety it could be provided by notice of intent to mine under the house. Since the promotion of public safety was a legitimate purpose, the precise means for achieving it was within the discretion of the legislature:

> The propriety of deferring a good deal to tribunals on the spot has been repeatedly recognized. . . . May we say that notice would afford adequate protection of the public safety where the legislature and the highest court of the State, with greater knowledge of local conditions, have declared, in effect, that it would not? If public safety is imperiled, surely neither grant, nor contract, can prevail against the exercise of the police power.[39]

To buttress his contention that compensation was not due, Brandeis likened the Kohler Act to a safety measure taken to protect the general public against poisonous fumes emanating from coal fields. "If by mining anthracite coal the owner would necessarily unloose poisonous gasses," he observed, "I suppose no one would doubt the power of the State to prevent the mining, without buying his coal fields. And why may not the State, likewise, without paying compensation, prohibit one from digging so deep or excavating so near the surface, as to expose the community to like dangers? In the latter case, as in the former, carrying on the business would be a public nuisance." [40]

[39] *Ibid.*, at 420.
[40] *Ibid.*, at 418–19.

In a contemporaneous comment on the *Mahon* case, Thomas Reed Powell suggested that the conflict between the "two intellectual masters of the Supreme Court" shed more light on the "reasoning" habits of each than on their conception of the "reasonableness" of public regulation. The two opinions, he went on to say, "afford such striking illustration of the comparative merits of reasoning and reasonableness that they merit the careful study of all who are interested in the mental processes that play such a part in directing the development of the law." [41] What Professor Powell did not explain was why the "mental processes" of a Holmes should have led him to a result so different from his usual position in similar cases. The really "striking" fact about the *Mahon* case is that the "reasoning" of both Brandeis and Holmes was obviously dictated by the attitude toward the legislation—whether it was constitutional or not—and not necessarily by their unique methods as judges.

Not long before Brandeis retired from the Court, he wrote an opinion which demonstrated that he could be just as vigorous as Holmes when he thought a state was going too far in destroying property values.[42] In an attempt to conserve the State's supply of natural gas, Texas adopted a statute in 1935 prohibiting the production of natural gas resulting in waste. It provided that production of natural gas in excess of transportation or market facilities, or reasonable market demands, constituted such waste. Acting under this law, the Texas Railroad Commission issued an order which restricted the owners of pipelines to a quota below amounts they needed if they were to fulfill their obligations under existing contracts. As a result, they were compelled to purchase gas from well owners who otherwise, for lack of a market, would have been prohibited from producing gas.

Brandeis wrote the Court's unanimous opinion, stressing that the producers against whom the order was directed were not guilty of waste and that they were being deprived of the normal advantages incident to the ownership and use of pipelines. "Our law reports

[41] Powell, "Reasoning, Reasonableness and the Pennsylvania Surface Subsidence Case," 1 *N. Y. Law Rev.* 242–43 (1923).
[42] Thompson v. Consolidated Gas Utilities Corp., 300 U.S. 55 (1937).

bear no more glaring instance of the taking of one man's property and giving it to another," said Justice Brandeis, and later added: "This Court has many times warned that one person's property may not be taken for the benefit of another private person without a justifying public purpose, even though compensation be paid." [43]

III

Even in cases concerned with economic issues on which his thinking was most at variance with prevailing attitudes, Brandeis had the support of Holmes. An outstanding instance is Brandeis' persistence in attacking the Court's approach to the economics of public utility regulation. His exhaustive opinions exposing the fallacies in the conventional formulas for determining whether rates fixed by regulatory tribunals met constitutional standards stand as a permanent monument to what is perhaps the most distinctive attribute of his skill as a judge—his unexcelled mastery of the complexities in the relations between law and economy. Holmes "hated" rate cases; [44] but Brandeis, who seemed to enjoy them immensely, met the challenge of their intricacies by drawing on his vast knowledge of business and finance to illumine and simplify the great public issues with which they were intertwined.

Brandeis brought to bear the full force of his command of fact and analysis to the task of releasing courts and commissions from

[43] *Ibid.*, at 79–80. Brandeis was also author of the Court's unanimous opinion which held The Emergency Farm Mortgage Act of 1933—also known as the Frazier-Lemke Act—to be unconstitutional, principally on the ground that it resulted in conferring on the debtor specific rights in property acquired by the creditor prior to the enactment of the statute. Louisville Bank v. Radford, 295 U.S. 555 (1935). Justice Brandeis concluded his opinion with these words: "For the Fifth Amendment commands that, however great the Nation's need, private property shall not be thus taken even for a wholly public use without just compensation. If the public interest requires, and permits, the taking of property of individual mortgages in order to relieve the necessities of individual mortgagors, resort must be had to proceedings by eminent domain; so that, through taxation, the burden of the relief afforded in the public interest may be borne by the public." 295 U.S. 555, at 602.

[44] "I fear me some cases for me that I don't want—there were several this week the kind I hate—rate cases and whatnot." Holmes to Laski, April 18, 1924. *Holmes-Laski Letters*, I, 610.

the incubus of Smyth v. Ames.[45] The decision in this case, handed down in 1898, was the climax in the doctrinal process by which the Supreme Court had come to interpret the constitutional provisions against the deprivation of property without due process of law to mean that privately owned utilities were entitled to charge rates which would yield a fair return on the value of the property. What constituted "reasonable rates" was a question ultimately to be decided by the courts.[46] In the *Smyth* case itself, Justice Harlan enunciated, for a unanimous Court, the rule that in ascertaining the "fair value" of the utility as a basis for determining a just rate of return, it was necessary to give "consideration" or "weight" to certain factors, among them, the original cost of constructing the property as compared with what it would cost to replace or reproduce it at the time of the rate hearing.[47]

So pervasive has been the influence of the "superstition which

[45] 169 U.S. 466 (1898).

[46] "If the company is deprived of the power of charging reasonable rates for the use of its property, and such deprivation takes place in the absence of an investigation by judicial machinery, it is deprived of the lawful use of its property, and thus, in substance and effect, of the property itself, without due process of law and in violation of the Constitution of the United States." Justice Blatchford, for the Court, in Chicago, Milwaukee & St. Paul Ry. Co. v. Minnesota, 134 U.S. 418, at 458 (1890). For an exellent recent account of this history, which deals with both the economic and legal complexities, see Robert L. Hale, *Freedom Through Law, Public Control of Private Governing Power* (New York: Columbia Univ. Press, 1952), pp. 461–538.

[47] "We hold, however, that the basis of all calculations as to the reasonableness of rates to be charged by a corporation maintaining a highway under legislative sanction must be the fair value of the property being used by it for the convenience of the public. And, in order to ascertain that value, the original cost of construction, the amount expended in permanent improvements, the amount and market value of its bonds and stock, the present as compared with the original cost of construction, the probable earning capacity of the property under particular rates prescribed by statute, and the sum required to meet operating expenses, are all matters for consideration, and are to be given such weight as may be just and right in each case. We do not say that there may not be other matters to be regarded in estimating the value of the property. What the company is entitled to ask is a fair return upon the value of that which it employs for the public convenience. On the other hand, what the public is entitled to demand is that no more be exacted from it for the use of a public highway than the services rendered by it are reasonably worth." 169 U.S. 466, at 546–47.

supported Smyth v. Ames"—to use Robert L. Hale's words [48]—that it took nearly half a century for the Supreme Court to free itself of it. As recently as 1939, Justice Frankfurter, in one of his first opinions, felt justified in criticizing the Court for giving "new vitality" to the "mischievous formula" of Smyth v. Ames.[49] Three years later, Justices Black, Douglas and Murphy sought to persuade the Court that it was time "to lay the ghost of Smyth v. Ames . . . which has continued to haunt utility regulation since 1898." [50]

In the meantime, Harlan's dictum had led to serious uncertainties and delays in the processes for fixing utility rates. Particularly troublesome was the problem of estimating the current reproduction cost of a utility. "In assuming the task of determining judicially the present fair replacement value of the vast properties of public utilities," complained Justice Stone in 1935, "courts have been projected into the most speculative undertaking imposed upon them in the entire history of English jurisprudence." [51] Leadership in the effort to rescue utility regulation from the resulting confusion fell preeminently to Justices Brandeis and Stone, supported most of the time by Holmes. Even before Brandeis became a member of the Court, Justice Holmes had spoken of the "delusive exactness" and the "speculative" character of the calculations on which utility valuations were made to depend.[52] On the same occasion he described the rate question the Court was being asked to decide as "too much up in the air." [53]

Though Brandeis did not hesitate to upset a rate order when

[48] Hale, *op. cit.*, p. 497.
[49] Concurring in Driscoll v. Edison Light and Power Co., 307 U.S. 104, 122 (1939).
[50] Concurring in a joint opinion in Federal Power Commission v. Natural Gas Pipeline Co., 315 U.S. 575, 599, at 602 (1942). These words were the inspiration for the title of Professor Hale's article, "Does the Ghost of Smyth v. Ames still Walk?" 55 *Harv. L. Rev. 1116* (1942).
[51] Dissenting in West v. Chesapeake and Potomac Telephone Co., 295 U.S. 662, 680, at 689 (1935).
[52] Louisville v. Cumberland Telephone and Telegraph Co., 225 U.S. 430, at 436 (1913).
[53] *Ibid.*

he thought the rates were so low as to be confiscatory, he seldom missed an opportunity to expose the ambiguities and economic absurdities inherent in the methods stemming from Smyth v. Ames. A relatively early but characteristic illustration is his concurring opinion, endorsed by Holmes, in the *Southwestern Bell* case, decided in 1923.[54] "For the first time," Thomas Reed Powell said of it, "a justice of the Supreme Court has ventured upon an explicit consideration of the folly of it all." Professor Powell was here referring to Brandeis' diagnosis of the results of Smyth v. Ames, and he described his *Southwestern* opinion as "the most signal judicial contribution to the problem that we have ever had."[55]

In reversing the Supreme Court of Missouri, which had upheld an order of the State's Public Service Commission reducing telephone rates, the Court held that inadequate weight had been assigned to the actual or "present" value of the property used in the business. That this deficiency was the primary basis for the decision, which was written by Justice McReynolds, can be gathered from these emphatic words:

It is impossible to ascertain what will amount to a fair return upon properties devoted to public service without giving consideration to the cost of labor, supplies, etc., at the time the investigation is made. An honest and intelligent forecast of probable future values made upon a view of all the relevant circumstances, is essential. If the highly important element of present costs is wholly disregarded such a forecast becomes impossible. Estimates for to-morrow cannot ignore prices of to-day.[56]

Justice Brandeis concurred in the reversal, but on different grounds. He had concluded that the order of the Commission prevented the utility from earning "a fair return on the amount prudently invested in it." From the very outset, however, he made it clear that in advocating "prudent investment" as the basis for utility

[54] Southwestern Bell Telephone Co. v. Public Service Commission of Missouri, 262 U.S. 276, 289 (1923).
[55] Powell, "Protecting Property and Liberty," *40 Pol. Sci. Quarterly 404,* 407 (Sept., 1925).
[56] 262 U.S. 276, at 287–88.

rates, he was in basic disagreement with the approach embodied
in the Court's decision. "I differ fundamentally from my brethren,"
he announced, "concerning the rule to be applied in determining
whether a prescribed rate is confiscatory. The Court, adhering to
the so-called rule of *Smyth v. Ames*, . . . and further defining it,
declares that what is termed value must be ascertained by giving
weight, among other things, to estimates of what it would cost to
reproduce the property at the time of the rate hearing." [57] The rest
of his opinion is an elaboration of the reasons why he considered
the doctrine of Smyth v. Ames to be "legally and economically
unsound."

By way of proving how unworkable the so-called rule of Smyth v.
Ames came to be, Brandeis recalled some of the influences which
had given rise to present value as the rate base. His summary of the
conditions which generated that rule helps to place the whole
problem in its proper historical perspective. He wrote:

The adoption of present value of the utility's property, as the rate
base, was urged in 1893, on behalf of the community; and it was adopted
by the courts, largely, as a protection against inflated claims based on
what were then deemed inflated prices of the past. . . . Reproduction
cost, as the measure, or as evidence, of present value was, also, pressed
then by representatives of the public who sought to justify legislative
reductions of railroad rates. The long depression which followed the panic
of 1893 had brought prices to the lowest level reached in the Nineteenth Century. Insistence upon reproduction cost was the shippers' protest against burdens believed to have resulted from watered stocks, reck-
less financing, and unconscionable construction contracts.[58]

At first, state commissions found reproduction cost as the measure
of present value useful in avoiding the exorbitant prices of the
original installations of the properties. Later, as prices rose, they
began to distrust both the estimates of the engineers and the
prophecies of the economists. Resistance to reproduction formulas
stiffened as the commissions discovered that under the greatly

[57] *Ibid.*, at 289–90.
[58] *Ibid.*, at 298.

inflated prices incident to World War I, estimates of replacement cost were way above the original investment in constructing the facilities.

Brandeis was able to show that fluctuations in general price levels were bound to make the search for present value an essentially vague and unstable process, unfair both to the public and the investor. "The most serious vice of the present rule for fixing the rate base is not the existing uncertainty, but that the method does not lead to certainty," he observed.[59] Thus, since the worth of a utility depended on its earnings and its earnings depended on the rates, the attempt to find present value made it inevitable that the commissions would move in a "vicious circle." Remarking that "Value is a word of many meanings," the Justice maintained that it has a "special" significance for rate-making purposes, and that it ought not to be confused with the concept of "exchange value" used in determining compensation when the community acquires private property for public use.[60] Public utilities are not bought and sold in the manner of merchandise or land. Brandeis' analysis of the wild uncertainties inherent in the replacement theory contained a prophecy which was also in the nature of a warning: "To require that reproduction cost at the date of the rate hearing be given weight in fixing the rate base, may subject investors to heavy losses when the high war and post-war price levels pass—and the price trend is again downward." [61]

There was more to Brandeis' opinion, however, than criticism of the futility of trying to value public utilities under the rule of Smyth v. Ames. He coupled his attack with a plea for a constructive substitute. What makes his opinion in the *Southwestern Bell* case a significant judicial landmark is his persuasive support for the theory of prudent investment. That theory was not his personal invention; it was an approach urged by experts in the field. James C. Bonbright reported in 1937 that "Justice Brandeis has been the

---

[59] *Ibid.*, at 308.
[60] *Ibid.*, at 310.   [61] *Ibid.*, at 302–03.

most distinguished exponent of the prudent investment principle, which has been favored by the majority of economists who have written recently on the subject." [62] In the *Southwestern* case, the Justice pointed out that some commissions were already using the new method: "Many commissions, like that in Massachusetts, have declared recently that 'capital honestly and prudently invested must, under normal conditions, be taken as the controlling factor in fixing the basis for computing fair and reasonable rates'."

While the prudent investment theory has its own complexities, Brandeis felt that it had the virtue of giving definiteness and stability to the procedures for fixing rates. "To give to capital embarked in public utilities the protection guaranteed by the Constitution, and to secure for the public reasonable rates," he asserted, "it is essential that the rate base be definite, stable, and readily ascertainable; and that the percentage to be earned on the rate base be measured by the cost, or charge, of the capital employed in the enterprise." [63] It was time and it was constitutional for the Court to adopt such a rule for measuring the rate base. All that a public utility is entitled to earn is a fair return on the cost or capital prudently invested in the business. Most of Brandeis' opinion was given over to a discussion of the advantages and the feasibility of this basis for determining reasonable rates. Improvements in accounting and in administrative methods since Smyth v. Ames made "prudent investment" an altogether workable standard. Guided by such a standard, both commissions and courts would be able to learn with certainty the cost of conducting a public utility as revealed by its operating expenses and capital charges—the two principal "factors" in rate cases:

The adoption of the amount prudently invested as the rate base and the amount of the capital charge as the measure of the rate of return would give definiteness to these two factors involved in rate controversies

[62] Bonbright, *The Valuation of Property* (New York: McGraw-Hill Book Co., 1937), II, 1085.
[63] 262 U.S. 276, 289, at 292.

which are now shifting and treacherous, and which render the proceedings peculiarly burdensome and largely futile. Such measures offer a basis for decision which is certain and stable. The rate base would be ascertained as a fact, not determined as matter of opinion. It would not fluctuate with the market price of labor, or materials, or money. It would not change with hard times or shifting populations. It would not be distorted by the fickle and varying judgments of appraisers, commissions, or courts. It would, when once made in respect to any utility, be fixed, for all time, subject only to increases to represent additions to plant, after allowance for the depreciation included in the annual operating charges. The wild uncertainties of the present method of fixing the rate base under the so-called rule of Smyth v. Ames would be avoided; and likewise the fluctuations which introduce into the enterprise unnecessary elements of speculation, create useless expense, and impose upon the public a heavy, unnecessary burden.[64]

Brandeis' sustained effort to win acceptance for the prudent investment formula took on the character of a campaign, though without the emotional fervor of the crusader. His special weapon was an awesome artillery of facts and figures. Some of his most impressive dissents were devoted to this cause. In his extraordinarily thoroughgoing study in the famous O'Fallon case [65]—a sixty-page dissent, concurred in by Justices Holmes and Stone—he succeeded in showing that if the nation's railroads were to be appraised on the basis of so-called present or reproduction costs, their valuation in 1920 would have been double their worth at the time they were built. This "veritable *tour-de-force*," as it has been characterized by his biographer, is reported to have undergone more than twenty revisions.[66]

The *O'Fallon* case arose as an attack on the valuation methods followed by the Interstate Commerce Commission under the Transportation Act of 1920. Congress directed the Commission to prescribe rates which would yield "a fair return upon the aggregate value of the railway property" of the United States. The Transporta-

[64] *Ibid.*, at 306–07.
[65] St. Louis and O'Fallon Ry. Co. v. United States, 279 U.S. 461, 488 (1929).
[66] Mason, *Brandeis: A Free Man's Life,* p. 553.

tion Act further provided that in ascertaining value, the Commission "shall give due consideration to all the elements of value recognized by the law of the land for rate-making purposes." A majority of the Supreme Court, again speaking through Justice McReynolds, found that the Commission had failed to give adequate weight to reproduction cost when it determined the property valuation of the railroad, thus vindicating the position taken by a minority of the Commission's members.[67] Brandeis maintained that the "weight" to be assigned to the various factors involved in the valuation process was entrusted by Congress to the discretion of the Commission.[68]

Writing in 1931, Henry Wolf Biklé—a distinguished railroad lawyer—described Brandeis' opinions in the *Southwestern* and *O'Fallon* cases as "the ablest available discussion of the so-called prudent investment theory of valuation." [69] As proof of the importance of Brandeis' ideas in this field, Mr. Biklé noted the fact that his opinions had become "the shining target at which those with contrary views undertake to aim their answering shafts—the best kind of compliment, it is believed, to their intellectual texture." [70] Though chiefly concerned with his high competence in railroad matters, Mr. Biklé's portrait of the Justice's specialized knowledge and profound social insights—including the intimate glimpse of his demeanor on the bench—conveys much that is significant in Brandeis' unique work as a judge:

[67] The same section of the statute—Section 15A—authorized the Interstate Commerce Commission to require the railroads whose earnings were in excess of six percent of their valuation to put one-half of the excess in a reserve fund and to turn over the other half to the Commission to be used for the benefit of the weaker carriers. The St. Louis and O'Fallon Railway Company insisted that if its property had been properly appraised, no excess profits would be found.

[68] Brandeis' chief antagonist in the valuation cases was Pierce Butler, the other railroad expert on the Court. For a discussion of their clashing viewpoints as well as of the cases in which they were on opposite sides, see Mason, *op. cit.*, pp. 550–53.

[69] Biklé, "Mr. Justice Brandeis and the Regulation of Railroads," *45 Harv. L. Rev. 4* (1931); reprinted in Frankfurter (ed.), *Mr. Justice Brandeis*, pp. 141, 162.

[70] *Ibid.*, pp. 162–63.

Indeed, this ready comprehension of the whole background of the situation makes it a peculiar pleasure to argue a railroad case before him. The questions he puts invariably serve to illuminate the picture, the apparently unconscious nods of comprehension infuse the eager advocate with renewed confidence, albeit he may know that these nods may signify clear understanding of the argument rather than agreement with it. It is always regrettable to lose a case, but there is some consolation to the vanquished when the court's opinion indicates that at least the trusted contentions have been fully understood. It is more difficult to be philosophic when the feeling persists that the court, like the lady celebrated by Mr. Kipling, "did not understand"—a fairly common complaint of defeated litigants, but one that the writer has never heard made in reference to the opinions of Mr. Justice Brandeis. And, at least in the matter of railroad cases, he has been in a position to hear them if any there have been.[71]

More than one interpreter, indeed, has pointed to Brandeis' valuation opinions as constituting the best examples of his distinctive contribution to modern jurisprudence. John Dickinson's comment on the *Southwestern* opinion is typical:

This opinion should be a landmark as a masterly example of a method of approach which is coming to be more and more necessary as the law expands to the measure of the modern business problems with which it must increasingly deal. It is an essay in legal economics which arrives at its conclusions not merely from a study of the cases, but from a study of the economic facts as well, in quite the same way in which the constructive opinions of our earlier law were based on a study of human conduct and political principles. To-day the law needs to understand the economic facts, because they are no longer so simple that they can be directly apprehended as a result of everyday experience, but have ramified into a tissue of elaborate organization which must be patiently analyzed if its significance is to be correctly grasped.[72]

There is yet another reason for the significance of Brandeis' valuation opinions. They showed him to have a most sympathetic appreciation of the administrative process as an essential instrument for coping with the ramifying effects of modern economic

[71] *Ibid.*, pp. 166–67.
[72] Dickinson, *Administrative Justice and the Supremacy of Law in the United States* (Cambridge: Harvard Univ. Press, 1927), p. 225.

problems. Of course, neither the substantive issues nor the administrative techniques were new to him; he had practiced before the Interstate Commerce Commission and had served it as special counsel in important cases. When the expert in the ways of public regulation became a judge, it was to be expected that this combination of knowledge and experience would incline him to be a friend of administrative agencies.

A consistently cordial attitude toward those charged with the responsibility of effectuating general policies was manifest throughout Brandeis' tenure on the Court. It was reflected in the main by the high degree of discretion he was prepared to allow them. He was not on the Bench for long before he disclosed that he was in fundamental disagreement with a majority of his colleagues over the extent to which courts should accord finality to the judgment of regulatory tribunals. His demand in the *O'Fallon* case that the Commission's findings should not be "disturbed" by the Court "unless it appears that there was an abuse of discretion" [73] had become a familiar theme in his opinions. It was but an echo of his insistence, in one of his earliest dissents, that the Federal Trade Commission's findings of the facts as to what constituted "unfair methods of competition," if based on the evidence, should "be taken as final." [74] The administrative machinery had to be upheld if Congress's program for regulating competition was to be made effective.

But if Brandeis usually voted to confirm the administrative decision, it was not because he was a partisan of bureaucracy. Deeper reasons could be discerned. His conception of the proper relationship between court and agency was never that of the technician or doctrinaire; it was the social consequences of excessive judicial intervention that were uppermost in his mind.

That this aspect of the matter was of chief concern to Brandeis

[73] 279 U.S. 461, 488, at 494 (1929).
[74] Federal Trade Commission v. Gratz, 253 U.S. 421, 429, at 437 (1920). Only Justice Clarke supported Brandeis in this case. Holmes was with the majority. See also Ohio Valley Water Co. v. Ben Avon Borough, 253 U.S. 287, 292, (1920).

was strikingly illustrated in his notable dissent in Crowell v. Benson [75]—an opinion which has been described by Louis L. Jaffe as "probably the greatest contribution of Mr. Justice Brandeis to the doctrinal side of administrative law." [76] A majority of the Supreme Court, with Chief Justice Hughes as their spokesman, had refused to regard as final a deputy commissioner's determination that the accident in question had occurred under conditions covered by the provisions of the Longshoremen's and Harbor Workers' Compensation Act. But Brandeis saw the judicial intrusion into the fact-finding process as a serious threat to the whole purpose of the statute as well as to its administration:

To permit a contest *de novo* in the district court of an issue tried, or triable, before the deputy commissioner will, I fear, gravely hamper the effective administration of the Act. The prestige of the deputy commissioner will necessarily be lessened by the opportunity of relitigating facts in the courts. The number of controverted cases may be largely increased. Persistence in controversy will be encouraged. And since the advantage of prolonged litigation lies with the party able to bear heavy expenses the purpose of the Act will be in part defeated. [77]

Brandeis was convinced that too much judicial control was bad for the courts as well as the agencies. As he put it in 1936:

In deciding whether the Constitution prevents Congress from giving finality to findings as to value or income where confiscation is alleged the Court must consider the effect of our decisions not only upon the function of rate regulation, but also upon the administrative and judicial tribunals themselves. Responsibility is the great developer of men. May it not tend to emasculate or demoralize the rate-making body if ultimate

---

[75] 285 U.S. 22, 65 (1932).

[76] Jaffe, "The Contributions of Mr. Justice Brandeis to Administrative Law," *18 Iowa L. Rev.* 213, 226 (1933). Both Brandeis' motivation and his method in this branch of constitutional law were summarized by Professor Jaffe in one succinct comment: "His devotion is not to doctrine; he is not primarily concerned to presume an artificial consistency with what he may have said in this or that case. Rather he seeks an intuitive judgment of what will be a just, a 'social' result, after a very elaborate and careful consideration of the pertinent realities." *Ibid.*, p. 224.

[77] 285 U.S. 22, 65, at 94.

responsibility is transferred to others? To the capacity of men there is a limit. May it not impair the quality of the work of the courts if this heavy task of reviewing questions of fact is assumed? [78]

Any suspicion that Brandeis' personal god was efficiency should have been dispelled by the earnestness of his dissent—reinforced by "exhaustive research" which impressed even Holmes—from Chief Justice Taft's dubious claim for an unlimited Presidential power of removal.[79] "The doctrine of the separation of powers was adopted by the Convention of 1787," we were reminded, "not to promote efficiency but to preclude the exercise of arbitrary power." [80]

Holmes did not always share Brandeis' view of administrative justice, nor did he always agree with everything Brandeis said when they voted the same way. Allowing for the differences between them with respect to both technical competence and social purpose, the record nevertheless indicates that they reached the same result in most of the really important divisions of the Court having to do with the scope of judicial supervision of administrative action. Few would question Judge Wyzanski's estimate of the comparative significance of their contributions to the development of administrative law in the United States:

Holmes' willingness to tolerate change, variety and experimentation accounts for his attitude toward another facet of orthodox democratic theory. He was as familiar as any statesman with the oft-proclaimed virtues of the separation of powers, and he was aware how many interpreters of our Constitution have found these virtues enshrined not merely in cer-

[78] Concurring in St. Joseph Stock Yards Co. v. United States, 298 U.S. 38, 73, at 92 (1936). It was in this opinion that Brandeis reduced the question as to the limits of judicial control of administrative action to two criteria: "The supremacy of law demands that there shall be opportunity to have some court to decide whether an erroneous rule of law was applied; and whether the proceeding in which facts were adjudicated was conducted regularly." (At 84.)

[79] Myers v. United States, 272 U.S. 52, 177, 178, 240 (1926).

[80] Ibid., at 293. Holmes also dissented, as did Justice McReynolds. "My brothers McReynolds and Brandeis have discussed the question before us with exhaustive research," Holmes began, adding, "and I say a few words merely to emphasize my agreement with their conclusion." Perhaps his real reason for filing a separate opinion was to be able to say that Taft's arguments were "spider's webs inadequate to control the dominant facts." (At 177.)

tain constitutional clauses but in the very textual structure of the document. . . . Yet Holmes was receptive to the needs of modern society to establish agencies of government which mingled these supposedly separate powers. He showed this in his votes in cases involving the Interstate Commerce Commission, the Federal Trade Commission and the government of the territories we acquired after the Spanish-American War. In many of these cases, however, he was less the pioneer than the second to Mr. Justice Brandeis, the chief judicial expositor of the most original affirmative powers of our twentieth century democracy—administrative agencies, governmental corporations and public authorities of mixed functions.[81]

[81] Wyzanski, *op. cit.,* in *The Holmes Reader,* p. 261.

12

"The quiet of a storm centre"

The recent spate of books exploring the anatomy of American conservatism and liberalism throws a good deal of light on the difficulty in assessing the stream of insurgent ideas of which Holmes and Brandeis were presumably the trail-blazers. Thus, one writer, though conceding at the outset of his scholarly journey that "conservatism is one of the most confusing words in the glossary of political thought and oratory," nevertheless concludes that "A definitive history of the post-Civil War Right would tell of . . . Oliver Wendell Holmes, Jr., a patrician skeptic whose doctrine of judicial self-restraint still leads some people to think of him as a Liberal." [1] Another scholar, primarily concerned with the ideological contradictions and "irrational compulsions" in American liberalism, poses an even more challenging question:

Brandeis, the Great Dissenter on the bench, was after all Brandeis, the great conformist in the realm of trustbusting Algerism. And if Holmes pursued a fine relativistic line, which might conceivably have sanctioned all sorts of things, including French Solidarism and German socialism, at least in the states, the fact was that these philosophies did not come to the bench for his judgment. The apparent bravery in the realm of legal institution did not carry over into the larger social outlook.[2]

[1] Clinton Rossiter, *Conservatism in America* (New York: Alfred A. Knopf, 1955), pp. 4, 169.
[2] Louis Hartz, *The Liberal Tradition in America* (New York: Harcourt, Brace and Company, 1955), p. 242.

Still another writer, who equates the liberal psyche with the urge
to reform, includes both Holmes and Brandeis as exemplars of that
mood.[3]

Yet the problem is not merely a semantic one. It is rooted in an
American dilemma as old as the whole tradition of judicial supremacy itself. More than a hundred years ago, Alexis de Tocqueville
perceived a basic truth about the political habits of the American
people. "Scarcely any political question arises in the United States,"
we read in *Democracy in America*, "that is not resolved sooner or
later into a judicial question." [4] Justice Frankfurter recently quoted
this observation and described it as "characteristic discernment." [5]
Another distinguished jurist—Charles E. Clark, now Chief Judge
of the United States Court of Appeals for the Second Circuit—not
so long ago expressed de Tocqueville's insight in terms more nearly
attuned to the temper of our own time:

> That an American judge in applying constitutional mandates is called
> upon to determine delicate matters of governmental polity beyond the
> scope of his professional competence is hardly news at this late date. In-
> deed, the dilemma thus posited for the judge may be thought of diminish-
> ing importance in the light of the present judicial tendency to avoid
> invalidation of legislation at almost all cost. But so strong is the popular
> tradition of judicial omniscience and power that the general public still
> looks to the courts for its protection against all sorts of feared dangers and
> oppressions from those in authority.[6]

The "reign of law and of lawyers" and the "legalistic approach
to governmental policy" of which Judge Clark also spoke on the
same occasion permeate public affairs in this country so extensively
that there probably is no way of assessing their exact impact on
either community policy or public thinking. What is clear is that

[3] Eric F. Goldman, *Rendezvous with Destiny* (New York: Alfred A. Knopf,
1952), pp. 134–40.

[4] de Tocqueville, *Democracy in America* (New York: Alfred A. Knopf,
1945; Phillips Bradley, ed.), I, 280.

[5] Frankfurter, "The Judicial Process and the Supreme Court," printed in *Of
Law and Men, Papers and Addresses of Felix Frankfurter*, edited by Philip Elman (New York: Harcourt, Brace, 1956), p. 34.

[6] Clark, "The Dilemma of American Judges: Is Too Great 'Trust for Salvation' Placed in Them?" 35 *Amer. Bar Assoc. J.* 8 (1949).

judicial review has cast upon American judges—especially those functioning at the constitutional level—the most difficult and delicate role in our system of popular government. It may be true, as Eugene V. Rostow has persuasively argued, that judicial review of legislation is no more "undemocratic" than are the other constitutional checks upon the exercise of governmental power in the United States. Professor Rostow writes:

> If one may use a personal definition of the crucial word, this way of policing the Constitution is not undemocratic. True, it employs appointed officials, to whom large powers are irrevocably delegated. But democracies need not elect all the officers who exercise crucial authority in the name of the voters. Admirals and generals can win or lose wars in the exercise of their discretion. The independence of judges in the administration of justice has been the pride of communities which aspire to be free. Members of the Federal Reserve Board have the lawful power to plunge the country into depression or inflation. The list could readily be extended. Government by referendum or town meeting is not the only possible form of democracy. The task of democracy is not to have the people vote directly on every issue, but to assure their ultimate responsibility for the acts of their representatives, elected or appointed.[7]

There may be "a look of logic," [8] as Holmes might have said, in the analogies suggested by Professor Rostow, but the great prerogative to annul the decisions of a community's policy-makers is not to be compared with the opportunities which other appointed functionaries may have for influencing the fate of a nation. "Why should a majority of nine Justices appointed for life be permitted

[7] Rostow, "The Democratic Character of Judicial Review," *66 Harv. L. Rev.* 193, 197 (1952). Professor Rostow rounded out his argument with this comment: "Where the judges are carrying out the function of constitutional review, the final responsibility of the people is appropriately guaranteed by the provisions for amending the Constitution itself, and by the benign influence of time, which changes the personnel of courts. Given the possibility of constitutional amendment, there is nothing undemocratic in having responsible and independent judges act as important constitutional mediators. Within the narrow limits of their capacity to act, their great task is to help maintain a pluralist equilibrium in society. They can do much to keep it from being dominated by the states or the Federal Government, by Congress or the President, by the purse or the sword." (At pp. 197–98.)

[8] Louisiana and Nashville R.R. v. Barber Asphalt Co., 197 U.S. 430, at 433 (1905).

to outlaw as unconstitutional the acts of elected officials or of officers controlled by elected officials?" [9] Implicit in this question, so challengingly phrased by Professor Rostow himself, is a glaring contradiction to the belief that ours is a system of popular representative government. The paradox has been deeply disturbing to many thoughtful Americans in every generation since the birth of the Republic. Judges, too, have been troubled by the discrepancy, especially in recent times. The subtle and therefore elusive connection between judicial power and governing policy is not without its historical irony, as Justice Frankfurter recently reminded us:

> In the light of their experience, the Framers of the Constitution chose to keep the judiciary dissociated from direct participation in the legislative process. In asserting the power to pass on the constitutionality of legislation, Marshall and his Court expressed the purposes of the Founders. . . . But the extent to which the exercise of this power would interpenetrate matters of policy could hardly have been foreseen by the most prescient. The distinction which the Founders drew between the Court's duty to pass on the power of Congress and its complementary duty not to enter directly the domain of policy is fundamental. But in its actual operation it is rather subtle, certainly to the common understanding. Our duty to abstain from confounding policy with constitutionality demands perceptive humility as well as self-restraint in not declaring unconstitutional what in a judge's private judgment is deemed unwise and even dangerous.[10]

Referring to the last sentence just quoted, Sidney Hook has suggested that "Justice Frankfurter's words . . . ought to be inscribed in letters of gold on the portals of the Supreme Court." [11] To some, however, it may seem misleading to cite as authority for the "right" attitude toward the exercise of judicial power the words of the judge who is generally recognized as the chief exponent of a special point of view—the so-called school of judicial self-limitation. Nevertheless, quite apart from one's estimate of the way in which Justice Frankfurter has applied the now well known precept in particular contexts, it cannot be denied that his

[9] Rostow, *op. cit.*, p. 193.
[10] Dennis v. United States, 341 U.S. 494, 517, at 552 (1951).
[11] Hook, *Heresy, Yes—Conspiracy, No*, p. 105.

counsel of restraint is but a variation of one of the oldest canons of constitutional construction. Its rationale was supplied by Justice Bushrod Washington as long ago as 1827 in a form which continues to be quoted as the classic statement of the basic principle: "It is but a decent respect to the wisdom, integrity, and patriotism of the legislative body, by which any law is passed, to presume in favor of its validity, until its violation of the Constitution is proved beyond all reasonable doubt." [12] Moreover, even in its more modern garb it has also served those reputed to be scornful of judicial self-abnegation. Thus, one of the clearest and most vigorous demands for respect for the legislative will has come from Justice Hugo L. Black, so often referred to as the leader of the Court's "activists." [13] "A century and a half of constitutional history and government admonishes this Court," he observed in 1945, "to leave that choice [among competing public policies] to the elected legislative representatives of the people themselves, where it properly belongs both on democratic principles and by the requirements of efficient government." And again: "Representatives elected by the people to make their laws, rather than judges appointed to interpret those laws, can best determine the policies which govern the people." [14]

But of course, everything depends on the implications a judge

[12] Ogden v. Saunders, 12 Wheat. 213, 254, at 270 (1827).

[13] Arthur M. Schlesinger, Jr. may have helped to popularize the labels in lay discussions with his widely read *Fortune* article on the Supreme Court. In it he differentiated the "judicial activists" from the "champions of self-restraint" in these words: "The Black–Douglas group believes that the Supreme Court can play an affirmative role in promoting the social welfare; the Frankfurter-Jackson group advocates a policy of judicial self-restraint. One group is more concerned with the employment of the judicial power for their own conception of the social good; the other with expanding the range of allowable judgment for legislatures, even if it means upholding conclusions they privately condemn. One group regards the Court as an instrument to achieve desired social results; the second as an instrument to permit the other branches of government to achieve the results the people want for better or worse. In brief, the Black–Douglas wing appears to be more concerned with settling particular cases in accordance with their own social preconceptions; the Frankfurter-Jackson wing with preserving the judiciary in its established but limited place in the American system." Schlesinger, "The Supreme Court: 1947," 35 *Fortune* 73, 201 (Jan., 1947).

[14] Dissenting in Southern Pacific Company v. Arizona, 325 U.S. 761, 784, at 789 and 794 (1925).

draws from the premise, as Justice Frankfurter expressed it in his
most criticized opinion, that judicial review is "a limitation on
popular government." [15] For some judges, it has served as a man-
date or excuse for acting as "saviors" of the people against themselves; all have used it as a basis for rationalizing their deference
to policies they were unwilling to disallow on constitutional grounds;
and all have invoked it in accusing colleagues of judicial imperial-
ism. "Every Justice," declared Robert H. Jackson in his extraordinarily candid lectures on the Supreme Court, "has been accused
of legislating and every one has joined in that accusation of others." [16]

That this discord may stem in part from the suspicion of the
Justices that the approach of their antagonists is serving an ulterior
purpose is suggested by something else Justice Jackson was prepared to say to his Harvard audience. We read in the third lecture:

> The question that the present times put into the minds of thoughtful
> people is to what extent Supreme Court interpretations of the Constitu-
> tion will or can preserve the free government of which the Court is a
> part. A cult of libertarian judicial activists now assails the Court almost
> as bitterly for renouncing power as the earlier "liberals" once did for
> assuming too much power. This cult appears to believe that the Court can
> find in a 4,000-word eighteenth-century document or its nineteenth-
> century Amendments, or can plausibly supply, some clear bulwark against
> all dangers and evils that today beset us internally. This assumes that the
> Court will be the dominant factor in shaping the constitutional practice of
> the future and can and will maintain, not only equality with the elective
> branches, but a large measure of supremacy and control over them. I
> may be biased against this attitude because it is so contrary to the doctrines
> of the critics of the Court, of whom I was one, at the time of the Roose-
> velt proposal to reorganize the judiciary. But it seems to me a doctrine
> wholly incompatible with faith in democracy, and in so far as it en-
> courages a belief that the judges may be left to correct the result of public
> indifference to issues of liberty in choosing Presidents, Senators, and
> Representatives, it is a vicious teaching. [17]

Writing at about the same time, Justice Douglas found himself
refuting this position:

[15] Minersville School District v. Gobitis, 310 U.S. 586, at 600 (1940).
[16] Jackson, *The Supreme Court in the American System of Government,* p. 80.
[17] *Ibid.,* pp. 57–58.

Judges like Brandeis, Cardozo, Hughes, Murphy, Stone, and Rutledge brought to the bench a libertarian philosophy and used it to shape the law to the needs of an oncoming generation. In that sense they were "activists," criticized by many. But history will honor them for their creative work. They knew that all life is change and that law must be constantly renewed if the pressures of society are not to build up to violence and revolt.[18]

On the long historical view, it is probably desirable that those who exercise the power of judicial review should on occasion feel a sense of guilt about the great authority they wield.[19] Too cavalier a disregard of the claims of the popular impulse may again produce the situation described by Justice Holmes shortly before he left the Bench: "As the decisions now stand, I see hardly any limit but the sky to the invalidating of those rights if they happen to strike a majority of this Court as for any reason undesirable."[20] In the particular case, Holmes was voicing his "more than anxiety" over the judicial erosion of the constitutional powers of the States, but his complaint was fundamentally applicable to the larger issue of the unrestrained use of judicial power. It should surprise no one that in an age in which—to borrow an apt comment from Justice Cardozo—"the process of psychoanalysis has spread to unaccustomed fields,"[21] those who accepted the diagnosis implicit in Holmes' criticism should have been led to explore the psychological roots of judicial error.

[18] Douglas, *An Almanac of Liberty,* p. 104.

[19] "A theme of uneasiness, and even of guilt, colors the literature about judicial review. Many of those who have talked, lectured, and written about the Constitution have been troubled by a sense that judicial review is undemocratic." Rostow, *op. cit.,* p. 193.

[20] Dissenting in Baldwin v. Missouri, 281 U.S. 586, 595 (1930). "I have not yet adequately expressed the more than anxiety that I feel at the ever increasing scope given to the Fourteenth Amendment in cutting down what I believe to be the constitutional rights of the States. As the decisions now stand, I see hardly any limit but the sky to the invalidating of those rights if they happen to strike a majority of this Court as for any reason undesirable. I cannot believe that the Amendment [Fourteenth] was intended to give us *carte blanche* to embody our economic or moral beliefs in its prohibitions. Yet I can think of no narrower reason that seems to me to justify the present and the earlier decisions to which I have referred." (At 595–96.)

[21] Dissenting in United States v. Constantine, 296 U.S. 287, 297, at 299 (1935).

Even as in the realm of human behavior generally, excessive preoccupation by judges with the limitations and risks of their labors is likely to result in confusion and lack of self-assurance. No one can quarrel with the judge who makes a conscientious attempt to remove some of the fog and mystery that have traditionally surrounded the adjudicatory process. The effort is particularly commendable and useful in the constitutional field. Nor is it difficult to account for the increase in self-analysis. The growing popularity of introspective jurisprudence was undoubtedly a reaction to the rampant self-indulgence in the 1920's and early 1930's. It was a necessary and salutary corrective. The trouble is, however, that this judicial catharsis has led to a kind of a cult, a cult of apologetics and negation. Self-examination seems to have led to self-contradiction. Semantic obscurantism and mutual recrimination are but part of the price we are paying for the Supreme Court's flirtation with modern psychology.

The more serious consequence is that the wrangles over attitudes and motives have tended to obscure the real nature of the judicial function under the American constitutional system. As John Raeburn Green has bluntly suggested, in the last analysis the "battle" of those who dwell on the undemocratic character of judicial review "is not with judicial review but with the Constitution." [22] In

[22] Green, Book Review: 32 *California L. Rev. 111*, 118 (1944). By way of indicating that the issue of judicial review versus democracy is not as simple as some might suppose, Mr. Green called attention to the special problem arising from the great diversities in the American federation: "The limitations which the Constitution, and in particular the Bill of Rights, impose, were and are an exercise of self-restraint by a national majority, intended to be permanent until changed by a subsequent national (not local) majority. So long as they remain unchanged, they may fairly be taken to reflect the continuing and present popular will of the nation, much more accurately than a school board's regulation, a town's ordinance, or even a State's statute. The essential principle of the Bill of Rights is certainly that the protection of the fundamental rights of minorities is a matter of national concern, necessary, as Mr. Chief Justice Hughes said, 'in order to save democratic government from destroying itself by the excesses of its own powers.' . . . In other words, the majority which makes and continues the constitutional compact, . . . is not identical with the local majority which . . . has indicated its will by local legislation. In a clamor of conflicting commands, ought not the Court, when it is ultimately required to act in a litigated matter, to make some inquiry as to which is the authentic voice of the people?" (At p. 117.)

claiming the right to have the final say as to the meaning of the Constitution, the Supreme Court assumed a power which was but a logical extension of the basic plan for subjecting governmental action to constitutional limits. When it is said that judicial review is an undemocratic feature of our political system, it ought also to be remembered that the architects of that system did not equate constitutional government with unbridled majority rule. Out of their concern for political stability and security for private rights, particularly property, they designed a structure whose keystone was to consist of barriers to the untrammeled exercise of power by any group. They perceived no contradiction between effective government and constitutional checks. To James Madison, who may legitimately be regarded as the philosopher of the Constitution, the scheme of mutual restraints was the best answer to what he viewed as the chief problem in erecting a system of free representative government: "In framing a government which is to be administered by men over men, the great difficulty lies in this: you must first enable the government to control the governed; and in the next place oblige it to control itself." [23]

While the question as to original intent will no doubt continue

[23] It may be of interest to recall the context in which this paradox is set forth: "But the great security against a gradual concentration of the several powers in the same department, consists in giving to those who administer each department the necessary constitutional means and personal motives to resist encroachments of the others. The provision for defence must in this, as in all other cases, be made commensurate to the danger of attack. Ambition must be made to counteract ambition. The interest of the man must be connected with the constitutional rights of the place. It may be a reflection on human nature that such devices should be necessary to control the abuses of government. But what is government itself, but the greatest of all reflections on human nature? If men were angels, no government would be necessary. If angels were to govern men, neither external nor internal controls on government would be necessary. In framing a government which is to be administered by men over men, the great difficulty lies in this: you must first enable the government to control the governed; and in the next place oblige it to control itself. A dependence on the people is, no doubt, the primary control on the government; but experience has taught mankind the necessity of auxiliary precautions." *The Federalist* (New York: The Heritage Press, 1945), pp. 347–48. For a discussion of Madison's influence in shaping the "core" of the Constitution, see Irving Brant, *James Madison: Father of the Constitution* (New York: Bobbs-Merrill Company, 1950), pp. 32–45.

to intrigue scholars and jurists, it is clear that the power proclaimed by Marshall for enforcing the "supremacy" of the Constitution is the most far-reaching of the manifestations of the grand design for preventing the popular will from having its way immediately or completely. When Alexander Meiklejohn recently spoke of "the paradoxical relation between free men and their legislative agents," [24] he was reminding us of a significant distinction between the American and the British systems of government. Unlike the legally unlimited position of Parliament, American legislators, though chosen by the people, have always been subject to fundamental limitations upon the powers they exercise. As a practical matter, the power of judicial review enables judges to impose upon the people's representatives, elected or appointed, restraints derived from the consensus of a bygone day. Inevitably, therefore, our "constitutional mediators" are compelled, by the very nature of their historic role, to weigh current public policies in terms of an established folklore. The claims of the past may be an influence shackling all men reared in a constitutional tradition; but for the American judge they are in essence the tests of his official responsibility. Torn between the old and the new—and the old has often meant the ways to which they had grown accustomed—judges can always invoke the Constitution to support their cherished notions of the public good.

If the Supreme Court of the United States is drawn, sooner or later, into all major public issues, the resulting strain is but an incident of its function as the ultimate arbiter of the fundamental conflicts which arise in the process of government. It is the ordeal of great political power free of direct accountability for its exercise, though wielded within a scheme of popular government. "We are very quiet there," Holmes reported after ten years on the Court, "but it is the quiet of a storm centre, as we all know." [25] The way in which a member of the Court meets this challenge of his difficult

[24] Meiklejohn, "What Does the First Amendment Mean?" *20 Univ. of Chicago L. Rev. 461, 463* (1953).
[25] Holmes, "Law and the Court," in *Collected Legal Papers*, p. 292.

office usually reveals not only his attitude toward present issues but also his whole conception of the Constitution and of the method for adapting it to needs not anticipated by the Founders.

Justice Owen J. Roberts, who served with Brandeis for nearly a decade, compared him to the old Hebrew prophets, though he also attested to the fact that his former associate was no Pharisee on the Bench. "We are teachers," Brandeis would occasionally say to his colleagues. He was apparently quite serious in urging that the Tribunal had a responsibility to teach and uphold moral principles.[26] Perhaps it is this lofty view of the Supreme Court's function which helps to explain what Judge Learned Hand has described as Brandeis' "almost mystic reverence" [27] for the Court as a national institution and his solicitude for its reputation. Who can doubt that Brandeis would have concurred in Charles P. Curtis' suggestion that the Supreme Court is the "conscience" of the American people.[28]

[26] Interview with Justice Roberts at Philadelphia, Sept. 19, 1951.

[27] "Before passing to my theme, I can therefore do no more than allude to much that I can ill afford to leave out: for instance, to his [Brandeis'] almost mystic reverence for that Court, whose tradition seemed to him not only to consecrate its own members, but to impress its sacred mission upon all who shared in any measure in its work, even menially. To his mind nothing must weaken its influence or tarnish its lustre; no matter how hot had been the dispute, how wide the final difference, how plain the speech, nothing ever appeared to ruffle or disturb his serenity, or to suggest that he harbored anything but regard and respect for the views of his colleagues, however far removed from his own." Judge Learned Hand, speaking at Proceedings in Memory of Mr. Justice Brandeis, 317 U.S. IX, at XI (Dec. 21, 1942).

One of Brandeis' secretaries points out that the Justice was acutely conscious of being part of an institution and that he drew a sharp distinction between the Supreme Court and the other branches of the Government. Brandeis seemed to believe that the really essential aspect of the Court's function was not the adjudication of individual cases but the dramatization of fundamental principles. The Court was a kind of Holy Synod, to be kept untouchable and unsullied. The Justice expected his law clerks to be most scrupulous and cautious in discussing Court business and particularly so in their relations with the press. (Interview with Willard Hurst, at New York City, Sept. 14, 1951.)

[28] "The Court had become potentially our conscience, the spiritual guide and father confessor of all our governments, state as well as federal, a court of honor as well as a court of law, our wise old uncle, the Hays office, if you please, of political behavior, or if you prefer, our daimon of Socrates; mediator, in brief, between man as an individual and man in society." Curtis, *Lions Under the Throne* (Boston: Houghton Mifflin Company, 1947), p. 284.

That Holmes had no such feelings about the Court's function may be inferred from his famous observation indicating that while he feared that "the Union would be imperiled" if local regulations could not be set aside, he did not think "the United States would come to an end if we lost our power to declare an act of Congress void." [29]

In the present century, it has become part of legal as well as psychological sophistication to believe that a Justice's constitutional slant is a mask for his convictions as a citizen. For this reason, the affinity between two men so different in background and social outlook as were Holmes and Brandeis continues to puzzle many. Personally doubtful of the possibility of social improvement through government direction, Holmes usually voted with the colleague for whom the achievement of greater freedom and justice was the final test of all social effort, including governmental activities. For Brandeis, it has rightly been said, "Law is not a system of artificial reason but the application of ethical ideals, with freedom at the core." [30] On the other hand, many an observer has seen in Holmes' deeply ingrained skepticism and his obsession with the logic of power an amoral philosophy akin to that of Hobbes and Hegel. Granted that there is both exaggeration and oversimplification in these careless ideological analogies, there is yet enough truth to them to lend mystery to Holmes' kinship with the great moralist and crusader on the Court. To the extent that their relationship on the Supreme Court helps to answer this baffling question, it sheds even more light on the nature of the American Constitution and on its interpretation by judges.

[29] "I do not think the United States would come to an end if we lost our power to declare an Act of Congress void. I do think the Union would be imperiled if we could not make that declaration as to the laws of the several States. For one in my place sees how often a local policy prevails with those who are not trained to national views and how often action is taken that embodies what the Commerce Clause was meant to end." Holmes, *op. cit.*, pp. 295–96.

[30] It was in these words that Felix Frankfurter and Nathan Greene dedicated their book, *The Labor Injunction*, to Justice Brandeis. (New York: The Macmillan Company, 1930.)

Venturing to assess Brandeis' "significance" shortly after Holmes left the Court, the late Harold J. Laski compared their individual attitudes toward the judicial function in terms which furnish one of the main keys for unlocking the mystery. Laski wrote:

President Wilson's nomination of Mr. Brandeis to the Bench in 1916 is not unlikely to rank as among the half dozen major acts of his period of office. It was significant enough in the opposition it aroused; no man can be better known than by the enemies he makes. It was even more significant by reason of the temper and method it brought to the work of the Supreme Court. Before 1916 Mr. Justice Holmes had been a liberal influence there because his mind was too skeptical to insist that his own judgment of what was desirable should be equated with constitutional truth. But Mr. Justice Holmes not only enjoyed a lonely eminence in this regard; he was content to accept the traditional affirmation by deduction as the proper judicial method; and the careful student of his opinions will find that his differences from his brethren lay less in the substance of their philosophy than in the refusal on his part to make it a final and unchallengeable way of life. Mr. Justice Holmes accepted the assumptions of the old capitalistic America, its confidence in the struggle for existence as the parent of the survival of the fittest, its distrust of social regulation, its belief that the great business man was the natural leader of America. Where he departed from the ancient ways was in his willingness to admit that other interpretations were not merely possible but, more important, constitutionally legitimate also.

It was the importance of Mr. Justice Brandeis' accession to the Court that where Holmes was a liberal by negation he was a liberal by positive affirmation. He brought to the court not only a willingness to doubt its traditional outlook but an alternative philosophy which might reasonably supersede it. The very fact that it was an alternative led his critics at once to the assumption that he was, in the special American sense, a radical. That is a mistaken view. There has been nothing in his analysis of social foundations which suggests any ultimate dissatisfaction with their primary assumptions. But whereas to most members of the Supreme Court the main purpose of the Constitution was to preserve the rights of private property from invasion by the popular will, to Mr. Justice Brandeis the control of their pathological results by state action was an inherent and desirable function of public power. It was the assertion that this function was both inherent and desirable, the insistence that no constitutional interpretation was justified which sought to put barriers in the way of its attainment, which has constituted the real innovation of Mr. Justice Brandeis in the years since he has sat upon the Court.[31]

The paradox perceived by Laski is obviously suggestive of more than one problem in the quest for an explanation of the judicial harmony between Holmes and Brandeis. It was not the first time that negative as well as positive values were made to serve the liberal tradition. The whole Bill of Rights heritage is, after all, liberalism "by negation" at its classic best. Indeed, in this respect both Holmes and Brandeis were true heirs of the Enlightenment. But the striking thing about the negative impulse in Holmes' liberalism is that it was directed against the assertion of judicial authority, an attitude all the more surprising because it came from one who was at heart an apologist for power. A positivist in matters of legal and political philosophy, he nevertheless was opposed to having judges use their office for positive purposes—in the sense, at least, of transmuting their private notions of public policy into constitutional mandates. As Daniel J. Boorstin has observed—in the course of suggesting that Holmes was more interested in law as a world of struggles than in the causes with which they are concerned— "The judge was a sort of *deus ex machina,* interested not so much in removing conflict as in resolving it."[32]

---

[31] Laski, "Mr. Justice Brandeis," *168 Harper's Magazine 209, 211–12* (Jan., 1934). Writing to Holmes, on August 12, 1933, Laski summarized the conclusions he had come to in the course of preparing this article: "The three things that emerge for me are that he [Brandeis] is really a Jeffersonian Democrat, trying to use the power of the State to enforce an environment in which competition may be really free and equal; this I take to be an impossible task. Secondly, his method of analysis does magnificently relate law to the life of which it is the expression; third his criterion for all action is an ethical individualism. I take him to be intellectually, as to ends, a romantic anachronism, but as to methods a really significant figure in the Court. I doubt whether he would have had the influence he has exerted if there had not been your thirteen previous years there to form the channel for its reception. But, granted that, I conclude that his contribution has been that of a good and big man. A prophet, I suspect, rather than a judge; a grand player for a side in which he believes both disinterestedly and with all his might." *Holmes-Laski Letters,* II, 1448.

[32] Boorstin, "The Elusiveness of Mr. Justice Holmes," *14 New Eng. Quar. 478, 482* (Sept., 1941).

Is it this detachment, then, that accounts for the fact that Holmes agreed so often with the colleague who felt deeply about the public side of the issues at stake in constitutional litigation? The late Felix S. Cohen had the courage to insist that this much celebrated Olympian aloofness was "perhaps the least admirable and the least distinctive of his qualities." After quoting a comment from Morris R. Cohen which spoke of Einstein and Socrates and Holmes as men who never outgrew "a childish curiosity about the universe," Mr. Cohen found in this judgment a clue to Holmes' most "distinctive" trait: "Resisting the common judicial assumption that omniscience is donned *ex officio* with the robes of office, Justice Holmes persisted, down to the last days of his life, in studying, reading, looking for new light on the ancient problems of law and life." [33]

Yet there is little proof that Holmes' ravenous appetite for books or his reflective bent of mind led him to revise old assumptions. The impression Edmond Cahn was candid enough to share with us after reading the published correspondence between Holmes and Laski—"There is no sign that this gargantuan bibliophagy ever modified a single important premise in the thought of either man" [34]—confirms a conclusion about Holmes' intellectual limitations which cannot be denied. His curiosity about the Cosmos did not include any hunger after knowledge concerning the wide implications of the problems coming before him for judgment, a preoccupation so characteristic of "Brother Brandeis." He was eighty-three when Brandeis was still criticizing him for the superficiality of his economic dogmas. "I came home with Brandeis who grew really eloquent on the evils of the present organization of society," Holmes wrote to Laski on January 6, 1923, continuing: "When I repeated my oft repeated views as to the economic elements he told me they were superficial and didn't deal with the real evil, which was not a question of luxuries or victuals but of power. . . . Then [he] said that I hadn't seen and knew nothing about the evils

[33] "Holmes-Cohen Correspondence," IX *Journal of the History of Ideas* 1, 3 (Jan., 1948).
[34] Cahn, Book Review: 28 *N.Y. Univ. L. Rev.* 764 (1953).

that one who had been much in affairs had seen and known. He
bullies me a little on that from time to time." [35]

It is one of the ironies of Holmes' respect for the modern scientific
spirit that it did not induce in him any desire to master the tools
for understanding social phenomena. He was frank to say that
"theory is all that I can bring even to the law," though he was
quick to add, "But theory sometimes leads one to keep in mind
fundamental facts that one more versed in detail may forget." [36]
To Brandeis "detail" mattered greatly. While he appreciated that
"The economic and social sciences are largely uncharted seas," [37]
he insisted on the fullest use of all that is known about the questions
with which judges must deal. His attitude was essentially that of
the scientist and the teacher—"the master of both microscope and
telescope," as Chief Justice Hughes once described him.[38] Hence
the deep inquiry into social and economic data and the elaborate
documentation of his opinions, particularly the dissents. One of his
law secretaries recalls the Justice's "disquieting" question after an
opinion had gone through numerous revisions: "The opinion is now
convincing, but what can we do to make it more instructive?" [39]
Since Holmes believed a judicial opinion should be "quasi an oral
utterance," [40] he saw no real need for Brandeis' heavy footnotage,
much as he admired his encyclopedic knowledge and his skill in
infusing it into his opinions. There is no reason to doubt the sincerity
of Holmes' tribute to him: "I think he has done great work and I
believe with high motives." [41]

The difference between the two Justices over the form in which
opinions should be cast was but a surface manifestation of a much

[35] *Holmes-Laski Letters,* I, 469.
[36] *Ibid.,* II, 949.
[37] Dissenting in New State Ice Co. v. Liebmann, 285 U.S. 262, 280, at 310 (1932).
[38] Hughes, "Mr. Justice Brandeis," in Frankfurter (ed.), *Mr. Justice Brandeis,* p. 3.
[39] Paul A. Freund, speaking at Proceedings in Memory of Mr. Justice Brandeis, 317 U.S. IX, XVI, at XIX (Dec. 21, 1942).
[40] *Holmes-Laski Letters,* I, 675.
[41] *Holmes-Pollock Letters,* II, 191 (Oct. 31, 1926).

deeper divergence. Brandeis made explicit the basic postulate of his juristic technique when he stated in one of his better known dissents, "Knowledge is essential to understanding; and understanding should precede judging." [42] In the atmosphere of judicial hostility to innovating social policy, this faith in facts was obviously much more than a matter of style or even intellectual conviction. Still, it is not necessary to consider it as a subtle façade in order to recognize that it was meant to serve a strategic role in constitutional adjudication. In the mind of a judge intent on showing that the new demands for social justice were entirely consistent with the underlying purposes of the Constitution, clarification of the complexity of the problems and of the reasons for the particular solutions naturally assumed the importance of an indispensable means toward a vital goal.

Seen in this light, Brandeis' lasting significance in American jurisprudence may be said to be represented by his effort to bend the judicial process to the task of preserving liberal democracy in an America whose traditions and institutions had come to be threatened by a pervasive industrialism. A major precept of the new liberalism, which the Justice championed both before and after coming to the Court, called for the use of the powers of government to prevent private interests from destroying the liberty of the individual and the welfare of the community.[43] One imbued with a philosophy which viewed government as the guardian of a free

[42] Burns Baking Co. v. Bryan, 264 U.S. 504, 517, at 520 (1924).

[43] That Brandeis had his doubts about the efficacy of reform by legislative fiat and that he was no doctrinaire "statist" was made clear in his famous letter to Robert W. Bruere, written in 1922—a document which Justice Robert H. Jackson thought "could wisely be the basic creed of the modern liberal." 9 *Vital Speeches of the Day* 664, 666 (Aug. 15, 1943). One paragraph in particular is pertinent: "Refuse to accept as inevitable any evil in business (e.g., irregularity of employment). Refuse to tolerate any immoral practice (e.g., espionage). But do not believe that you can find a universal remedy for evil conditions or immoral practices in effecting a fundamental change in society (as by State Socialism). And do not pin too much faith in legislation. Remedial institutions are apt to fall under the control of the enemy and to become instruments of oppression." The Justice spoke of the responsibilities of democracy and remarked that it "demands . . . more exigent obedience to the moral law than any other form of government." The whole letter is reprinted in Mason, *Brandeis: A Free Man's Life*, p. 585.

and progressive society could not be expected to remain indifferent
to the devitalizing effects of a judicial attitude which was unmind-
ful of the challenge of the times. It was this concern with the practical results of decision-making which has led some of the interpreters to suggest that Brandeis may have had less in common with
Holmes and much more with a McReynolds or a Sutherland.
"Brandeis, like his conservative colleagues," writes Professor Mason,
"was inclined by the pressures and drives of his own nature to
translate his own economic and social views into the Constitution."[44]
Holmes' suspicions in this regard seem to have lessened as he came
to know his colleague better: "I told him once that when he had
strong economic convictions I thought that he sometimes became
the advocate and ceased to be detached—but it isn't often."[45]

Implicit in Brandeis' conception of the judicial function is the
belief that judges have a creative role to play in molding constitutional law to meet the needs of social change—in essence, a responsibility of statesmanship. After Brandeis had completed fifteen years
on the Court, an astute foreign observer of our legal system was
able to discern that his work as a judge, in and of itself, helps to
illumine the Supreme Court's unique position in American society.
His incisive words are worth recalling:

It is characteristic of the political system of the United States that the
type-figure of a great revolution in political thinking should occur . . .
among the members of the judiciary. Such a condition could not, perhaps,
occur in any other country, for the simple reason that there is no other
country in which the permissible directions of self-development of the
living body politic are so largely determined by the courts. A judge in any
other country may be a great judge; in few countries can he be at the
same time a great exponent of statecraft.[46]

Given the Supreme Court's province to speak as the authoritative
voice of the Constitution, there devolves upon the individual Justice

[44] Mason, *op. cit.*, p. 580.
[45] *Holmes-Laski Letters*, I, 556 (Nov. 5, 1923).
[46] B. K. Sandwell, Book Review: *18 Amer. Bar Assoc. J.* 805 (1932). A distinguished Canadian academician and journalist, Mr. Sandwell was for twenty
years editor of *Saturday Night* and for several years Rector of Queens
University.

the inescapable duty of making the generalities of another age relevant for the problems of his day. Thus inevitably pulled into the conflicts of principle and policy which generated the law suits, he is afforded a tempting opportunity to endow with constitutional sanction his own social, economic and political ideals. That Holmes and Brandeis responded quite differently to the responsibility of judicial power is by now commonplace. Controversy is likely to persist, however, over the question as to whose attitude was the more enlightened and useful contribution.

Holmes' imperturbable confidence in the capacity of society to defy artificial meddling with its natural evolution enabled him to maintain equanimity and poise in the presence of drastic changes and grave evils. His tolerance was born of skepticism and apathy, and it made it easy for him to "transcend" his own "convictions." [47] So it happened that the "great dissenter" on the Court was actually— as America's other eminent skeptic exclaimed after discovering the Justice's essential conservatism—"no more than an advocate of the rights of law-makers." [48] This inclination to let the legislature have its way brought him nearly always to the same result as Brandeis, even though the particular case was concerned with measures of which he was dubious and which Brandeis thought to be both wise and necessary. Where Brandeis was saying that the country's commitment to democracy required the fulfillment of the aspirations

[47] "We [judges] too need education in the obvious—to learn to transcend our own convictions and to leave room for much that we hold dear to be done away with short of revolution by the orderly change of law." *Collected Legal Papers,* p. 295.

[48] H. L. Mencken, Book Review: *20 American Mercury 122* (May, 1930). See also Mencken's "The Great Holmes Mystery," *26 American Mercury 123* (May, 1932). Horace Chapman Rose, whose year with Holmes included the Justice's last four months on the Court, insists that Holmes was no H. L. Mencken type of cynic. Indeed, according to Mr. Rose, emphasis on Holmes' skepticism would result in a completely wrong appraisal of him. If by cynicism is meant the annihilation of values, Holmes was no cynic. He may have been skeptical of precise formulations, but rebellion against absolutes is not inconsistent with a devotion to values. (Interview with Horace Chapman Rose, at Washington, D.C., May 17, 1951.) In the sense of a "lifelong dissent from the American creed," as Edgar Kemler has described Mencken's heresy, Holmes certainly was no cynic. See Kemler, "The Bright Twilight of H. L. Mencken," *The New York Times Magazine,* p. 14 (Sept. 11, 1955).

sought to be realized by legislation, it was enough for Holmes that the Constitution did not forbid the experiments. Even Brandeis' interest in strictly limiting the Supreme Court's jurisdiction probably stemmed from his desire to enable it to perform more effectively its historic function of constitutional statesmanship. "In order to give adequate consideration to the adjudication of great issues of government," he declared in 1929, the Court "must, so far as possible, lessen the burden incident to the disposition of cases which come here for review." [49]

As long as the Supreme Court retains its right to abort the decisions of the popularly constituted branches of the government, the Holmesian gospel of judicial forbearance will remain a valuable legacy to the American people. Situations are bound to arise when deference to the community's primary policy-makers will be the course of wisdom. But it is doubtful whether the rarefied objectivity typified by Holmes, even if it were attainable, is the best equipment for the arbitration of constitutional issues. His ability to rise above the clamor of contending forces and the demands of ephemeral interests may be a great asset in a judge deciding purely private disputes. This kind of personal insulation may give him that "high maturity" which Judge Jerome Frank deems to be the mark of "the completely adult jurist," as he has admiringly described Justice Holmes.[50] "I have said to my brethren many times," Holmes wrote to John C. H. Wu in 1929, "that I hate justice which means that I know if a man begins to talk about that, for one reason or another he is shirking thinking in legal terms." [51] Holmes was seldom moved by the issues before the Court; when matters of social policy were at stake, Brandeis was incapable of summoning the moral neutrality in which his older colleague gloried. Does this difference between

[49] Dissenting in Railroad Commission of California v. Los Angeles Railway Corp., 280 U.S. 145, 158, at 166 (1929).

[50] Frank, *Law and the Modern Mind* (New York: Tudor Publishing Co., 1930), pp. 253, 257.

[51] Harry C. Shriver (ed.), *Justice Oliver Wendell Holmes: His Book Notices and Uncollected Letters and Papers* (New York: Central Book Company, 1936), p. 201.

the two Justices lend support to the conclusion to which Max Lerner came after comparing their contributions to the legal profession?—"Perhaps by the very fact of his indirections and his lesser urgency Holmes may ironically prove the more enduring voice." [52]

The detachment idealized by Holmes is a potential hazard in constitutional adjudication; it could lead to the form of social irresponsibility with which history has charged the Court's erstwhile conservatives. Today practically all of the cases coming before the Supreme Court deal with matters of public concern, whose outcome is of moment to persons and interests beyond those involved in the immediate court wrangle. The Justices should not be expected to do their work in an intellectual vacuum, which is what would happen if they somehow were able to divest themselves of their deepest convictions on donning their black robes. Their attitude toward the values of our society—ethical, political and economic— must surely condition their approach to the controversies they hear. No one has expressed this basic truth better than Holmes himself: "The felt necessities of the time, the prevalent moral and political theories, intuitions of public policy, avowed or unconscious, even the prejudices which judges share with their fellow-men, have had a good deal more to do than the syllogism in determining the rules by which men should be governed." [53]

However labeled—judicial, political, or super-legislative—the fact is that the power enjoyed by the Supreme Court of the United States is fraught with fateful consequences for the nation. More is needed for its responsible exercise than legal acumen.[54] While the Court may not be the sole custodian of the fundamental principles of our

[52] Lerner, *The Mind and Faith of Justice Holmes*, p. 29.

[53] Holmes, *The Common Law* (Boston: Little, Brown and Company, 1881), p. 1.

[54] Writing in 1931, Walton H. Hamilton remarked that Brandeis' "realistic bent has led many to overlook the significant fact that he is probably the ablest technical lawyer on the bench." *33 Current History 654, 657* (Feb., 1931). Justice Sutherland is reported to have said of Brandeis: "My, how I detest that man's ideas. But he is one of the greatest technical lawyers I have ever known." See above, p. 295, n. 26.

system of government, their application is largely within its keeping. Its services as umpire between Nation and States and its guardianship of property rights and personal liberties help to maintain the Constitution as a living force for each generation of Americans. So long as the need for the performance of these functions remains, the Court will be in a position to influence the direction of public policy.

Perforce one is compelled to agree with Justice Holmes that "Constitutional law like other mortal contrivances has to take some chances."[55] Awareness of human fallibility is no justification, however, for moral indifference on the part of those holding high public office. Man's basic ills may be eternal, but the key to their dimensions in the modern world is their complexity. In his lectures on the Supreme Court, Charles Evans Hughes had observed that the proper discharge of the Court's function depends less on "formulas" and more "on a correct appreciation of social conditions and a true appraisal of the actual effect of conduct."[56] Guided by this criterion, it would have to be conceded that Brandeis was far more successful than Holmes in adapting law and its techniques to the stark realities of life in the twentieth century. The fusion of richly informed judgment and high social purpose is his legacy to the judicial process.

Because decisions on constitutional questions necessarily have far-reaching effects, it is of the utmost importance that those who make them not only understand the problems they have been asked to resolve but that they care deeply about the fruits of their labors. It is Brandeis' extraordinary gifts as a student of American society as well as the strength of his attachment to the imperatives of the democratic creed which make him the authentic leader of modern constitutional jurisprudence. Unless the fate about which Walt Whitman sang is as inexorable as it sounds—"How all times mischoose the objects of their adulation and reward"[57]—it may be

[55] Blinn v. Nelson, 222 U.S. 1, at 7 (1911).
[56] Hughes, *The Supreme Court of the United States*, p. 166.
[57] "Beginners" in *Leaves of Grass* (Philadelphia: David McKay, 1884), p. 15.

predicted that Louis D. Brandeis will continue to be honored as a model of judicial statesmanship. It has taken a warm and eloquent admirer of Holmes to state most clearly the superior claim of Brandeis to the homage of posterity:

The premises of [Holmes'] individual decisions are often far from modern. For the rest, the striking expression remains: "My agreement or disagreement has nothing to do with the rights of a majority to embody their opinions in law," with only the qualification of vigilance against attempts to check *opinions* that we loathe. These views were obsolete or obsolescent when the young Holmes took his commission in the Twentieth. The *modern* need which began then and has rolled up bewilderingly since was the need for the social technician, for him who in the whirring, clanging maze of modern economic life could find sense, see out-of-gearness, invent remedy. A Brandeis sustains a new industrial or business regulation because he sees and demonstrates its utility. A Holmes sustains it in mild wondering approval, patient tolerance, magnificent disinterest. Modern in any sense of a man of the industrial era, or of a man equipped to deal with its peculiar needs, Holmes is not.[58]

But each Justice, in his own way, has come to symbolize the never-ending struggle to infuse law and balance into the processes by which the people of the United States are governed. They differed greatly in intellectual taste, social perception, political ideals, and juristic method. Yet they were able to achieve almost complete accord in their exposition of the Constitution. The harmony between Justices Holmes and Brandeis is as illuminating a commentary upon the essentially flexible nature of America's fundamental charter as one can expect to find in the whole field of judicial biography.

[58] Karl N. Llewellyn, Book Review: *31 Col. L. Rev. 902, 905* (1931).

Index

Dennis v. United States, 193, 222, 240–56, 288
Depression of the 1930's, 179
Di Santo v. Pennsylvania, 156
Dickinson, John, 280
Dictatorship of the proletariat, 223, 226
Dilliard, Irving, 92
Dirlam, Joel B., 173
Dissents, role of, 102–105
District of Columbia Minimum Wage Case. *See* Adkins v. Children's Hospital
District of Columbia Minimum Wage Law, 142, 145–47, 149
Dodd, William E., 68
Donnell v. Herring-Hall-Marvin Safe Co., 5
Douglas, Justice William O., 172, 236, 237, 240, 242, 250, 253, 256, 273, 289, 290–91
Dr. Miles Medical Co. v. Park and Sons Co., 58–59
Driscoll v. Edison Light and Power Co., 273
Due process of law, 30, 32, 34, 36, 41, 63, 130, 188, 227, 239, 262, 265, 272, 290–91
Duplex Printing Press Co. v. Deering, 120, 121–27, 129, 137, 138

Eastern States Retail Lumber Dealers' Association v. United States, 121
"Economic elements," 25, 299
Ege, Warren S., 257
Ehrlich, Eugene, 12
Eighteenth Amendment, 160
Einstein, Albert, 299
Elman, Philip, 286
Emergency Farm Mortgage Act of 1933. *See* Frazier-Lemke Act
Emerson, Ralph Waldo, 181
Eminent domain, 271
Employment agencies, 100–102
Equal protection, 130, 164, 166
Erdman Act, 62
Espionage Act of 1917, 190, 194, 195, 196, 198, 200, 204–05, 214, 217, 219–20, 244
Exchange value, 276

Fact finding. *See* Administrative finality
Fair procedure and criminal trials, 262–263
Fair value, 272, 273
Falbo v. United States, 238
Farnum, George R., 6, 116
Farrand, Max, 106
Federal Employers' Liability Act, 97–99
Federal Power Commission v. Natural Gas Pipeline Co., 273
Federal Reserve Board, 287
Federal Trade Commission, 281, 284
Federal Trade Commission v. Gratz, 281
Federalist Papers, 46, 106, 107, 108, 293
Fellman, David, 240–241
Fellow servant's negligence, 98
Field, Justice Steven J., 32–33, 60, 61
Field, Judge Walbridge Abner, 20
Fifth Amendment, 62, 144, 147, 264, 271
Finkelstein, Maurice, 159, 162
First Amendment, 181, 182, 186, 187, 191, 192, 193, 196, 210, 236, 237, 238, 244, 253, 254
Fisher, H. A. L., 9
Flag salute cases, 202, 235, 240, 290
Ford, John C., 184
Fourth Amendment, 264
Fourteenth Amendment, 29, 31–33, 36, 38–39, 42, 43, 85, 130, 133, 148, 150, 151, 153, 160, 164, 166, 179, 181, 218, 238, 259, 269, 291
Fox v. Washington, 189, 193
Fraenkel, Osmond K., 69
Framers of the Constitution, 181, 288
Frank, Judge Jerome N., 171, 304
Frank, John P., 241
Frank v. Mangum, 262
Frankfurter, Justice Felix, 7, 8, 9, 12, 14, 30, 84, 88–89, 92, 104, 108, 131, 137, 138, 140, 142, 143, 147, 156, 161–62, 202, 210, 222, 235, 236, 238, 240, 242, 243, 253, 254, 265, 273, 286, 288, 289, 290, 296, 300
Frazier-Lemke Act, 271

Index

Judicial review, purpose of, 41, 105–08, 291, 292, 294
Judicial self-restraint, 3, 16, 32, 42, 57, 66, 116, 234, 288, 289, 292
Just compensation, 268, 271

Kahn, Alfred E., 173
Kemler, Edgar, 303
Kent, Chancellor James, 14, 83
Kipling, Rudyard, 280
Kirchwey, George W., 103
Knox, Philander C., 49
Kohler Act, 268, 269
Konvitz, Milton R., 201, 233
Kovacs v. Cooper, 238, 265

La Follette, Robert M., 73
Labor injunctions, 119, 126, 130, 135
Laissez-faire, 31, 36, 39, 42, 144, 249, 266
Landis, James M., 92
Laski, Harold J., 34, 60, 69, 93, 95, 97, 103, 176, 183, 257, 265, 268, 271, 297–98, 299
Lawlor v. Loewe, 121
Left Wing Manifesto, 223–25, 247
Lerner, Max, 9–10, 13–14, 24, 48, 57, 74, 110, 143, 176, 207, 258, 261, 305
Liberalism, 8–9, 59–60, 65, 73–74, 93–96, 139–42, 232–34, 258, 285–86, 297–98, 301
Liberty of contract, 31, 33, 36, 37, 40, 50, 62, 63, 144, 148, 233, 238, 259
Liberty of contract, 31, 33, 36, 37, 40, 50, 62, 63, 144, 148, 233, 238, 259
Lief, Alfred, 70, 71, 77
Liggett v. Baldridge, 170–71
Liggett v. Lee, 166–69
Lilienthal, David E., 172–73
Llewellyn, Karl N., 117, 307
Lloyd, Henry Demarest, 47
Lochner v. New York, 35–44, 64, 85, 109, 143, 144, 146, 147, 150, 259
Lodge, Henry Cabot, 15
Loewe v. Lawlor, 121–22
Longshoremen's and Harbor Workers' Compensation Act, 282
Lorenzo v. Wirth, 5
Lottery Case. See Champion v. Ames

Louisiana and Nashville R.R. v. Barber Asphalt Co., 287
Louisville and Nashville R.R. v. United States, 96
Louisville Bank v. Radford, 271
Louisville v. Cumberland Telephone and Telegraph Co., 273
Luce, Henry R., 184
Lucey, Francis E., 184
Lyons, Louis M., 94

McAuliffe v. New Bedford, 185
McCloskey, Robert G., 241
McKenna, Justice Joseph, 112, 143, 174, 210–11, 216, 220
McKinley, President William, 223
McKinnon, Harold R., 184
MacLeish, Archibald, 131
McReynolds, Justice James C., 60, 100, 136, 143, 150, 163, 233, 259–60, 274, 279, 283, 302
Madison, James, 46, 196, 293
Maitland, Frederick William, 9
Malthus, Thomas R., 24
Manchester School, 249
Maple Flooring Manufacturers' Association v. United States, 176
Marbury v. Madison, 107
Marke, Julius J., 262
Marshall, John, 3, 7, 14, 83, 106–107, 109, 288
Martial rule, 188
Marxist-Leninist ideology, 224, 247
Mason, Alpheus Thomas, 6, 7, 67, 73, 79, 84, 102, 152, 278, 279, 301, 302
Massachusetts Bill of Rights, 16
Massachusetts Commission on the Minimum Wage, 90
Massachusetts General Court, 19
Massachusetts Supreme Judicial Court, 17
Masses Publishing Co. v. Patten, 194
Medina, Judge Harold R., 246–47, 250
Meiklejohn, Alexander, 182, 192, 254, 294
Mencken, H. L., 303
Mendelson, Wallace, 193
Mermin, Samuel, 122

Index

315

Privacy, right of, 263–64
Progressive movement, 43, 47, 69, 73, 74, 78
Property, constitutional protection of, 63, 77, 132, 136, 259, 266–67, 269, 306
"Prudent investment," 274, 277–78
Pusey, Merlo J., 169, 262

Quaker City Cab Co. v. Pennsylvania, 163–65, 170

Railroad Commission of California v. Los Angeles Railway Corp., 304
Realism in law, 60–61
Reasonableness, test of, 40, 42, 64, 91, 267–70
Reed, Justice Stanley F., 236
Reproduction cost, 275, 278
Respondeat superior, 98
Richardson, Elliot L., 254
Riesman, David, 6, 163
Roberts, Justice Owen J., 137, 150–51, 166, 233, 236, 295
Rockefeller, John D., 25–26
Rodell, Fred, 258
Roosevelt, President Franklin D., 9, 10, 105
Roosevelt, President Theodore, 15–16, 48–49, 55
Roosevelt Court, 10, 136, 232, 235
Roosevelt Court Reorganization Plan, 105, 290
Rose, Horace Chapman, 303
Ross, Charles G., 94
Rossiter, Clinton, 285
Rostow, Eugene V., 254, 287–88, 291
Rule of reason, 52
Russian Revolution, 203, 205
Rutledge, Justice Wiley B., 236–37, 240, 291

St. Joseph Stock Yards Co. v. United States, 283
St. Louis and O'Fallon Ry. Co. v. United States, 278, 279, 281
Sandwell, B. K., 302
Sanford, Justice Edward T., 223, 226, 227
Savings-bank insurance, 74

Schaefer v. United States, 210–11, 213, 225, 244
Schenk v. United States, 181, 187, 189–96, 197, 200, 201, 206, 211, 216, 220, 225, 244
Schlesinger, Arthur M., Jr., 289
Schmidinger v. Chicago, 154
Seagle, William, 9
Secondary boycott, 121, 124, 128, 137
Sedition Act of 1918, 202–03
Senn v. Tile Layers Union, 136–37
Separation of powers, 283–84
Shaw, Judge Lemuel, 83
Sherman Anti-Trust Act, 49–50, 51, 52, 54, 55, 56, 57, 121, 122, 129, 137, 169, 172, 174, 176
Shriver, Harry C., 304
Shulman, Harry, 232
Skepticism, 103, 110–11, 140, 303
Slaughterhouse cases, 32–33
Smith, Adam, 24, 31, 45
Smith Act, 219, 242–43, 246, 249, 250, 251
Smyth v. Ames, 272–75, 276
Socialism, 66, 78, 198, 213, 285, 301
Socialist Party, 196, 213, 223, 247
Sociological jurisprudence, 40, 92
Socrates, 295, 299
Southern Pacific v. Arizona, 289
Southern Pacific Co. v. Jensen, 118
Southwestern Bell Telephone Co. v. Public Service Commission of Missouri, 274, 277, 280
Spanish-American War, 284
Spencer, Herbert, 31, 39, 42, 145
Standard Oil Co. of New Jersey v. United States, 52
Stare decisis, 265
Stettler v. O'Hara, 89, 92, 144
Stimson, Henry L., 94
Stone, Justice Harlan Fiske, 111, 138, 149, 150, 151, 158–59, 164, 175, 177, 233, 234–35, 236, 273, 278, 291
Story, Joseph, 3, 7, 13, 83
Sugar Trust Case. *See* United States v. E. C. Knight Co.
Supremacy of law, 283
Sutherland, Justice George, 60, 108,